OBJECT-ORIENTED ANALYSIS AND SIMULATION

OBJECT-ORIENTED ANALYSIS AND SIMULATION

David R.C. Hill

Blaise Pascal University, France

Translated by K International, Beds., LU6 2DN, England.

▲▼ **Addison-Wesley Publishing Company**
Harlow, England • Reading, Massachusetts • Menlo Park, California
New York • Don Mills, Ontario • Amsterdam • Bonn • Sydney • Singapore
Tokyo • Madrid • San Juan • Milan • Mexico City • Seoul • Taipei

© 1996 Addison-Wesley Publishers Ltd.
© 1996 Addison-Wesley Publishing Company Inc.

Cover designed by Op den Brouw, Design & Illustration, Reading
and printed by The Riverside Printing Co. (Reading) Ltd.
Translated from the French by, and typeset by K International, Bedfordshire
Printed and bound by The University Press at Cambridge.

First printed 1996

ISBN 0–201–87759–7

British Library Cataloguing-in-Publication Data
A catalogue record for this book is available from the British Library.

Library of Congress Cataloging-in-Publication Data applied for

PREFACE

◁ Presentation

The work presented in this book concerns both software engineering and modelling. It is intended for advanced undergraduate and postgraduate students, and for qualified engineers and computer scientists who are faced with the analysis and design of complex systems and who feel the need to master modelling techniques. It offers an introduction to modelling as well as different states of the art concerning the object models, concepts, object-oriented analysis and design methods and techniques for animating simulation results. This book also proposes an object-oriented analysis and design method for modelling discrete flow systems (where the modelling tool is discrete event simulation). In addition, we propose and use graphics software tools for modelling.

◁ Introduction to complex system modelling

The design and operation of complex systems (manufacturing systems, data processing systems, transportation systems, administrative systems, ...) pose a certain number of problems, such as understanding their operation (in normal or in crippled mode), their dimensions, improving their productivity or evaluating their performance. To resolve these problems, discrete events simulation is almost essential, especially to study transient phenomena. However, the mastery of this technique is not obvious despite the availability of powerful simulation software whether dedicated or general purpose. The dedicated tools (SEEWHY/WITNESS, CADENCE, MICROSAINT ...) deal with a restricted number of the problems that exist in industry: those for which they have been designed. General-purpose simulation software and languages (GPSS, SIMAN, SIMSCRIPT, MODSIM II,

QNAP2, ...) are based on a formalism which is difficult to acquire rapidly, but they do allow the modelling of very complex systems. It is therefore useful to design user-friendly modelling environments, using general software as a base. Such an environment should make it possible to construct a knowledge model of a system easily, and automatically deduce a valid simulation program which corresponds to an action model. A modelling environment comprises:

- performance evaluation software (constituting the kernel of the environment);
- graphics tools;
- statistics and operational research tools;
- a decision support system;
- a database management system;
- a networking management system;
- an analysis method;
- specification tools;
- a set of modelling methods;
- software interfaces to link up these tools.

The proposed modelling methods use an object-oriented approach.

These methods apply to the phases of analysis, specification, design and implementation (Kellert, 1992).

The principal objectives for a modelling environment are as follows:

- Supply the user with specification tools for the system, allowing him or her to construct a knowledge model.
- Construct a methodology making it possible to avoid preparing a dedicated simulator for each system.
- Automatically translate this knowledge model into an action model (which can be considered here as a simulation program).
- Assist in checking and validating the action model.

Concerning the last two points our objectives are:

- to find an object-oriented analysis and design method adapted to the modelling problems of discrete systems in order to construct quality simulation programs;
- to design graphics verification and validation tools using object animation techniques.

The complexity of knowledge models and simulation programs in industry is such that it is necessary to produce these models using the techniques and tools of software engineering. According to the Lehman classification of software, simulation models fall into the highest category in terms of difficulty (Lehman, 1980). One of the major objectives of this book is to bring together software engineering and simulation. Right at the start, we will try to give an inventory of the advanced techniques of software engineering which may be used for simulation, then we will propose software engineering tools for the analysis, design, verification and validation of simulation models. We will undertake this inventory on the basis of the object model used by the software engineering and simulation communities. This model, most of the concepts of which were introduced with SIMULA-67, allows access to an industrial software production stage. One of the numerous interests of object techniques is that they facilitate links between, on the one hand, the analysis and specification of a real system and, on the other, the design and implementation of an action model. Thus, Dahl and Nygaard presented SIMULA in these terms: '...a programming language designed to provide a systems analyst with unified concepts facilitating a concise description of discrete event systems' (Dahl and Nygaard, 1966). This description of SIMULA brings together the two essential components of performance evaluation research described by Potier (1977): 'on the one hand to prepare methods and tools for measuring and analysing the behaviour of systems, and on the other to arrive at a description and the clearest possible understanding of these forms of behaviour'.

The simulation world's object model finally conquered the software engineering community in the past decade, by proving that it could improve the productivity and quality of software.

The idea of considering the object design of a software system as coming within the sphere of modelling is not new. We must, moreover, quote Bertrand Meyer:

> 'Nowhere perhaps is [this] view of the software as inescapable as in the area of simulation. Thus it is not an accident that since Simula 67, simulation has been one of the choices of application domains of object-oriented techniques.' (Meyer, 1988, pp. 51).

The object model is not limited to programming techniques since it is now used by software systems analysis and design methods. This subject of research is currently in fashion, as witnessed by the substantial recent bibliography on the subject. The choice of an object model is all the more justified, as it allows consistent and unified concepts as well as a seamless process for all the modelling phases, from analysis to implementation via specification and design.

◁ Our main lines of research

Our first line of research arises from the realisation that the simulation community is somewhat lagging behind in the matter of object analysis and design methods. A part of this book will describe object-oriented analysis and design methods as well as software development life cycles. Amongst all the methods and processes studied, it is not currently possible to find one object modelling method really adapted to the problems encountered in simulation. On the other hand, a search for the constant elements in existing methods, those associated with the tasks specific to the analysis and design of complex systems, with a view to studying them by simulation, permits us to propose and define guidelines for an adapted object modelling method. We include a domain analysis in this object modelling method in order to have realistic reusability tools at levels which are much more abstract than those of software components. Furthermore, the experience of simulation specialists can help in providing a better understanding of the modelling of the dynamic aspects of systems. We must therefore take advantage of the contributions of the two communities by adopting, on the one hand, the results which have arisen from the static modelling of software systems and, on the other, the experience gained by the simulation community through taking account of the dynamic aspects of real systems (details of the transactions in the systems modelled, the internal behaviour of objects, dynamic classification, ...).

Following a second line of research, we will tackle the graphics techniques for simulation model verification and validation. Simulation models are often used to assist in taking critical decisions, involving certain objectives concerning generally expensive projects. Potential users therefore require valid models which allow them to have confidence in the results supplied. It is consequently necessary to verify and validate the models produced to the greatest possible extent.

A great deal of software engineering research work has made it possible to improve software verification techniques. The majority of these techniques may be applied to simulation software, which is, of course, computer programs. The fact that these software engineering techniques are seldom used may be explained by the terminology gap between the language of software engineering practitioners and that of simulation practitioners, something Balci highlighted: 'The overwhelming majority of simulation practitioners are not software engineers, do not speak the software engineering language and thus do not reap the benefits of verification technology available from the software engineering field' (Balci and Withner, 1989). From all the existing verification techniques, we have chosen to invest in graphic model animation techniques. These techniques may be used effectively to develop simulation programs while remaining at a level of abstraction close to that of the objects of the domain.

In most cases, it is possible to include the behaviour of an entity in the real world in an object-oriented simulation code, since the effectiveness of this approach no longer has to be proven. To allow graphic animation of simulation results it is advisable to implement, in the graphic object, the visual behaviour of the objects of the real system as well as the mechanisms allowing verification of the consistency of the simulation execution. It is then possible to obtain animation by means of communication between the simulation objects and the graphic objects corresponding to them. Each graphic object, knowing its state and its field of action, may test what is required of it and react in the event of any inconsistency. It also seems natural to envisage the automatic generation of simulation code from the graphic objects captured. If the automatic translation of the knowledge model into a simulation program is correctly verified, some of the human errors in the coding are eliminated.

We therefore recommend that the object model be used to propose a modelling method as well as to build graphics tools which offer not only a verification potential greater than those of existing tools but also possibilities of validating knowledge models of complex systems. The modelling method must use the major concepts of the object-oriented approach and domain analysis and must also take account of the actual needs of complex systems simulation, such as decomposition into three subsystems (physical, logical and decisional) and the highlighting of dynamic aspects as well as details of the transactions.

◁ How to read this book

We have divided this book into seven chapters which may be read either sequentially or in a less orderly fashion. It is thus possible to go straight to Chapter 2 to gain a view of the state of the art of the object model, its cycles of development and its analysis methods; or go to Chapter 4 to learn the M2PO object-oriented modelling method. Chapters 5 and 6 and the appendices introducing C++ and various simulation languages may be used as course material.

Chapter 1 specifies the context of complex system modelling. We present the class of systems studied as well as the problems they pose, involving an evaluation of their performance. After setting out the principles of performance evaluation making use of discrete event simulation, we study the techniques of validating and verifying simulation models. We then endeavour to define and describe modelling environments in order to place our objectives within these environments.

Chapter 2 presents a description of the state of the art of the object model as well as the object analysis and design methods. Following an introduction to software engineering, we set out the various concepts of the object model.

Chapter 3 relies on the concepts of the object model in order to deal with the various object development cycles of software and studies the main object-oriented analysis and design methods currently used.

Chapter 4 proposes an object modelling process and a method (M2PO) adapted to the needs of simulation which uses simple graphic notation. Initially, we present the constant elements of current methods, then we explain our modelling process. This process makes it possible to understand domain analysis and includes a distinction between knowledge models and action models. Finally, we deal with the various aspects of our object modelling method. M2PO remains independent of any object-oriented language (whether for simulation or not) and separates the static and dynamic aspects of the real system to be modelled. This method makes use of domain analysis and also uses decomposition into three subsystems (physical, logical and decisional), a technique which has been validated in a great many industrial cases. M2PO also helps in establishing a set of paths and phases for flow elements; this enables us to understand the operation of complex systems with a view to effecting object-oriented simulations using a transactional approach.

Chapter 5 begins with a presentation of simulation animation graphics techniques, then it describes the analysis, design and implementation of a multi-domain toolbox for animating simulation results.

A separation between animation objects independent of the domain of the animated systems and the objects dependent on the domain makes it possible to include, within the latter, aids for the validation and verification of the models. The functions of the kernel of the object animator are explained both for the version on microcomputer and for the version running under UNIX.

Chapter 6 gives examples of the use of the C++ version of the toolbox proposed in the previous chapter. The first example leads to the production of an industry software for animating the simulation results of flexible assembly systems: VIEWMOD. We show how it is possible to produce an object code for the QNAP2 simulation software from a graphics specification automatically. We explain how to extend the QNAP2 algorithmic language by adding polymorphism and dynamic inheritance. The second example involves the graphic specification of stochastic and communicating Petri nets and the generation of the corresponding simulation code for the QNAP2 and SIMAN IV software and for the Occam 2 language.

Chapter 7 assesses the work carried out and reviews the prospects for the two main lines of research described.

◁ Acknowledgements

This book is dedicated to my parents and also to Leia. First of all I thank God whose amazing grace has allowed me to be still alive.

I wish to express special gratitude to Patrick Kellert, 'Maître de Conferences' (Associate Professor at ISIMA (Computer Science and Modelling Institute, Blaise Pascal University)), for the quality of his supervision, the excellence of his teaching, his wise advice, his encouragement and for having passed on to me a taste for scientific research.

Amongst the people who contributed to forming my conception of the object model, I especially thank Andre Flory, Professor at the INSA of Lyon, and Jean Bezivin, Professor at the University of Nantes, for the time they spared me to help polish up this work, for the interest they showed in this study, for the research paths that they opened up for me and for the advice they gave me.

And 'last but not least' I would also like to thank all the people who assisted me in all kinds of jobs, from the loan of laptops to photocopying. They all contributed to creating and maintaining a warm and friendly working environment. I take this opportunity to express to them my deepest and most sincere gratitude.

David Hill
December 1995

CONTENTS

Preface   v

1   The context of complex system modelling   **1**
   1.1   Introduction   1
   1.2   The class of systems studied   4
   1.3   The contribution of modelling   5
            1.3.1   The problems posed   5
            1.3.2   Determination of system performance by measurement   6
            1.3.3   Evaluation of system performance   7
   1.4   Validation and verification of simulation models   9
            1.4.1   Definitions   9
            1.4.2   Validation of models   10
            1.4.3   Verification of action models   12
            1.4.4   Other forms of verification and validation   14
   1.5   Definition of a modelling environment   14
   1.6   How to model a system   18
   1.7   Conclusion   21

2   The object model   **25**
   2.1   Introduction   25
   2.2   Elements of software engineering   26
            2.2.1   Software as complex systems   26
            2.2.2   The aims of software engineering   26
            2.2.3   Reusability and the concept of software components   28
   2.3   Evolution towards objects   30
            2.3.1   The origins   30
            2.3.2   Subroutines   31
            2.3.3   Modules   31
            2.3.4   Abstract data types   32
            2.3.5   The notion of object   33

	2.4	The concepts of the object model	35
	2.4.1	Introduction	35
	2.4.2	Abstraction	35
	2.4.3	Encapsulation	36
	2.4.4	Sending messages	37
	2.4.5	Modularity	38
	2.4.6	Typing	39
	2.4.7	Classification	40
	2.4.8	Dynamic classification and dynamic inheritance	49
	2.4.9	Polymorphism and dynamic binding	51
	2.4.10	Persistence	54
	2.4.11	Concurrency and actor models	55
	2.4.12	Memory management	58
	2.5	Conclusion	59

3 Software development life cycles and object-oriented analysis and design methods — **61**

	3.1	Studies of software development life cycles	61
	3.1.1	Description of a few cycles	61
	3.1.2	Consistency between the various stages of a development life cycle	64
	3.2	Studies of analysis and design methods	65
	3.2.1	General presentation	65
	3.2.2	Various categories of methods	65
	3.2.3	The need for object-oriented analysis and design methods	66
	3.2.4	Some object-oriented analysis and design methods	67
	3.3	Conclusion	80

4 Proposal of an object modelling method — **83**

	4.1	Introduction	83
	4.2	The work required for an object-oriented analysis and design method	84
	4.2.1	Introduction	84
	4.2.2	Identification of classes	86
	4.2.3	Establishing the relationships between classes	86
	4.2.4	Classification	89
	4.2.5	Organization of the tasks of objects	90
	4.2.6	The choice of attributes and methods	91
	4.3	Definition of an object modelling process	93
	4.3.1	Introduction	93
	4.3.2	Proposal for an object modelling cycle	93
	4.4	Proposal for an object modelling method	98
	4.4.1	General presentation	98
	4.4.2	Stages of main M2PO phases	100
	4.4.3	Results provided by the application of M2PO	103
	4.4.4	The choice of a graphic and textual notation	105
	4.4.5	Taking static aspects into account with M2PO	106
	4.4.6	The dynamic aspect	115
	4.5	Conclusion	124

5 Analysis and design of a multi-domain toolbox for the animation of simulation results **128**

5.1 Introduction 128

5.2 Graphic animation of simulation results 130

    5.2.1 Background history 130

    5.2.2 The contributions of graphics and animation in a simulation project 132

    5.2.3 Various techniques for animating simulation results 137

    5.2.4 Technical problems of simulation animation 139

    5.2.5 Visual interactive simulation 142

5.3 Description of the GIGA toolbox 145

    5.3.1 Presentation of the general concepts 145

    5.3.2 Analysis and design 147

    5.3.3 Debugging techniques 161

    5.3.4 Hypergraphics 162

    5.3.5 Technical characteristics 162

5.4 Limitations of the proposed toolbox 162

5.5 Conclusion 164

6 Generation of code and animation of simulations **167**

6.1 Introduction 167

6.2 Generation of object-oriented simulation code and animation of manufacturing systems 168

    6.2.1 The editing and animation of discrete flow assembly system models 168

    6.2.2 Generation of object-oriented simulation code from a graphic specification 179

6.3 Implementation of polymorphism and dynamic classification in QNAP2 195

    6.3.1 The choices made: a compromise between inheritance and delegation 195

    6.3.2 Implementation of method lookup 197

    6.3.3 Performance 198

    6.3.4 Constraints 200

6.4 Generation of simulation codes from a graphic Petri net specification 200

    6.4.1 Introduction 200

    6.4.2 Identification of the object classes 201

    6.4.3 Simulation of Petri nets 201

    6.4.4 Production of code to simulate a Petri net 203

6.5 Conclusions 211

7 Conclusions and prospects **214**

7.1 Conclusions concerning the possibilities of the tools designed 214

7.2 Prospects 216

Appendix A Introduction to C++ **218**

A.1 Introduction 218

A.2 The modelling of a problem by means of classes 219

	A.2.1	Abstraction and encapsulation	219
	A.2.2	Declaration of classes	220
	A.2.3	Methods	221
	A.2.4	The construction and destruction of methods	222
	A.2.5	Class declarations and modules	223
A.3	The notion of inheritance and hierarchy		224
	A.3.1	General aspects	224
	A.3.2	Extension of a class and simple inheritance	224
	A.3.3	Multiple inheritance	227
A.4	Polymorphism and virtual functions		229
	A.4.1	General aspects	229
	A.4.2	Implementation at machine level	230
	A.4.3	The technique of redefinition (or substitution)	233
	A.4.4	Pure virtual functions and abstract classes	234
A.5	Complements and special C++ features		235
	A.5.1	References	235
	A.5.2	A simple form of polymorphism: function overloading	236
	A.5.3	The recovery of the address of overloaded functions	237
	A.5.4	Overloading operators	237
	A.5.5	Overloading the new and delete operators	239
	A.5.6	Friend functions	240
	A.5.7	Genericity	241
	A.5.8	Streams	242
	A.5.9	Explicit 'inline' declarations	242
	A.5.10	Static members	243
	A.5.11	Automatic generation of the assignment operator and the copy constructor	243
	A.5.12	The tasks	243
	A.5.13	Exceptions	244
	A.5.14	Pointers and members	245
A.6	References forming part of the C++ appendix		246

Appendix B   A number of simulation languages   **248**
B.1	Introduction		248
B.2	GPSS		248
	B.2.1	History of GPSS	248
	B.2.2	Modelling with GPSS	249
	B.2.3	Animation and interactivity	251
B.3	SIMAN, CINEMA and ARENA		252
	B.3.1	History	252
	B.3.2	Modelling with SIMAN	252
B.4	SLAM II and SLAMSYSTEM		254
	B.4.1	History of SLAM (O'Reilly and Lilegdon, 1987)	254
	B.4.2	Modelling with SLAM II (Hammesfahr *et al.*, 1989)	255
	B.4.3	Modelling with SLAMSYSTEM (O'Reilly and Nordlund, 1989)	256
	B.4.4	The animation possibilities (Pritsker, 1989)	256
B.5	Simula-67		257
	B.5.1	History	257

		B.5.2	Modelling with Simula-67	258
B.6		ModSim III		260
		B.6.1	History of ModSim (Bryan, 1989) (now ModSim III)	260
		B.6.2	Modelling with ModSim II (Herring, 1990)	260
		B.6.3	Editing of results in the form of graphics and animation	262
		B.6.4	Simulation and parallelism with ModSim (Bryan, 1990)	263
B.7		QNAP2		263
		B.7.1	History	263
		B.7.2	A few elements of the QNAP2 language (Pistre, 1991)	264
		B.7.3	Other features of the QNAP2 language	269
B.8		Bibliographical references to the tools and simulation languages presented		269
		B.8.1	GPSS	269
		B.8.2	ModSim II	269
		B.8.3	SIMAN	270
		B.8.4	SIMULA	270
		B.8.5	SLAM/SLAMSYSTEM	270
		B.8.6	QNAP2	270

Glossary	272
Bibliography	278
Index	288

1

The context of complex system modelling

◁ OBJECTIVES

The aim of this chapter is to provide an introduction to modelling. Complex systems, because of their size or operation, are frequently the object of modelling. (Complex does not designate here the chaotic aspects of certain systems.) For many years it has been difficult to imagine the design of a boat or an aircraft without building a model. These models should resemble the system to be designed and be intended to simplify its study.

The modelling technique we use in this book is discrete event simulation and we are interested in the modelling of any type of system whose flows may be considered as discrete. One of the main objectives we set ourselves concerns the performance evaluation of the systems studied with a view to improving them. We present various techniques for determining the performance of a system, then we concentrate on the verification and validation of simulation models. The latter part of this chapter presents the notion of a modelling environment.

◁ 1.1 Introduction

Complex systems are increasingly used in a great many areas (software systems, manufacturing systems, computer systems, transport systems, administrative systems, ecological systems, ...). The complexity of these systems may be linked both to their size (number of elements in a system) and to their operation (type and number of interactions between the elements of a system). The main problems posed by complex systems are their dimensions, understanding their operation, improving their productivity and determining their performance.

Studying a system in order to evaluate its performance leads to the notion of a model and to a modelling process. Minsky (1968) states that a model's interest for a particular observer is to be able to learn something useful concerning the operation

1

of the system modelled. Popper (1973) suggests three concepts relating to the notion of a model:

- A model must have some resemblance to the real system.
- A model must constitute a simplification of the real system.
- A model is an idealization of the real system.

In practice, a model is constructed on the basis of observations of the real system to be modelled, but it also takes account of the objectives to be achieved by the model (the questions to which answers are required). It is therefore ridiculous to build a Formula 1 car model in plastic to scale 1/15, if the aim is to test the strength of this Formula 1 car in the event of a lateral collision against a wall at 230 km/h. On the other hand, if the aim is to give information about the wheelbase, this model will be found useful. With the same objective, a model to scale 1/2 would turn out to be too expensive for the accuracy required. The detail level of a model is therefore an economically important criterion, which may or may not involve extra time and effort.

Two approaches may be distinguished for modelling complex systems. The first is used in designing systems which do not yet physically exist, in order to determine their main characteristics (a priori modelling). The second consists in improving, adapting or modifying existing systems (a posteriori modelling). Whether we deal with a priori modelling or a posteriori modelling, the principles set out above remain valid. It is, however, advisable to generalize the term 'real system' (used by Popper), so that it applies both to the notion of a system which does not yet exist and to the notion of an existing system.

In this study we include the concepts of knowledge model, action model and modelling process proposed by Gourgand (1984) (Figure 1.1). We will define the meaning of these two concepts more precisely.

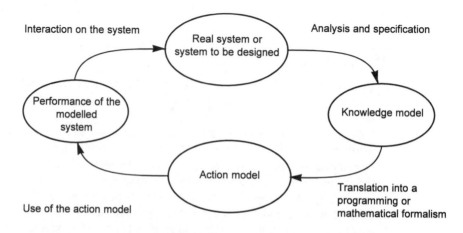

Figure 1.1 Modelling process (Gourgand, 1984).

The knowledge model of a system is a formalization in a natural or graphic language of the structure and functioning of the system. If the system exists, the knowledge model will contain all of the knowledge acquired during the observation phases. If the system does not exist, the knowledge model contains the topology and operating specifications of the designers.

There are two approaches to the design of a model: the station approach and the transaction approach. In the station approach, the observer (or the designer) describes, in the formalism chosen, the operation of each active resource of the system. In fact, he or she defines the relations which link an active resource to the various entities that visit it. In the transaction approach, the operation is described by the routing and successive processing undergone by the clients of the system which are then considered to be the dynamic entities of the system, whereas processing entities are considered passive.

The action model is a translation of the knowledge model into a mathematical formalism (for example, an analytical method which uses the theory of queueing networks) or into a programming language (for example, a simulation language). It may be used directly on a computer and supplies the performance of the modelled system without resorting to direct measurement.

The use of the knowledge model and action model is called the modelling process. This process is generally iterative. Figure 1.1 is a diagram of this process.

For Potier, modelling should be considered as an experimental procedure 'similar to that of a physicist who, faced with a little-known phenomenon, has to construct appropriate measuring instruments, to observe the phenomenon, analyse it and attempt by means of a model to explain and forecast its behaviour ...' (Potier, 1977). We distinguish four large families of available modelling tools:

- the exact or approximated analytical methods
- continuous simulation
- Monte Carlo simulation
- discrete event simulation.

The advantage of analytical models lies in their low operating cost; however, their hypotheses are very restrictive, thereby limiting their field of application. Discrete event simulation, however, has an almost unlimited field of application, but remains financially very expensive (in both human and machine time). Discrete event simulation is not based on any mathematical theory, so it is advisable to be careful when using it (paying attention to the quality of the pseudo-random number generators, validity of the synchronizing kernels, ...).

Nevertheless we are interested in discrete event simulation (Leroudier, 1980), which remains one of the best-adapted methods of solving the problems posed by the performance evaluation of complex systems (problems of synchronization, the study of transient behaviour, ...). Simulation is carried out by causing an abstraction of a real system (the action model) to evolve in real time in order to assist the understanding of the functioning and behaviour of this system and to understand certain of its dynamic characteristics, and with the aim of evaluating different decisions. This technique therefore allows simulation of the operation of existing or

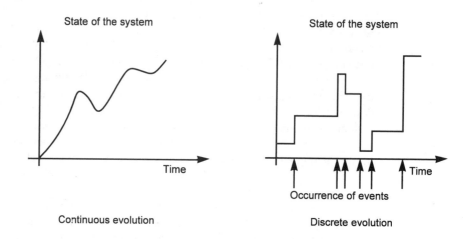

Figure 1.2 Continuous or discrete evolution of a system.

non-existing systems, for a given work load (studies of transient operations, testing of different strategies, ...). Discrete event simulation (the system evolves discretely in time) is often opposed to continuous simulation (the system continuously changes state) (Figure 1.2). The principles of causality (the future cannot influence the past) and determinism (the future of the system may be determined from its present and its past state) must be guaranteed in order to allow consistent evolution of the entities of the action model.

◁1.2 The class of systems studied

The class of systems we will study is the complex system with discrete flows (which evolves discretely in time); that is, there is a strictly increasing succession of positive real numbers $t(i)$, $i = 0, 1, 2, ...$, called moments, such that during the quantity $d(i) = ti + 1 - t(1)$ units of time, the state of such a system does not evolve. The state of a discrete system is only modified when certain events occur. For example, the chronological order of the starting and finishing dates of a set of machine tools operations in a manufacturing system has this characteristic.

To ensure it functions correctly, a discrete flow system has active and passive resources. The active resources carry out the operations. These resources are entities which have a certain autonomy in relation to the system to which they belong; that is, their state may evolve independently of the other entities which make up the system. The passive resources do not participate directly in the operations, but they are essential for an active resource to be able to carry out its operations. The passive resources in general are critical resources.

◁1.3 The contribution of modelling

1.3.1 The problems posed

All systems, of whatever type, pose a certain number of problems, during both their design and their operation, and an effort must be made to solve these. The following may be mentioned:

- The determination of their dimensions: if we consider three types of systems, namely manufacturing, computer and administrative systems, the problems to be resolved concern finding the number of machines, processors or officials that must be provided, the size of the buffer stock areas, the cache memory, waiting rooms, and so on.
- An understanding of their functioning: are there any bottlenecks? How can priority requests be taken into account without causing too many disturbances?
- An improvement in their productivity: how can we make sure that the resources are used to the best advantage? Are there any active resources that spend more time waiting than producing?
- The maintenance problems: must an active resource be stopped for preventive maintenance or can we wait until it breaks down to take action (is it necessary 'to force' a person to take holidays and how often?).
- The problems of risks or lack of resources: it is interesting to be familiar with the behaviour of a system when it is operating in crippled mode; are there any critical resources that risk blocking all or part of the system if they break down?
- The problems of scheduling flows in systems: are there one or more schedules that improve the output of a system?

To understand the behaviour of a system, and therefore detect and quantify the consequences of the problems mentioned above, the values taken on by the performance criteria variables are analysed. The term performance means what the system is capable of accomplishing, for example the flow rate of the system, the rates of utilization of the resources, the response time of the system, and so on. These performance criteria allow us to understand the behaviour of the system under various permissible loads, a load being all of the service demands undergoing execution at any given moment. The determination of the performance criteria is a problem. If the system exists, a solution is to take measurements of the system and process the resulting data by means of statistical tools. Where the user does not wish to or cannot determine the performance criteria of the system by means of measurements, he or she may construct a model to evaluate the performance of an existing or non-existing system. In this context, the user may apply the process shown in Figure 1.1.

1.3.2 Determination of system performance by measurement

If this technique is one of the most reliable for determining the values of the performance criteria (for it does not depend on simplified hypotheses concerning the operation or structure of the system), its implementation must be effected with a great deal of care and stringency. We must, for example, make sure that the system, by its very design, allows the taking of measurements: it is imperative that the measurement sensors, whether physical or abstract (measuring software), only disturb the behaviour of the system slightly. Another problem is verifying that the load to which the system is subject is typical of its usual behaviour: what interest would there be in measurements of an administrative system taken on the day when a third of the human resources are all struck down by a flu virus?

Another disadvantage of the measuring technique is that the series of measurements is often long: the development of certain complex systems in terms of time (for example, ecological systems, manufacturing systems, hospital systems, and so on) is generally slow (compared with the human scale). In this case, obtaining performance criteria might turn out to take even more time as the system is subject to random disturbances and/or significant fluctuations in its load. We must however point out that if all the necessary precautions are taken, the series of measurements, although difficult to take, still remain the most reliable technique when it comes to obtaining performance criteria (Figure 1.3).

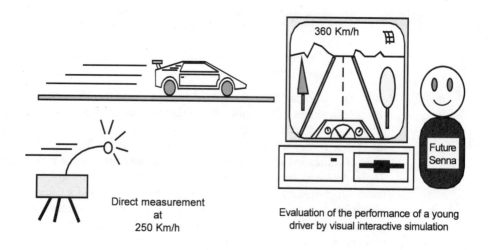

Figure 1.3 Measuring/performance evaluation.

1.3.3 Evaluation of system performance

To evaluate means 'to determine a quantity by calculation without direct measurement'. Evaluation is therefore always effected by means of models. We will therefore offer a possible classification of various approaches to modelling complex systems (Gourgand and Kellert, 1991) (Figure 1.4).

A POSTERIORI   Amongst all the existing systems, we should distinguish two types: those that do not
MODELLING   satisfy their operators, and those that operate correctly.
OF A SYSTEM

Experts solve the operating problems by modifying the topology and/or rules of management of their system. However, we find that most of the time their actions are not convincing, because it is difficult for them to know the reason or reasons why the functioning of the system is unsatisfactory. The number of events to be understood, the correlation between most of these events, the dynamic behaviour inherent in a system and the complexity of the analysis of the behaviour of a system are such that we must have methods and tools allowing a quantitative and rational analysis of a system. The action model, obtained from the knowledge model, must allow us to detect the main causes of incorrect functioning.

Various hypotheses may be tested and evaluated. If the operation of a system is not satisfactory and the experts cannot find a solution, or show that there is no solution to improve its operation, then the implementation of the modelling process shown in Figure 1.2 is quasi-imperative.

A posteriori modelling of a system which is operating satisfactorily is always difficult to justify, if only for reasons of time and costs. Most existing systems

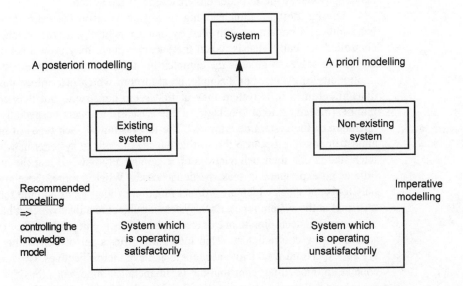

Figure 1.4 Classification of the possible approaches to system modelling.

operate without posing any major problems to their operators, as long as they are not subject to significant variations in their load. If the topology and/or rules of management are fixed for ever, and if the load on the system is absorbed at any moment, then the need to construct a model of the system is not always justified. However, if the system or its load is forced to evolve, it would seem a good idea to construct at least one knowledge model of the system. It must be stressed that the knowledge of a system is not in general held by a single person. Not knowing your system is the same as not controlling its operation if an unforeseen event arises (breakdown, substantial increase in load, ...) or if a physical development (such as the addition or replacement of resources) or decisional factor (such as modification of the management policy) is programmed. If the load on the system increases, for example, and the system cannot absorb it satisfactorily, the implementation and operation of an action model may assist in solving the problems caused. This procedure is only meaningful if the knowledge model exists, and if it can be easily modified to include the new characteristics. A posteriori modelling may therefore have a beneficial contribution to make in assisting the reconfiguration of an existing system, or quite simply in improving its operation.

A PRIORI MODELLING OF A SYSTEM
The design of a system is tricky and expensive. Current design methods are based mainly on experience. The procedure generally consists of proposing several possible configurations and dimensions and then determining the configuration and dimensions which seem best to satisfy the future load of the new system. This choice is often made on the basis of subjective criteria which can only be verified afterwards (a posteriori), when the system is operating. In this context, modelling may contribute an aid to better dimensioning of the system.

During design, dimensioning is not necessarily the main problem. The behaviour of a system is controlled by management algorithms which, if they are controlled statically, that is, when they are designed, may pose a set of problems difficult to solve, so great is the complexity of the operation of the system and the multiplicity of events. For example, an algorithm which determines the routing of dynamic entities in a system may at first seem consistent, but it is common for famine (indeed, a total blockage of the system) to occur, especially when the operation of the system deteriorates. The forecasting of such types of behaviour is almost impossible because the distinctive feature of the systems in which we are interested is that their behaviour is often completely new, so that the experts have little or no experience in these particular cases. What is more, these systems have only transient states which are a direct function of their loads and the scheduling of the flows at the system input. Each system is subject to a load which it has to absorb 'as best it can' according to one or more criteria (economic, technical, ...) which may sometimes be contradictory. This load formalizes a set of constraints which the system experts must take into account to achieve their objectives. Obviously, in this context, a modelling contribution is financially important, for if it does not contribute a financial gain directly, it does at least make it possible not to lose by avoiding the construction of a system whose operation would be doomed to failure.

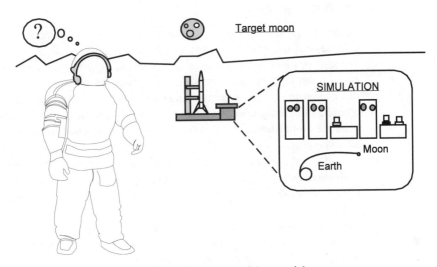

Figure 1.5 Seeking the confidence of the user.

Simulation models are often used as an aid in taking decisions concerning expensive projects. The users of these models must therefore be in a position to trust the models (Figure 1.5).

For this confidence to be justified, it is necessary to verify and validate these models on the basis of the objectives which have been set.

1.4 Validation and verification of simulation models

1.4.1 Definitions

The terms validation and verification as defined by simulation experts essentially relate to simulation models and programs. It is useful to distinguish the notion of validation from that of verification, the distinction between these two notions often being confused according to Balci and Sargent (1981). The validation of a model consists in recording that its results have an adequate margin of accuracy consistent with its expected utilization within its framework of application. The verification of an action model consists in making sure that the program is functionally correct, and that it properly translates the choices and hypotheses made.

A simulation study has to be carried out with a precise aim and for a properly defined utilization. The validation and verification of a model must therefore be effected within the framework of this objective and their importance must not be underestimated.

1.4.2 Validation of models

To demarcate the anticipated utilization framework of a model it is necessary to have several sets of experimental conditions (Zeigler, 1976; Sargent, 1979). In fact, a model may be considered valid for one set of experimental conditions and not for another. To be considered valid for one given set of experimental conditions, the results that the model generates must be within an acceptable margin of accuracy, considered as the necessary degree of accuracy to achieve the objectives which have been set. In practice, several action models are produced iteratively so as to obtain a valid model.

The validation of a model is a separate process, which consists of carrying out evaluation tests which allow us to assume the validity of the model. It is in fact impossible to show that a simulation model is completely valid over the full extent of its field of application.

There is a great variety of validation techniques. Unfortunately there is no procedure or algorithm to choose the technique to be used according to the type of model and type of application. We include at this point a summary of the main techniques set out by Sargent (1984) and Leroudier (1980), some of which can only be used to produce a posteriori models. More recent techniques can be found in Balci (1994) and Pace (1995).

(1) The validity of repetitiveness (compared with other models or with reality). It is sometimes possible to compare the results of simulation models of simple cases with other valid models (analytical or Markov models) or with reality (Figure 1.6).

(2) Comparison tests. These consist in asking the system experts whether the model and its behaviour are consistent. This technique is used to determine empirically whether the operating logic is correct and whether the relationships between the model inputs and the results are acceptable.

(3) Turing tests. With this type of test, the experts in the system modelled try to distinguish the results of the system from those obtained with the model.

(4) The validity of events. The events generated by the model are compared with those of the system.

(5) Tests of extreme conditions and of degeneration. The structure and results of a model must be plausible for any extreme or undesired combination of the parameters of the model. The degeneration of the behaviour of the model is tested by eliminating portions of the model.

(6) The use of constants. Values may be fixed for all the internal and input variables of a model in order to allow verification of the results of the model by comparing them with manual calculations (if possible).

(7) Internal validity. Several replications of a stochastic model are made to determine the internal stochastic variability of the model.

(8) Sensitivity analysis. This technique consists in acting on the parameters

identified as sensitive for the model in order to verify that the behaviour of the model still remains consistent.

(9) Tracking. The behaviour of various entities of the system are tracked during a period of execution to determine whether the logic of the model is correct and whether the necessary accuracy is achieved.

(10) Predictive validity. The model is used to predict the behaviour of the system. Comparisons are made to determine whether the behaviour of the system and the predictions are consistent.

(11) Graphics and animation. The actual operation of the system is displayed in the form of curves, histograms, and pie charts showing the state of certain entities of the system (Figure 1.7). As regards animation, the evolution in real time of certain entities of the system can either be requested by the latest virtual reality tools or displayed by shifting icons against a background representing the topology of the system.

(12) Structural validity. An action model is structurally valid not only if it supplies satisfactory results but also if the internal structure of the action model corresponds to the operating structure of reality.

For a particular model, it is advisable to select, from this set of tests, those which best apply. Some of them are inapplicable in the case of a priori modelling. In all cases, it is necessary (Shannon, 1975):

- to carry out comparison validity tests,
- to test the hypotheses of the model,
- to verify the 'model inputs/model results' transformations.

Validation remains one of the most difficult problems facing a simulation expert.

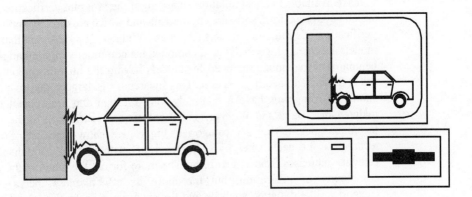

Figure 1.6 Validity of repetitiveness with reality.

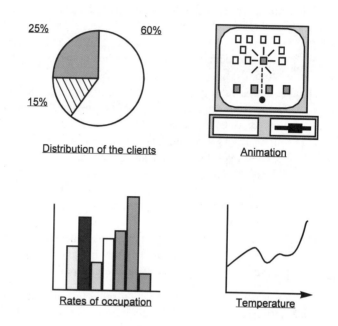

Figure 1.7 Graphic techniques.

1.4.3 Verification of action models

The verification of simulation software must not be neglected, for it assists in proving that an action model is a correct translation of the corresponding knowledge model into a programming language. A study by Balci and Whitner has shown how to make available to the simulation expert all of the program verification techniques which have come from software engineering and which are directly applicable to the verification of simulation models (Balci and Withner, 1989). Aware that simulation models are increasingly bulky and complex, the community of simulation experts is beginning to recognize the need for models having the qualities recommended by the software engineering experts. This awareness is largely due to the fact that simulation programs have a relatively long lifespan and are subject to frequent maintenance. Balci and Whitner (1989) present a classification of the verification techniques, identifying six categories. Figure 1.8 shows the list of verification techniques for each category. The level of mathematical formalism for each category increases from left to right. The more formal the method, the greater the complexity of utilization, but the more its effectiveness increases. Certain categories, like dynamic analysis and the analysis of constraints, are based on the use of software tools which in turn make use of the information presented in the code. These techniques increase the costs of computation resources but reduce the costs of human resources.

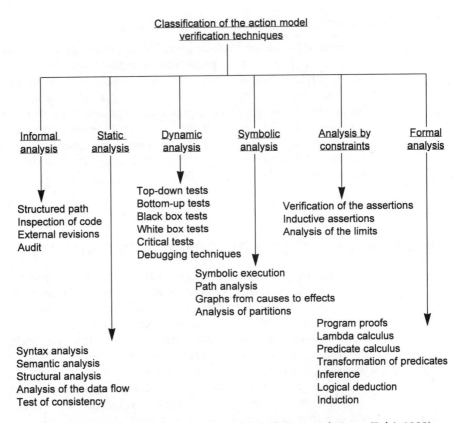

Figure 1.8 Classification of the action model verification techniques (Balci, 1989).

Without going into the detail of the various techniques, which are described in the Balci and Whitner (1989) paper, we give below the six categories identified:

(1) Informal analysis takes account of the reasoning capacity of human beings and evaluates the models while taking human subjectivity into account.
(2) Static analysis verifies the action model on the basis of obvious characteristics of the source code.
(3) Dynamic analysis studies the behaviour of the action model when it is executed. The analysis criteria are collected during this execution (study of the profiles of programs, control and data streams, finalization of symbols, and so on).
(4) Symbolic analysis examines the transformation, by the action model, of symbolic input data all along the execution path.
(5) Analysis of constraints verifies the conformity of the execution of the programmed model with the hypotheses made. It serves as the reference for validation by guaranteeing that the designed model operates in its domain.
(6) Formal analysis concerns the complete verification of software of every kind (proof of programs, and so on).

1.4.4 Other forms of validation and verification

We believe that the validation and verification processes should be applied not only after the implementation phase but throughout the modelling cycle. More particularly, we consider it essential to validate the knowledge model in conjunction with the system experts, or with the experts of the domain to which the system belongs in the case of a posteriori modelling. The design choices and the hypotheses made must be valid; certain validation techniques presented may also apply to the knowledge model of a system. Furthermore, verification must be applied at all phases of the modelling process. Further reading can be found in the following papers: Sheng (1993) and Pace (1995).

◁1.5 Definition of a modelling environment

The exact or approximate analytical methods and the discrete event simulation method are tools which are widely used for modelling systems (Bel and Dubois, 1985; Buzacott and Yao, 1986). The hypotheses of the analytical methods are, however, too restrictive to be able to effect a detailed study of a complex system. Discrete event simulation has proved that it is a method very well adapted to solving this type of problem. None the less, mastery of this technique is not obvious, despite the availability of powerful simulation software.

There are two large categories of software or software tools for simulation modelling and performance evaluation. It is advisable to distinguish dedicated software from general software.

The tools of the first category (CADENCE, HOCUS, SEEWHY/WITNESS, SIMULFLEX, ...) offer users, who are not specialists in modelling, facilities for constructing models, for the formalism used is very close to that used in industry. Their main limitation is that they only know how to deal with a restricted number of the problems which exist in real systems: those for which they have been designed.

In the second category, we find the general software or languages such as Simula, GPSS, QNAP2, SIMAN, SIMSCRIPT, SLAM, ModSim and so on. The major disadvantage of these is that they are based on a degree of formalism which is difficult to acquire rapidly. The writing of an action model is therefore not that easy and calls for a high capacity for abstraction. On the other hand, they do allow the modelling of very complex systems and their power is broadly greater than that of dedicated software. Moreover, these are tools which have existed for one, two or three decades, which are widely used in industry and which are maintained.

It is therefore interesting to design, using a general simulation software or language as a base, a user-friendly environment which will enable non-specialists to construct a knowledge model of their system easily, and to use the action model deduced from it. Figure 1.9 is a diagram of the development time to be expected in terms of the complexity of the system modelled and the type of software chosen, and sets the objective to be achieved for a modelling environment.

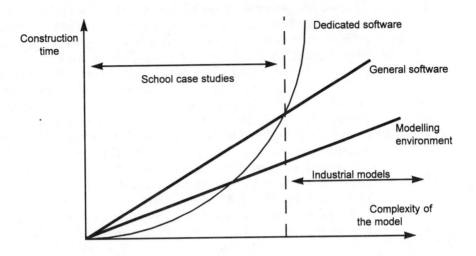

Figure 1.9 Ratio of construction time to difficulty (Kellert, 1992).

We can define a modelling environment as comprising:

- performance evaluation software (constituting the kernel of the environment);
- graphic tools;
- data analysis tools;
- networking tools;
- a decision support system;
- a database management system;
- analysis and specification methods;
- modelling methods;
- software interfaces to link up these tools.

The main objectives for a modelling environment are as follows:

- to supply users with the specification tools for their system, enabling them to construct the knowledge model of this system;
- to construct a set of methods making it possible to avoid preparing a dedicated simulator for each system;
- to translate this knowledge model into an action model automatically;
- to assist the verification and validation of the action model.

The design of a modelling environment for discrete flow assembly systems was achieved in the Computer Laboratory of Blaise-Pascal University at the time of the SIGMA (Breugnot *et al.*, 1990) project. This project was financed by the French Ministry of Research and Technology. We were interested in the design and implementation of modelling methodology for the class of discrete resource sharing systems.

We will present a number of choices made at the time of the design of this methodology. To construct the knowledge model, it was necessary to determine the entities making up the system to be studied and to describe the relationship linking them together. To this end, a conceptual model of the entity/relationship type (Chen, 1976) (abbreviated E/R hereinafter) was proposed for the class of discrete flow assembly systems. The analysis and specification method, designed for SIGMA, is based on the conceptual model which is transparent to the user. Using this method, which is included in the modelling environment, the expert constructs the knowledge model of his or her system. With an object-oriented approach, a system is seen as a set of related objects forming a structured whole and collaborating so as to allow the system to fulfil its function. This approach is consistent with the formalism and concepts proposed by the systemic (Le Moigne, 1977; Von Bertalanffy, 1987; Simon, 1991).

The dynamic functioning of a system is modelled by message sending between the various objects of the system; it corresponds to the execution of an action model generated automatically from the knowledge model. The kernel of the SIGMA environment, which makes use of action models, must be a powerful and validated performance evaluation software. The software retained was QNAP2 (Potier, 1983) which proposes an object-oriented language for discrete simulation. In addition, this software provides exact or approximate analytical methods (BCMP theorem, MVA method, diffusion methods and so on) and Markovian analysis.

The continuation of the design is oriented towards the solving of two types of problems:

- organic problems such as the inclusion of a library of data analysis tools and its interface assisting the expert to make use of all these techniques;
- theoretical problems concerning the decision system layer (communication between simulator and decision support system) (Kieffer and Khrifech, 1989; Shannon, 1985) and the modelling methods layer (decomposition methods / aggregation of models, hybrid modelling, ...).

The concepts put forward at the time of preparing SIGMA were generalized in order to take account of domains other than that of discrete flow assembly systems.

Figure 1.10 gives the composition of a modelling environment for the performance evaluation domain. Details of the composition of such an environment are to be found in Breugnot *et al.* (1990), Gourgand and Kellert (1991) and Kellert (1992); however, we will explain some of the components of the environment.

The **performance evaluation software** must be validated to guarantee that the results obtained are not spoiled by errors due to bugs in the software. The **Graphics** layer consists of tools allowing use of the most user-friendly environment possible. For example, the acquisition of the knowledge model, the specification of the operation of the system under study and the presentation of results by means of graphics techniques such as animation will be used and implemented by means of software with user-friendly interfaces. The **Decision Support** layer must allow the expert to gain easy access to tools aiding the taking

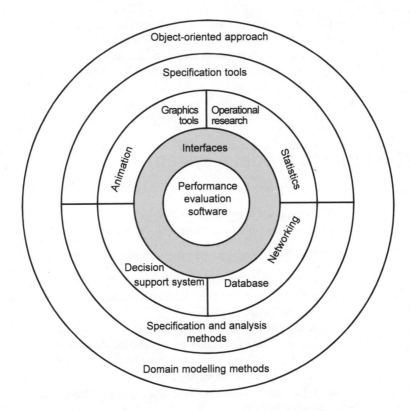

Figure 1.10 Definition of a modelling environment (Breugnot, 1990).

of decisions. For example, the coupling of a simulator and an expert system to improve the operation of a system is a very active field of research at the moment. If such communications turn out to be useful, the environment must use them. The **Data Management** layer concerns access to technical databases allowing, for example, the collection of the characteristics of the various elements of the systems being modelled, in order to obtain the processes and lists of operations carried out by these systems.

The **Data Analysis** layer must allow the user to make easy and effective use of data analysis techniques to determine, for example, the laws which govern various stochastic processes. The **Networking** layer provides tools and protocols enabling remote data exchanges and management, distributed simulation, remote display of results, and so on. The **Analysis and specification** layer is very important because it contains methods and tools for analysis and specification to describe the flows in the system and to specify the system management rules. Finally, **Modelling Methodology** will be useful when we are interested, for example, in the problems of the hierarchical decomposition of the system studied, the implementation of iterative processes for evaluating performance or the problems of the calculation time required to obtain the results. A typical example is the problem of aggregating part of the action model of a manufacturing system. When simulating the functioning of a complex system, billions of events are generated: if it is possible to aggregate a part of the complex model to a simpler equivalent model which requires the generation of fewer events to obtain equivalent results, the simulation times will be reduced significantly.

◁1.6 How to model a system

The modelling process of Figure 1.1 raises two questions which must be answered:

- How do we construct a knowledge model?
- How do we obtain an action model from this knowledge model?

The first question alone raises a multitude of underlying problems, such as:

- What must the structure of the knowledge model be?
- Are there methods or specification tools which make it possible to construct the knowledge model?
- What is the desired degree of detail of description of the operation?
- What information is lacking to describe the system satisfactorily?
- What simplifying hypothesis may be made without distorting the description of the operation too much?
- What entities characterize the system studied and what relations link them together?

The answer to the second question depends on the tool we wish to use and therefore on the simplifying hypotheses concerning both the structure and/or the operation of the system, and the description of the load on the system.

It is therefore necessary to reach a compromise between a model which is over-simple and a model which is too detailed (thus being difficult to construct, maintain and use).

The construction of the knowledge model of a system begins with an analysis of the system. If this analysis turns out to be complex and time-consuming, the Cartesian approach proposes breaking down the initial problem into a set of problems which are easier to analyse. By analogy with the studies carried out for manufacturing systems within the framework of the SIGMA project, we consider that a discrete flow system may be broken down hierarchically into:

- A logical subsystem made up of the flows which the system must handle and the sets of operations concerning these flows.
- A physical subsystem, broken down hierarchically into units consisting of physical entities. The topology of the physical subsystem defines all of the physical means, their geographical distribution and their interconnections.

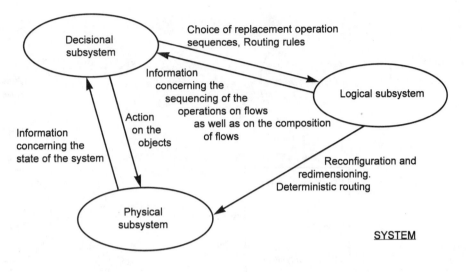

Figure 1.11 Communications of the three subsystems.

- A decisional or management/control subsystem which must specify the system management and operating rules.

Although these three parts seem to function separately, they are none the less linked to each other. The decisional subsystem acts both on the physical subsystem (management rules, attribution of resources, ...) and on the logical subsystem.

The knowledge model of a system is therefore broken down into three additional submodels with which the experts will be able to formalize their knowledge totally. The generic interactions between these subsystems are shown in Figure 1.11 by analogy with Kellert (1992).

The diagram in Figure 1.12 shows that the overall E/R model is one of the results of the analysis of one class of system from which three views are extracted:

- view 1, allowing the construction of an analysis guide and a glossary;
- view 2, specifying that the decisional subsystem uses vital information for the control of a system and returns the decisions to the physical subsystem;
- view 3, from which it can be deduced that the input data of a modelling environment must be structured into three parts: physical, logical and decisional.

Views 1 and 2 define what the structure of a knowledge model must be for a system belonging to the class of discrete flow systems. The environment assists the experts in constructing their knowledge model by providing them with a glossary, an analysis guide and a flow specification method. The glossary is essential, for there must be no ambiguity concerning the terms used by the experts. The entities of the analysis guide are those deduced from the E/R diagram. This guide assists

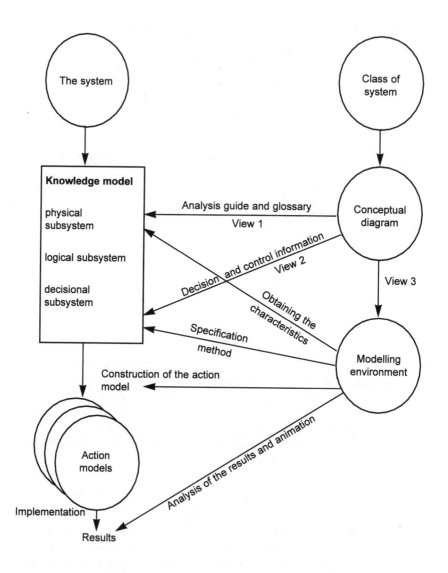

Figure 1.12 Diagram showing how knowledge and action models are obtained from an overall E/R diagram and a modelling environment (Gourgand, 1991).

the experts in recognizing the entities representing their system and in placing their entities in one of the three parts (physical, logical or decisional). The description of complex entities is effected by breaking them down hierarchically into simpler entities. This process is iterated until no further decomposition is possible.

◁1.7 Conclusion

The production of a modelling environment, as described in Section 1.5, constitutes the equivalent of software engineering 'case tools' for modelling and simulating complex systems. We wish to bring together the advanced techniques of software engineering and simulation by means of the object-oriented techniques shared by both communities. The object model is not limited to the simple techniques of programming since it is now retained to put together the analysis and design methods of software systems. This research subject is at present in full swing as witnessed by the significant recent bibliography on the subject. It seems to us that despite the introduction of Simula, the simulation community is to some extent lagging behind in the matter of object-oriented analysis and design methods. To model complex systems, we believe that it is necessary to have analysis and specification tools which take into account the techniques of software engineering, not forgetting the specific features peculiar to performance evaluation by simulation. The principal objectives which may be set are as follows:

- the use of all the major object-oriented concepts;
- separating the static and dynamic aspects of the systems to be modelled;
- the promotion of reusability, not only at the level of the codes produced, but also at analysis and design level;
- taking into account decomposition into three subsystems (physical, logical and decisional);
- highlighting the dynamic aspect of systems (interactions between objects, internal behaviour of the objects, transactions within the systems, and so on).

We have also mentioned the problems of validating and verifying simulation models. Software engineering research has produced a great many software verification techniques.

These techniques may be used mainly to verify simulation software, which is of course computer programs. Amongst the existing verification techniques, we wish to concentrate on the graphic animation of models (these techniques are included in a modelling environment). The techniques of animating simulation results are often used for commercial purposes and do not always allow for necessary verifications. Most of the existing animation tools are satisfied with shifting bitmaps on the screen, without bothering about the consistency of the animation with the model in progress. Moreover, the verification potential of these tools is often limited, because they are content to follow the orders given by a simulator, without trying to verify the consistency of the system dynamics.

We envisage developing graphic animation software based on systems of objects. Thus it is advisable to determine the possible contributions of the object model to the validation and verification of models by animation.

In order to be included as a reusable component within a modelling environment, a tool for simulating animation results must remain independent of the

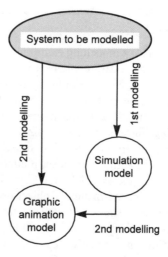

Figure 1.13 Modelling for graphic animation.

simulation software. It is then necessary to envisage communication between an animation tool, which must generate the graphic models of the system, and an environment kernel which takes charge of the action models. This procedure requires additional modelling in order to obtain a robust graphic animation model which takes into account the pertinent visual characteristics of the real system (Figure 1.13). The first stage consists in modelling for simulation, the second stage consists in modelling for animation.

When specifying the structure and operation of a system by using a modelling environment, it is possible to envisage part of this specification in an object-oriented graphic form so as to generate the simulation code automatically. The automatic translation of the knowledge model into a simulation program must improve the reliability of programs.

Our main objectives, which include all the points already stated, are to be able to analyse a complex system and specify its behaviour in order to build a knowledge model, then to design and automatically generate an action model, and finally to animate it. We distinguish several levels of difficulty in terms of the degree of complexity of the decisional subsystem of the real systems.

Figure 1.14 shows the objectives we set. In the case of real systems with a decisional subsystem limited to local rules, we must be capable of carrying out all these tasks. For systems with global operating rules, it is necessary to carry out all the aforementioned tasks properly, in order to have a complete environment (the development of such an environment is way outside the scope of this book). There is a last category of systems, those which are so special and peculiar that they cannot be taken into account by modelling environments. They require complex and specific modelling work, calling upon specialists and all the power of general-purpose simulation software.

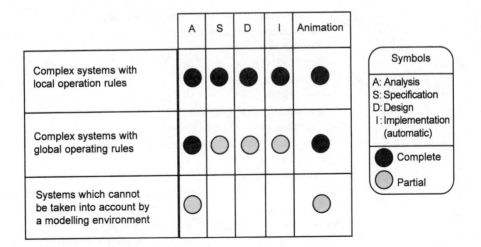

Figure 1.14 The objectives in terms of the category of system to be modelled.

To succeed in achieving our objectives, we are going to propose and use software tools for modelling. We must therefore first of all invest in software engineering, taking a particular interest in the object model. We will study the basic concepts as well as the advanced techniques of object-oriented analysis and design. Any reader interested in further details concerning simulation techniques may refer to the following excellent works: Shannon (1975), Zeigler (1976), Kobayashi (1978), Gordon (1978), Ferrari (1978), Fishman (1978), Leroudier (1980), Law and Kelton (1982), Mitrani (1982), Pritsker (1986), Banks and Carson (1984), Zeigler (1984, 1990), Cellier (1991), Law and Kelton (1991), Fohwich (1995).

◁ KEY POINTS

- The study of a system with a view to evaluating its performance leads to the concept of a model and a modelling process.
- A distinction is made between a priori modelling for the design of systems which do not yet exist and a posteriori modelling where the idea is to improve or modify an existing system.
- A knowledge model of a system makes it possible to formalize the structure and operation of a system in a natural or graphic language.
- An action model is a translation of a knowledge model into a mathematical formalism or into a programming language (for example, a simulation program).

- A modelling environment can be defined as a set comprising:
  - performance evaluation software (constituting the kernel of the environment)
  - graphic tools;
  - data analysis tools;
  - networking tools;
  - a decision support system;
  - a database management system;
  - analysis and specification methods;
  - modelling methods;
  - software interfaces to link up these tools.
- A discrete flow system, by definition, does not evolve continuously in time, as there are time periods (between two occurrences of events) during which we consider that the system does not change state.
- The performance of a system may be either evaluated or determined by measurement.
- It is a fundamental requirement to verify and validate simulation models.
- A modelling environment must provide users with tools and methods allowing them to construct the knowledge model of a system easily and to implement the action model deduced from it.

◁EXERCISES

1.1 Are the critical resources considered as passive or active resources?

1.2 What are the principles which must be guaranteed for a simulation model to evolve consistently in time?

1.3 What is the difference between the verification and validation of a model?

1.4 What is the role of the validation techniques of a simulation model?

1.5 What can the graphic techniques of verifying simulation models contribute?

1.6 Compare analytical methods with discrete event simulation in terms of performance.

1.7 Is it possible to mix continuous simulation (on the basis of differential equations) and discrete event simulation?

2

The object model

◁ OBJECTIVES

This chapter presents an introduction to software engineering and attempts to describe the state of the art as regards the concepts of the object model. The object-oriented approach allows a pronounced analogy between the production of a simulation model and the development of object-oriented software. In this chapter we will study a number of elements which enable a better comprehension of software complexity and an understanding of the aims of software engineering. We will then discuss the evolution of data processing towards object technologies. Finally, the main concepts of the object model will be studied using the class/instance relationship and the concepts of encapsulation, inheritance and polymorphic messages.

◁ 2.1 Introduction

We have shown that we intend to use an object-oriented approach both for the analysis and design of models of complex systems and for the design of graphic software for the animation of simulation results. We will study the main concepts of the object model. These concepts arise, mainly, from programming techniques for the production of high-quality complex software, whether simulation software (Dahl and Nygaard, 1966) or general software (Booch, 1987; Meyer, 1988). Cox and Novobilski (1986) state that the development of software engineering makes it possible, by means of object techniques, to reach the industrial stage of software development.

A software system developed using an object-oriented approach may be considered as a system of objects communicating by messages, each object being responsible for the accomplishment of certain tasks which depend on its state.

This view of a software system is similar to that used with discrete event simulation to model the various entities of a real system and to describe their interactions during simulation. There is therefore an important analogy between the object-oriented development of software and the production of a simulation model.

◁2.2 Elements of software engineering

2.2.1 Software as complex systems

The development of software may turn out to be very complex. The majority of industrial applications require teamwork, which is often difficult to manage. Software engineering reference works for the object-oriented approach are produced by Meyer (1988, 1990), Booch (1987, 1991, 1992) and Sommerville (1988, 1992). We will attempt here to provide a brief summary of the principal concepts provided by these authors. According to Grady Booch (1991), the complexity of large software systems arises principally from four elements:

- the size of the problem domain to be dealt with;
- the difficulty in managing the development process;
- the flexibility constraints required for the final software;
- the problems caused by the compilation and fine analysis of the characteristics of the software system which is being designed.

This complexity is the cause of the numerous faults attributed to software products, despite the work of large development teams. The main complaints are as follows (Booch, 1991; Meyer, 1988; Sommerville, 1992):

- The software designed does not satisfy the requirements and is delivered late.
- The development costs are excessive, and the maintenance costs (evolutionary or curative) are even higher (difficulties, introduction of new errors, and so on).
- The software cannot easily be run on other hardware and does not make effective use of the resources available. Moreover, it frequently falls foul of programming errors.

2.2.2 The aims of software engineering

Software engineering attempts to master problems involved in software complexity and thereby to reduce the development and maintenance costs which are often prohibitive (Figure 2.1).

External factors	Internal factors
reliability, robustness validity ease of utilization validity integrity compatability effectiveness	reusability intelligibility, readability modularity modifiability, extensibility portability verifiability

Figure 2.1   Good software properties.

Surveys have shown that for various projects, the maintenance costs are between 45% and 75% of the total cost of the software project. Maintenance consists in both making modifications and correcting the various design or implementation errors. Software engineering techniques must therefore propose a set of solutions giving control of the design phase while taking future maintenance into account.

Booch and Sommerville express the aims of software engineering by means of four properties (Booch, 1987; Sommerville, 1988; Meyer 1988), namely modifiability, effectiveness, reliability and intelligibility. We will examine them briefly.

Modifiability: a software system is likely to be modified for one of two reasons:

(1)   to respond to a change in the specifications of a system;
(2)   to correct an error introduced previously into the development process.

In order to modify software effectively, it is necessary to assimilate all the design decisions which have been taken; if this is not done, the modifications are only rough, indiscriminate repairs which are independent of the original choices. To be judged 'modifiable', software must also allow changes without increasing its overall complexity.

Effectiveness: this implies that the system designed uses the available resources to the best advantage. These resources can be classified into two groups: time resources and space resources, corresponding respectively to the use of the calculation power and the use of the available memory.

Reliability: this is absolutely essential for any software system. The reliability of the final software must be taken into account from the beginning of design. It is therefore necessary not only to avoid design faults, but also to be in a position to make the necessary corrections if dysfunctions occur (tolerance of failures).

Intelligibility: this means making the software understandable by means of various factors situated at several levels. At the lowest level, the software must be readable as a result of a good coding style. At a higher level, we should be able to isolate easily the data and operations to be carried out on this data. Intelligibility depends to a large extent on the programming language chosen to implement the software.

The principles which have just been stated are not the only quality criteria that we find in the literature. Bertrand Meyer (1988) proposes a set of external and internal factors to quantify the quality of software.

The external factors are those detected by the user of the product, such as ease of utilization, speed of execution or ease of adaptation to specification changes. The internal factors correspond to those perceived by computer scientists, such as **readability, modularity** and so on. If the internal factors are the most important for maintenance, they can only be taken into account through the external factors.

Bertrand Meyer proposes a set of qualities which software should possess, five of which are essential, namely: **validity** in relation to the specifications, **robustness** (use under abnormal conditions), **extensibility**, **reusability** and **compatibility** which offers the possibility of combining with other software. Other qualities specified by Bertand Meyer are the effectiveness already mentioned above, **portability**, **verifiability** (suitability for testing), **ease of utilization** and **integrity** (protection of the information handled) (Meyer, 1988).

These qualities are not all compatible with each other. It is therefore advisable to establish compromises by defining explicitly the weight to be given to the internal and external factors. Amongst the qualities mentioned, it seems to us that reusability is fundamental, which is why we will study it in the following section.

2.2.3 Reusability and the concept of software components

Any developer will recognize that he or she has coded the same algorithms many times, due to certain variants which it was not possible to parametrize in the programming language used. This happens frequently with algorithms for handling data structures such as tables, lists, trees or dynamic hashing tables. The algorithms that manage these structures are often rewritten to manage entities of different types.

There are also algorithms which must be modified whenever a new abstract type is added to the software.

An inventory of the known fundamental algorithms is given in books such as Knuth (1975), Sedgewick (1985) or Aho et al. (1989). These algorithms are always being rewritten, since the majority of the languages in which they are implemented do not allow access to a sufficient degree of abstraction. Moreover, financial obstacles slow down the distribution of reusable components.

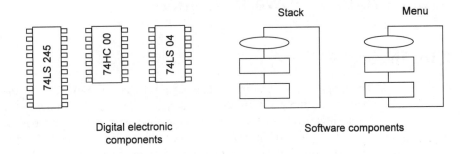

Figure 2.2 Digital electronic and software components with their interfaces.

The classic analogy, which proposes the concept of software components which are as widely usable as electronic components, is detailed by Brad Cox (Cox and Novobilski, 1986) (Figure 2.2). In order for these libraries of components to be used, it will be necessary for them to be as well known (as 'data books' of electronic components). A user (potential client) could thus consult the characteristics of the software components and choose the one which satisfies his or her requirement. Contrary to their electronic counterparts, it is possible to load the desired software components remotely on the Internet.

If reuse of the source code of components is envisaged, the same applies to the work of analysis and design. Software engineering techniques recommend total consistency between analysis and implementation. It is a very praiseworthy principle, but its application is generally Utopian. If it is necessary, during design, to understand the architecture of a project clearly and consistently, it is necessary to recognize that the analyses are mostly based on documentation outside the software code. The ideal position would be to be able to undertake the design phase within the code of the actual software: this would guarantee consistency between design and implementation. This procedure is now beginning to become feasible with object languages and a great many authors now wish to see the generalization of languages authorizing the presence of a maximum of design components in source code (Dahl and Nygaard, 1966; Cox and Novobilski, 1986; Meyer, 1988).

One of the other advantages concerning reuse of the code, or of the design or analysis work, is the increase in the degree of reliability. The more an element is used, the greater the opportunities for discovering errors. As elements which are reused have already undergone tests, the maintenance costs may be reduced.

We will now present the process of evolution which led to the object concept. Like Budd (1991), we choose to follow the progression from subroutines to modules to abstract data types and finally to objects.

◁2.3 Evolution towards objects

2.3.1 The origins

The origin of programming languages brings us back to machine languages, then to assembly languages in which most of the first programs were written by a single person; the size of these programs rarely exceeded some tens of thousands of lines (Figure 2.3). To solve the problems caused by increasing size, the first so-called high-level languages were introduced (Cobol, Fortran, ...). This increased the development possibilities, and further requirements followed as the problems to be solved could now only be solved by teams of developers, combining their efforts to end up with the required solution. This introduced a further degree of complexity into the design and production of software systems. In fact it is public knowledge that ten programmers do not work ten times quicker than a single programmer. Team working introduces complex communications problems both at the human level and at the level of protocols connecting up various software components written by various members of a team. The tool selected to tackle this type of difficulty is abstraction. This is the faculty, possessed by human beings, of ignoring the characteristics of a problem that are not significant to its solution in order to concentrate on those that are.

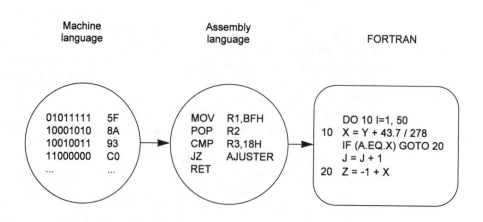

Figure 2.3 The first evolutions of programming techniques.

2.3.2 Subroutines

The first level of abstraction used was the concept of a subroutine (or procedure, routine, function, ...). The subroutine mechanism made it possible to manage all the repetitive tasks, in a simple and effective manner (Figure 2.4). Subroutines were one of the first means of both structuring a program and 'hiding information'. In fact a programmer may use a subroutine written by another programmer, and needs to know only its name and parameters. It is a waste of time to learn the details of its implementation. This decomposition mechanism has been used since Descartes, who advised that difficulties should be split up into as many packages as were needed to solve them. None the less, Timothy Budd highlights at least one of the essential reasons for the inadequacy of the level of abstraction offered by subroutines: the visibility problems of certain identifiers are only partially resolved (Budd, 1991). Indeed, let us suppose that a developer wishes to develop a set of functions to handle a stack. The example of a stack has very often been used (Booch, Meyer, Cox, Budd, ...) because it allows the different concepts to be used synthetically. Our developer will therefore have written a set of stack management routines (stack, unstack, clear the stack, ...). These routines must all have access to both the stack and the stack pointer, which must, for obvious reasons of effectiveness, be declared as global variables. Now, if these are global data, they become accessible from other parts of the program: data protection is therefore not guaranteed.

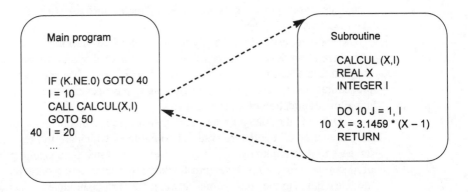

Figure 2.4 Mechanism for calling a subroutine and returning from it.

2.3.3 Modules

The notion of modules (Figure 2.5) was introduced to solve the problem mentioned previously. A module is separated into a visible 'public' part and a 'private' part. The public part, currently called an **interface**, is accessible from outside the module while the private part is only accessible from inside the module. The

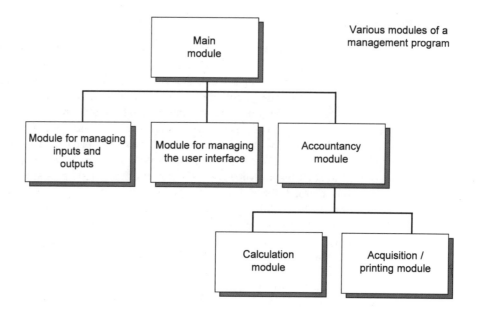

Figure 2.5 A module diagram using only structured programming.

techniques for determining the modules and their interfaces are clearly explained by David Parnas (1972).

Modules respond effectively to the problem of masking information and the implementation details. It is possible to create a stack management module where the data is masked from the outside world which only has access to the interface procedures. However, it may be interesting to have several stacks, but modules do not allow duplication of their data zones.

One of the dangers associated with the concept of modules is the decomposition of a software system into modules which are too big, leading to an increase in its complexity. For any problem, therefore, there is an 'optimum' level of decomposition. This level must take into account not only the number of modules, but also the connections between the various modules.

2.3.4 Abstract data types

Abstract data types are an extension of the concept of modules for they allow duplication of the data zone. The developer designs a new type with its various associated operations, allowing the programmer to handle this abstract type in the same way as a predefined type. Let us take the classic example of handling complex numbers. A programmer decides to describe a new 'complex' type as

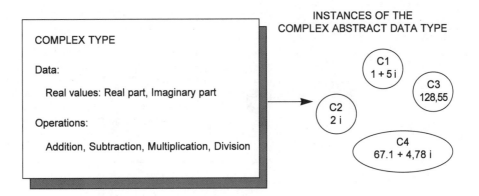

Figure 2.6 Example of instances of an abstract data type.

being made up of two real values (Figure 2.6) and then wants to implement the operations of addition, subtraction, multiplication and division. Only the operations specified in the interface of the abstract data type will be able to handle data of a complex number: data is therefore protected. It also becomes possible, with this abstract data type for complex numbers, to declare a multitude of variables of the 'complex' type, for not only are abstract types defined then known to the system, but it is possible to produce copies of abstract data type zones. All new variables are **instances** of the 'complex' type which share the operations defined on the abstract data type, each possessing its protected data zone. Abstract data types have been implemented with the 'package' concept in the Ada language (Booch, 1987; Barnes, 1988), for instance.

2.3.5 The notion of object

The premisses of the notion of object date from the Minuteman missile project in 1957 (Ten Dyke and Kunz, 1989). The design and simulation of the functioning of this missile were based on a handful of software components taking over the physical part of the missile, the trajectories, the various flight phases, and so on. The operation of the overall system was based on the exchange of information messages between the various components. Each software component was designed by a specialist and had private data. The component was also virtually isolated from the rest of the program by all of its methods serving as an interface.

During the 1960s, the need to find more general solutions to simulation problems led Ole-Johan Dahl and Kristen Nygaard to introduce the SIMULA and SIMULA-67 languages, which propose and implement a set of concepts which were revolutionary at the time (Dahl and Nygaard, 1966). These concepts were only to be

State	Behaviour
Brand: L'ADA Registration: 95 Speed: 0 km/h Fuel level: 35l DIN power: unknown	Start Accelerate Brake Stop Drain ...

Figure 2.7 An object of the car class.

used much later. The first concept proposed is the unification of data and codes into a **class of objects**. The second concept put forward by Dahl and Nygaard consists of separating a class from its instances. A class forms a model for the creation of instances which are only individual representations of this model. The third concept relates to the organization of the classes (this was called prefixing). Prefixing allows us to make the characteristics of certain classes common to other classes by using an **inheritance graph**. The 1970s saw the appearance of the Smalltalk language in the Xerox Corporation PARC. Alan Kay, imbued with Simula, formalized the concept of a **message** in Smalltalk as being the only technique for interaction between objects (Goldberg and Robson, 1983).

The concept of a complete object supplements the concept of an abstract data type at several points. An object **encapsulates** a **state** (the value of its data or **attributes**) and a **behaviour** (its operations or **methods**) (Figure 2.7). An object-oriented approach is not limited to a set of new concepts; rather it proposes a fresh way of thinking which leads to a new process of breaking down problems. This approach contrasts with a classic approach which gives more priority to the functions of software than to the data. Experience shows that, generally, during the evolution of software, the data handled by the software is more stable than the processes associated with it. The object-oriented approach therefore gives priority to the data handled by the software. With this approach, the problems tackled may be modelled by a collection of objects, each of which takes over a specific task. The solution to the problem is provided by object interaction.

The possible states and behaviour of objects are defined by the **classes** which are models for the construction of objects. Each object constitutes an **instance** of a class. All the instances of one and the same class have the same characteristics and the same reactions, but each instance is identified by the value of its attributes (Figure 2.8).

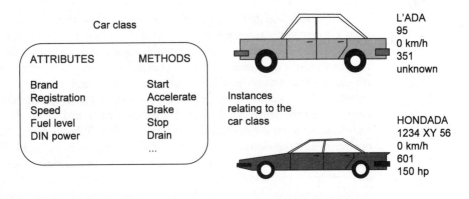

Figure 2.8 Creation of two instances of the same class.

◁ 2.4 The concepts of the object model

2.4.1 Introduction

We have just seen that the object-oriented approach arose from the slow evolution of abstraction mechanisms. It is a concept which unifies the data-oriented approaches and those based on functional decomposition. The object-oriented approach applies to numerous fields of data processing, from pure algorithms to databases through graphics and user interfaces. The object-oriented approach is, however, still in its early days and is accompanied by a heterogeneous terminology which is full of synonyms. Below we will present the main concepts of this approach as well as the associated terminology.

2.4.2 Abstraction

Abstraction was previously presented as one of the fundamental tools which we strive to use in order to deal with the complexity of the world surrounding us. It is now appropriate to give a few definitions proposed by various authors:

> An abstraction denotes the essential characteristics of an object that distinguish it from all other kinds of objects and thus provide crisply defined conceptual boundaries, relative to the perspective of the viewer. (Booch, 1991)

> Abstraction; a principle consisting in ignoring the aspects of the subject which are not significant to the objectives in progress so as to concentrate completely on those which are. (Coad and Yourdon, 1991)

Abstraction is therefore an operation of the mind which isolates one element from a concept by ignoring the others. It concentrates on the external view of an object so as to separate the essential behaviour of an object from its implementation. The objects may communicate with each other by means of messages. The set of messages which an object may receive constitutes the protocol of the object. This protocol corresponds totally to the concept of an interface already presented for the abstract data types and for modules. We shall therefore use **protocol** or **interface** indiscriminately. What is more, the concept of operations in Ada (Booch, 1987; Barnes, 1988), of methods in Smalltalk (Goldberg and Robson, 1983) and of member functions in C++ (Stoustrup, 1986) are identical and represent various forms of behaviour of the object. Considering only the possible behaviour of an object, without bothering about the implementation details, corresponds to the use of **procedural abstraction** which may be defined as follows:

> Procedural abstraction: a principle by which any operation which results in a well determined effect may be considered by its users as a single entity, despite the fact that this operation may be broken down into a set of lower level operations. (Coad and Yourdon, 1991)

This form of abstraction is not the only one used by the object-oriented approach which is also based on **data abstraction**. Indeed, if the architecture of a system may be obtained either from functions or from data, the latter offers better stability during the software lifetime. Experience shows that a classic top-down functional design does not facilitate maintenance activities (Booch, 1991; Coad and Yourdon, 1991). Bertrand Meyer gives numerous examples, showing that to achieve aims such as reusability and extensibility of software, it is preferable to base the architecture of a system on its data (Meyer, 1988). Since this has to be protected, here is a definition of data abstraction:

> Data abstraction: a principle which consists in defining a type of data in terms of operations applying to the objects of this type, with the constraint that the actual data of these objects can only be modified or consulted via these operations. (Coad and Yourdon, 1991)

This definition states that when an object is defined by its attribute values (the data which constitutes its state) and the services it can render, the only means of gaining access to the attributes is to use the methods which the object proposes to us. Moreover, this constitutes a good style of programming in software engineering. There is a complete set of instructions for this programming style and even a 'law' (the law of Demeter) to obtain a correct object-oriented style of coding (Liberherr and Holland, 1989; Budd, 1991).

2.4.3 Encapsulation

Encapsulation consists in integrating the code and data of an entity within an object. Encapsulation also prevents client users of an object from learning the details of its

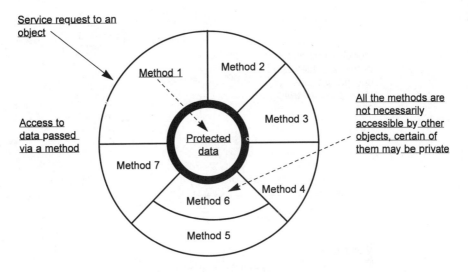

Figure 2.9 Classic representation of encapsulation.

implementation by supplying only an external view (information hiding).

Encapsulation may be considered as a generalization of data abstraction coming within the following definition (Figure 2.9):

> Encapsulation is the process of hiding all the details of an object that do not contribute to its essential characteristics. (Booch, 1991)

Only the interface (or protocol) of an object must be visible to the eyes of a potential client. David Parnas (1972) shows how encapsulation makes it possible to minimize maintenance operations. In fact, modifications of the implementation details have no effect on the clients of the object. Only a change in the interface affects clients.

2.4.4 Sending messages

The sending of messages is the only means of communication between objects. A message constitutes a request to activate one of the methods of an object. The message must correspond to a part of the behaviour of the object, otherwise an error occurs.

Let us take an example to illustrate the type of situation which may be encountered. If a 'stack' object receives a message asking it to remove an object from the stack, this object reacts to the message by activating the appropriate method. However, if the stack removal message is sent to a car object, obviously it cannot be dealt with. Expressions like 'sending a message', 'request for service', or 'activation of a method' are equivalent when it comes to specifying that an object

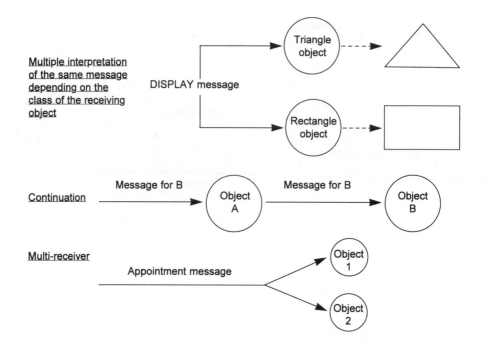

Figure 2.10 Different methods of message transmission.

procedure or function forming part of its behaviour. After touching on a number of additional concepts, we shall subsequently detail the following points (Figure 2.10):

- the interpretation of a message, which may differ depending on the receiving object;
- the concept of continuation, which authorizes the sending of a message response to an object other than the one transmitting the request;
- the concept of multi-receiver, which specifies several addresses for a message.

2.4.5 Modularity

Breaking down software into individual components makes it possible to reduce its complexity (Parnas, 1972). But modularity is also one of the key elements of reusability and extensibility. Composition into modules is taken into account during analysis, then during design, and finally affects the programming.

A summary of the various pieces of advice compiled by Grady Booch (1991) recommends the construction of modules which are as independent of each other as possible. Each module must group together the maximum amount of data linked to the same abstract data type. Booch then proposes the following definition:

> Modularity is the property of a system which has been broken down into a set of cohesive and loosely coupled modules. (Booch, 1991)

Bertrand Meyer proposes five criteria to evaluate the degree of modularity of the design methods: decomposability, composability, comprehensibility, continuity and protection (Meyer, 1990).

Bertrand Meyer also presents the concepts of the opening and closing of modules. A module is described as closed as soon as it can be used by client modules. A module is described as open when it can still be extended. The two concepts are both necessary simultaneously during development projects. Only the object-oriented approach, with the techniques of inheritance, allows simplified opening/closure of modules during software construction, and this is due to the low degrees of dependency of the various objects on each other.

2.4.6 Typing

THE CONCEPT
OF TYPE
AND CLASS

The notion of type is linked to the concept of abstract data type. The man in the street may liken class to type but there are nuances which may be consulted in Booch (1991). We do, however, subsequently consider that classes may be viewed as types. Grady Booch gives the following definition of **typing**:

> Typing is the enforcement of the class of an object, such that objects of different types may not be interchanged, or at most they may be interchanged in very restricted ways. (Booch, 1991)

Booch considers that typing is only a minor element of object modelling. As far as implementation is concerned, a strongly typed language, a slightly typed language or a language which is not typed at all may still be an object-oriented language.

In strongly typed languages, assignments or operations which might not be consistent with the types of the objects concerned are detected at compile time (Figure 2.11). This function is desirable for reasons of software validity. However, it is possible with numerous typed languages to make **varying records** in order to handle variables which may have different types. This feature, included in most major languages, shows a real need for flexible typing.

$$18 \text{ km} / 3° = ?$$

Figure 2.11 Consistency checking may be effected by means of strong typing.

STATIC AND
DYNAMIC
TYPING

To distinguish a language with static typing from a language with dynamic typing it is sufficient to know whether the types are associated with identifiers of the variables or with the values (representing the content of a variable at a particular instant). In languages with static typing such as Eiffel, Simula and C++, types are associated with identifiers by means of declarative instructions or when a dynamic allocation is made. On the other hand, in languages with dynamic typing such as Smalltalk, Objective-C and CLOS, types are associated not with variables but with the contents of these variables. Each content is capable of determining its class, for it possesses all the necessary information. With this concept, the object references are no longer typed, and it is therefore no longer possible to make illegal assignments. This greatly facilitates the construction of highly reusable components.

The problem of choice between static and dynamic typing is linked to the replies we wish to obtain to the following questions. At what moment do we verify the consistency of a message? When is it necessary to determine whether object O has method M? Is it at compile time or at runtime? If this verification is effected at compile time, the typing is static; if it is during execution the typing is dynamic. In the first case greater safety is provided, in the second greater flexibility.

The main arguments compiled by Booch and Meyer in favour of static typing remain, however, as follows:

- Without verifying the type on compilation, simple programming errors will only be detected at runtime;
- Type declarations are used for the documentation of software.
- Compilers may generate a much better code if the types are declared.

The flexibility lost by using a statically typed language may be offset by the safety gained, especially in large software developments; prototyping still remains very much associated with dynamically typed languages.

2.4.7 Classification

THE CONCEPT
OF HIERARCHY

The decomposition of a complex system may lead to large sets of objects. To manage these objects simply, it is advisable to determine the relationships which exist between them. Certain of these relationships may be tackled with the concept of hierarchy which will make it possible to ensure an order for the set of abstractions obtained. The methods used to organize a set of objects may be either decomposition or taxonomy, by analogy with biology.

GENERICITY

Genericity is a technique designed to obtain reusable software components to guarantee the consistency of the types. It is frequently used to handle general data structures comprising elements of the same type. Genericity comes from the Algol 68 language which made it possible to define modules where the type of entities handled is parametrized. This technique was taken up again by the Ada language

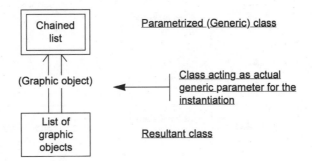

Figure 2.12 Example of genericity.

with the notion of a 'generic package'. The development of parametrized classes is also present in the Eiffel language and corresponds to the concept of 'template' in the C++ language. Generic parameters are simple elementary types or classes. We consider that genericity is a relationship between a parametrized class and its instances which are themselves classes (and not objects). This leads us to consider parametrized classes as being in fact **parametrized metaclasses**. It is principally for this reason that we place genericity amongst the classification techniques (Figure 2.12).

When static verifications are effected on the types of generic parameters (which must satisfy certain conditions, possess certain operations ...) we talk of **constrained genericity**. If the verifications are inhibited, then this is **unconstrained genericity**.

THE CONCEPT
OF SIMPLE
INHERITANCE

The concept of inheritance is one of the key concepts of object modelling. Coad and Yourdon (1991) propose the following definition:

> Inheritance: a mechanism intended to express the similarities between classes, by simplifying the definition of classes possessing similarities to those previously defined. Inheritance makes use of the principles of generalization and specialization by explicitly sharing the common attributes and services by means of a hierarchy of classes.

Let us take an example of simple inheritance between two classes, one called the 'parent' class and the other the 'child' class. The 'child' class **inherits** characteristics from its 'parent' class (attributes and methods) but is distinguished by its own characteristics. The 'child' class is called a **subclass**, and is more specialized than its parent which is called a **superclass** and is more generalized. The inheritance relationship is also known as **generalization/specialization**. The 'object-oriented' terminology also talks of **base classes** for superclasses and **derived classes** for subclasses. The **derivation** action consists of creating a new class by enrichment of a base class (new methods, new attributes). When this concept

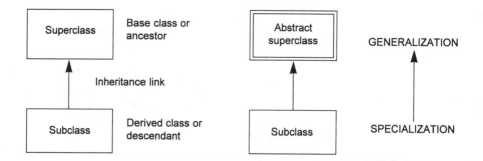

Figure 2.13 Graphic presentation of the inheritance concept.

is extended to a family of objects, we obtain an inheritance tree. The hierarchy of classes arising out of this is called an inheritance hierarchy (an inheritance lattice or graph also exists). It is also advisable to present another terminology used by Bertrand Meyer for whom the superclasses are called **ancestors**, the subclasses being called **descendants** with the nuance of **personal descendants** of an ancestor when these are the direct descendants. The concept of inheritance also brings in the concept of **abstract class**. An abstract class is a class which cannot have any instances. These classes are used as superclasses in an inheritance hierarchy.

They make it possible to reason at a higher level of abstraction than that of the classes intended to produce objects. Because of the role of the abstract classes, we frequently use the term **abstract superclass** to name them (Figure 2.13).

We should supplement the terminology given with that introduced by the 'purest' of the object languages: Smalltalk (Goldberg and Robson, 1983). In a Smalltalk system, everything is an object, including the classes which are instance objects of higher-level classes called **metaclasses. Metadata** is data which describes other data. The definition of a class corresponds to a metadata, for a class describes the attributes and methods of objects. Simulation models themselves are metadata for they describe the systems they model.

The conceptual consistency of the object model naturally brings with it the definition of a metaclass which describes the attributes and behaviour of a class. We talk of **class methods** or **factory methods** as well as **class variables** or **class attributes** as opposed to **instance methods** and **instance variables**. Class methods turn out, with experience, to be very useful for a whole category of services. The method of creating an object is not an instance method. Likewise, let us assume that a software component makes it possible to specify a manufacturing system by means of graphic objects. If we wish to generate the simulation code for the manufacturing system specified, we can associate with each class of graphic objects a particular simulation code, according to the object simulation language used. All the graphic instances representing the manufacturing system are stored

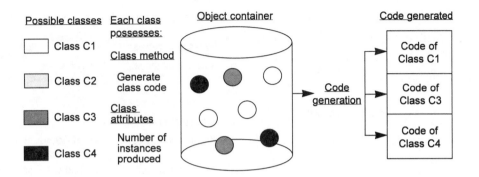

Figure 2.14 Example of class method and variable.

in a set of objects called a container. Whatever the simulation language retained, the simulation code corresponding to each class of object need not be generated for each instance encountered in the collection, but just once for each class having instances. The method to be applied is a class method and not an instance method. This method must use a class variable to count the number of instances generated, or at the very least indicate whether a class has produced instances (Figure 2.14). On the other hand, if we wish to generate the part of the simulation code which causes the instantiation of all the simulation objects corresponding to the graphic objects present in the container, then we will call this an instance method.

Let us give a classic example of a simple inheritance tree corresponding to the domain of the animation of flexible manufacturing systems. The abstract base class we consider in this example is a transporter comprising an identifier, two pairs of graphic coordinates and methods used to initialize and consult the coordinates and the identifier. A conveyor class is then defined which inherits all the characteristics of the transporter class, but which possesses a speed and a length. The methods peculiar to a conveyor concern the initialization and consultation of the speed and the length, and the loading and unloading of parts. It should be noted that a conveyor possesses, by inheritance, the following attributes: graphic coordinates, identifier, ... as well as the methods for consulting and initializing these attributes (Figure 2.15).

According to Brad Cox, inheritance is not a primordial function for object modelling. However, he states that it is an extremely powerful and useful organization technique for constructing and using a set of reusable classes (Cox and Novobilski, 1986). Cox also stresses that an inheritance-based design is natural and substantially reduces the development time. Budd (1991) agrees with Cox on a great many points, and he also specifies that inheritance is not a central concept of object modelling, but rather constitutes an implementation technique offering numerous advantages. This point of view is in slight conflict with the ideas of other

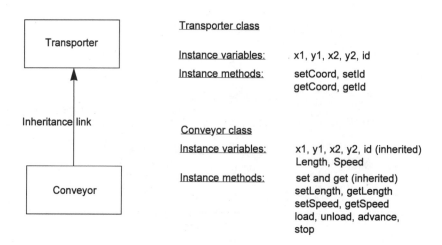

Figure 2.15 Simple example of inheritance of attributes and methods.

authors such as Booch (1991) and Coad and Yourdon (1991) for whom encapsulation, inheritance and communication by messages are key parts of object-oriented analysis and design. For our part, we consider inheritance, for the same reason as composition, as one of the preferential and fundamental relationships between classes as far as object modelling is concerned. We believe that inheritance is a powerful and natural concept, which is found in numerous branches of science. Inheritance, as a simple implementation technique (code sharing without common semantic), may however lead to aberrations such as **construction inheritance** which seems to us to be the worst possible use of inheritance.

If properly used, inheritance makes it possible to preserve a conceptual view at code level. It therefore seems to us rather bizarre to wish to use this concept at the time of implementation to share the code when no real semantic of the inheritance relationship can be implemented; this can advantageously be achieved by delegation.

ADVANTAGES AND DIS-ADVANTAGES OF SIMPLE INHERITANCE

We will show how inheritance leads to a certain number of advantages in the following fields: reusability, reliability, code sharing, incremental development of software components, rapid prototyping and polymorphism.

When a class inherits a certain number of methods from its superclass, this code has not been rewritten. We have previously stressed that many designers and developers spend their time writing portions of code already known; the inheritance of methods makes it possible to avoid this redundancy.

Let us take another look at the example of the classification of conveyors: the methods and attributes of the abstract class 'transporter' may be reused. The reusability of the code is an additional reliability gain. Let us now examine the

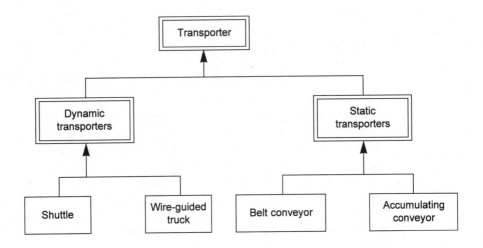

Figure 2.16 Example of classification by inheritance.

shuttles and conveyors which inherit from the 'transporter' superclass. The two classes 'shuttle' and 'conveyor' share the code of the methods of the superclass 'transporter'. It may also be interesting to create an intermediate abstract superclass which takes into account characteristics and behaviour common to 'static transporters' (the specific features peculiar to 'accumulating conveyors' or to 'belt conveyors' being specified in the subclasses).

Again, the classes 'shuttle' and 'wire-guided truck' may be considered as a specialization of an abstract superclass 'dynamic transporter' (Figure 2.16). When we increment an object model by adding new classes with a few small differences (their own specific features) from the existing superclasses, this is called differential programming.

Amongst the advantages of inheritance from the example proposed is the fact that the source code of the model is smaller than it would be with a classic approach which does not factor out the common characteristics. Also, maintenance is easier because, with inheritance, maintenance problems are more quickly located and relate only to small portions of code. We can briefly give two examples of maintenance favouring the use of inheritance, one relating to curative maintenance and the other to evolutionary maintenance:

(1) Let us assume that we wish to correct an implementation error on the 'shuttle' class (for example, the storage of the stopping points in a different data structure). It is sufficient to modify the code specific to the 'shuttle' class without having to worry about the inherited code. This code, peculiar to the shuttle class, is shorter and therefore simpler than if all the characteristics of the shuttles (attributes and methods) were stored in one and the same module.

(2) If we wish to add a stocking capacity (in number of parts) on transporters, it is sufficient to add a capacity attribute to the abstract superclass 'transporter' together with the corresponding methods of initialization, access and modification. After this operation, all the subclasses inherit these modifications and therefore have a capacity attribute and the associated methods.

Rapid protyping (Jordan *et al.*, 1989) is a technique based on the notions of inheritance and reusable components. The design and development effort may be concentrated on what is new and unusual in the problem to be dealt with. Therefore only this new part is added to the hierarchy of the existing classes of components. System development is thereby accelerated. These techniques are called **rapid prototyping** or **exploratory programming**. This style of iterative programming based on a succession of prototypes is also very useful when the objectives of the system to be designed are only vaguely mastered and/or understood at the beginning of a project.

Having stated the advantages of inheritance, we now examine the cost. It may be calculated as execution time: it is more expensive in terms of time to search a hierarchy of class describers to look up the address of the method than to call this method up directly. None the less, the gain in time during design and maintenance remains an asset which is far more important than the nanoseconds lost in managing the inheritance mechanism. What is more, the gain in quality at design level may easily lead to better overall performance. (This type of reasoning will not, however, convince certain diehard assembler language programmers ....)

Another drawback is the often substantial size of the resulting programs. This 'waste' is very slight with certain object languages (such as C++), which only keep a small amount of information about the classes at runtime. However, certain implementations, particularly those using a dynamic typing model, are fairly greedy for memory (Smalltalk, CLOS or, to a lesser degree, Objective-C). However, we must admit that the ability to control the development costs and to produce high-quality code rapidly are well worth some financial sacrifices in favour of dynamic memory vendors.

Amongst the faults blamed on inheritance is the possibility of violating the principle of encapsulation. Indeed, with a primary inheritance mechanism, a subclass may gain access to an instance variable of its superclass and call up one of its private operations, or again access directly the superclasses of its superclass. This can be avoided, as the current concept of inheritance also introduces the notion of information hiding. A superclass may thus mask certain attributes and certain methods which will not be inherited by its subclasses. In certain cases, it may also be useful not to inherit certain functions: we then talk of **selective inheritance**, **inheritance exception** or **constraints on inheritance**. The classic example for knowledge representation is the ostrich, which is a bird but does not fly (Figure 2.17). It may often be possible to get round selective inheritance by a careful design of abstract classes.

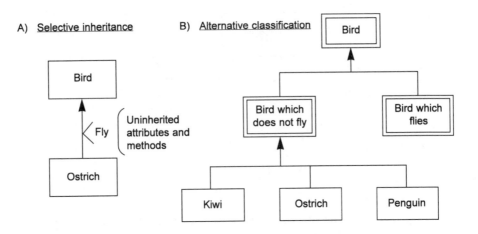

Figure 2.17 Selective inheritance with filtering of a method.

By analogy with the notion of a module which, when used to the extreme, leads to complex solutions, the wrong utilization of inheritance may also lead to another form of complexity. Understanding software which uses 20 levels of inheritance may require numerous traversals of the inheritance graph, which also limits the performance of certain object languages in searching for methods.

Any reader interested in the theoretical aspects of inheritance may refer to the work of Ducournau and Habib (1989). In addition, the differences between **subtyping** and inheritance are set out in Cook *et al.* (1990).

MULTIPLE AND REPEATED INHERITANCE
Multiple inheritance allows a class to inherit several superclasses. An example is the description of an amphibious vehicle which is both a car and a boat, or an 'industrial robot' class which inherits the classes 'stock', 'machine' and 'static transporter'. Conflicts and collisions may occur when two methods or two attributes bearing the same identifier are inherited. For example, the class 'car' has a method 'advance' which uses the wheels via the engine of the car, and the class 'boat' also has a method 'advance' which uses the propeller via the engine of the boat. The classes 'stock', 'machine' and 'static transporter' all have an identifier; the robot class then has three identifiers (Figure 2.18). In certain implementations, these conflicts are resolved explicitly, by stating from what superclass methods or attributes come (for example, C++ (Ellis and Stroustrup, 1990)).

Conflict may also be resolved by allowing the system to choose the most appropriate version of the method. Another technique involves renaming conflicting names when declaring the inheritance. This solution is proposed by Bertrand Meyer (1988) for the Eiffel language. In most cases, collisions which are not resolved by the developer are reported by compilers.

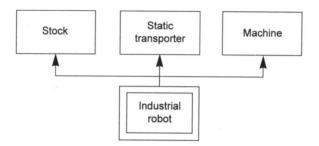

Figure 2.18 Example of multiple inheritance.

The robot example is simplistic and highlights the problems of too many duplications of attributes (a robot does not possess three identifiers). It seems that it would be advisable to define a common abstract 'graphic manufacturing object' superclass for the classes of stocks, machines and transporters (Figure 2.19). If this appears to be a better solution, the duplication problem is still there. We talk of **repeated inheritance** when a class inherits twice (or more) from one of its superclasses (in this case, graphic manufacturing object). The solutions proposed to manage repeated inheritance duplications involve renaming and virtual derivation (C++). Originals that are not renamed are shared and those that are renamed are duplicated.

Many object-oriented languages do not propose multiple inheritance in their original specification and some people consider it a bad design. Anyway, we view multiple inheritance as an annex feature in a Swiss army knife, that is, not vital but can be found useful.

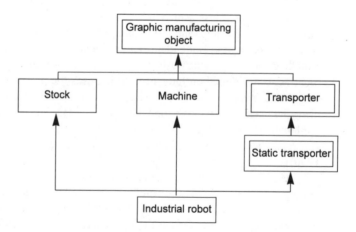

Figure 2.19 Repeated inheritance.

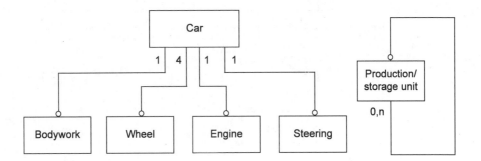

Figure 2.20 Examples of composition relationships.

THE NOTION
OF
COMPOSITION
OR
AGGREGATION The composition or aggregation relationship is a fundamental relationship of the classification process. Here is an example of composition: let us model the following problem in terms of classes and objects. A car consists of a certain number of elements (bodywork, engine, steering, transmission, wheels, and so on). Considering these elements as classes of objects, it is advisable not to make the mistake of saying that the class 'car' inherits from superclasses 'wheel', 'bodywork', ... This type of relationship is not multiple inheritance but **composition**. The object 'car' is an assembly consisting of parts (the wheels, the bodywork, the steering, the engine, ...) (Figure 2.20). We also talk of **aggregation**, the car being an aggregation of the other classes. The hierarchies which come from aggregation lead to the notion of **abstraction levels**. With this notion, the class 'car' is situated at a level of abstraction greater than the classes 'wheels', 'bodywork', ... The aggregation relationship is therefore used as a hierarchical decomposition tool.

Let us give another classic example to distinguish between composition and inheritance relationships. In this case we are dealing with AWACS aircraft which have the special feature of behaving like a sort of radar. With this view, we may therefore effect a multiple inheritance, the AWACS class inheriting both the class radar and the class aircraft (Figure 2.21). Let us now assume that an AWACS has several identical radars. It is now necessary to bring in the two relationships: an inheritance of the superclass aircraft and a composition with the class radar (an AWACS being 'made up of' from one to n identical radars).

2.4.8 Dynamic classification and dynamic inheritance

Dynamic classification corresponds to the possibility of changing an object's class during its lifetime. With dynamic classification, an object may be an instance of different classes at different moments. An object of the 'motorbike' class may be

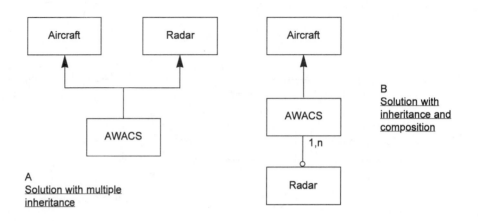

Figure 2.21 Example of possible inheritance and composition.

transformed into a motorbike of the 'chopper' class on a manufacturer's premises, or a simple employee can become a manager. We separate three types of class changes:

- the simple transtyping of an object of a class into an object of another class;
- the assembling of different objects (which may be of different classes) into an object of another class;
- the breaking up of an object of a particular class into several objects which may be of different classes.

The notion of dynamic classification obviously includes the possibility of adding or deleting attributes to or from a class during the life of a system of objects.

Dynamic inheritance means that the information peculiar to a class only exists in a single location on the inheritance graph and is used by a dynamic mechanism. Static inheritance implies, on the other hand, the recopying of information inherited from the direct superclass. It is more effective and often used for the management of the variables of a class (variables peculiar to the class and variables inherited from the direct superclass). Dynamic inheritance is used to share the methods in certain implementations inspired by Smalltalk 80. Complete dynamic inheritance facilitates the addition or deletion of inheritance links during the life of a system of objects. This contributes interesting flexibility but is more expensive in execution time, because managing the effects on the inheritance hierarchy requires the inherited information to be searched for dynamically. This flexibility is also paid for in the sense that it becomes impossible to verify the validity of calls on methods at compile time; the reliability of software systems is then entirely the responsibility of the programmer.

2.4.9 Polymorphism and dynamic binding

INTRODUCTION TO POLYMORPHISM We have just seen that inheritance is mainly used for reusability. It is also for this reason, together with the aim of extensibility, that **polymorphism** and **dynamic binding** are complementary to inheritance. These concepts provided power and flexibility which had not yet been achieved with other development techniques. Polymorphism makes it possible to define several forms of a method common to one hierarchy of object classes. It is at runtime that we determine what form to call up, depending on the class of the current object, using dynamic binding. The notion of a **polymorphic method**, highlighted by inheritance, constitutes one of the most powerful characteristics of object-oriented languages.

Let us immediately establish our ideas properly with an example. We have a base class 'graphic manufacturing object' and subclasses 'machine', 'stock' and 'transporter'. The instances of the manufacturing objects are stored in a collection of objects which groups together all the objects of a manufacturing system (Figure 2.22).

We wish to display all the objects of a manufacturing system on a screen. It is particularly interesting to be able to specify, by means of a general code, that each object in the collection, whatever its class, receives a message requesting it to activate its display method. In this context the code could be of the style:

```
For all the objects of the collection
        DISPLAY object
End for
```

A code which did not use polymorphism could use a multiple choice instruction depending on the class of objects encountered. Such a code would therefore have to be modified whenever a class was added or deleted. Here is an

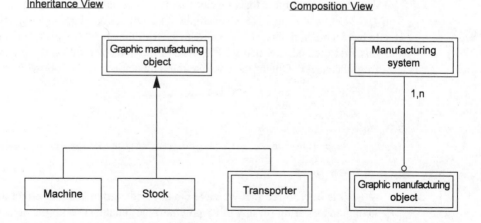

Figure 2.22 View of inheritance and composition as an example of pure polymorphism.

example of code that does not use polymorphism:

```
For all the objects of the collection
          case MACHINE             : display_machine
          case CONVEYOR            : display_conveyor
          case STOCK               : display_stock
          case SHUTTLE             : display_shuttle
          ...
End for
```

What we have just described is called pure polymorphism. The DISPLAY message is polymorphic. In a static typing model we talk of virtual methods, or deferred methods when the methods have the faculty of taking on different forms depending on the execution context. With a dynamic model, the messages are always considered as being capable of polymorphism. In both cases (static or dynamic) polymorphism is available, thanks to dynamic binding. The graphic representation of a machine is different from that of stock or a conveyor; however, in our example, the right display method will be called up. This assumes, of course, that each class has its own method called DISPLAY.

Polymorphism may be constrained by inheritance, as is the case in static typing languages such as Simula, C++ and Eiffel. This means that in our example the compiler verifies that the 'graphic manufacturing object' class does in fact have an original virtual DISPLAY method and that any descendant of the 'graphic manufacturing object' class possesses or inherits an implementation of this method. For example, it is impossible and inconsistent to ask a car to take off and then fly at 3000 feet. In dynamic typing languages, this type of inconsistency can only be detected at runtime. This seems incompatible with the objectives of validity, robustness and reliability. But looking at it in another way, the flexibility provided by this lack of strict checking is likely to promote better reusability and better extensibility. With static typing languages, the compiler verifies that a programmer does not ask an object for a service that it cannot render.

Let us look again at the example of the collection of graphic objects. We wish to have a method making it possible to save all the objects on disk. Quite apart from this first method, we also wish to have a method for clearing the graphic objects from the screen. One of the possible implementations is the following:

```
First method:For all the objects of the container
     SAVE object
End for

Second method:For all the objects of the collection
     CLEAR object
End for
```

It is easy to see that we have clumsy code redundancy to effect the display, saving and clearing (or any other polymorphic function). With the object model, it is possible to have a single procedure for consulting all the objects of the collection.

This method must accept a polymorphic method as parameter, which would give:

```
Procedure (POLYMORPHIC METHOD)
For all the objects of the collection
    Apply POLYMORPHIC METHOD to the current object
End for
```

Certain object-oriented languages which have static typing, such as SIMULA, do not allow the implementation of such components. Others, such as C++, authorize it but at the expense of heavy syntactic expressions.

THE VARIOUS FORMS OF POLY-MORPHISM

We have just mentioned pure polymorphism. We are now going to look at **overloading** which is a very simple form of polymorphism, whereas **redefinition** and **multiple polymorphism** are sophisticated forms.

It is appropriate to clarify certain aspects which distinguish pure polymorphism from method overloading. Overloading is a primitive form of polymorphism which only makes it possible to have several meanings for the same method identifier. Overloading distinguishes two functions with the same name by their **argument signatures** (number and type of arguments) which must be different; we speak of **parametrized overloading**. Method overloading does not allow software extensibility. On the other hand, with pure polymorphism, a code such as that written for the display of graphic objects no longer has to be amended. However many subclasses of graphic objects we add to or withdraw from the software, methods using pure polymorphism must have the same argument signatures.

In the case of dynamically typed languages, **message selectors** make it possible to identify methods. The argument signature is integrated into the selector (genericity may also be considered as a form of parametrized overloading).

Polymorphism with redefinition or substitution is used when certain subclasses of an inheritance hierarchy need to 'redefine' an inherited polymorphic method, redefinition being capable of integrating a call on an inherited implementation and substitution making no call on the superclass methods (Figure 2.23).

Multiple polymorphism brings about the intervention of several objects (of different classes) to determine the right method to be called up. We may quote the example of polymorphic diadic mathematical operators; the addition of a real and a complex number is not dealt with in the same way as the addition of a vector and a complex number. Similarly, a graphic display method may be polymorphic depending on the class of display device and on the class of graphic object. Multiple polymorphism is associated with the multi-receiver notion introduced in CEYX, which is a system of objects developed under Le Lisp by Jean-Marie Hullot (1983), the great NeXT developer.

With the exception of overloading, the various forms of polymorphism allow the developer to create components with a high degree of reusability and

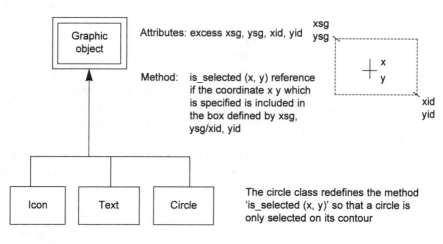

Icon and Text inherit the method 'is_selected
(x, y)' as specified in the superclass

Figure 2.23 Example of the redefinition of a polymorphic method.

extensibility. Without this assistance, a developer would have to write a code consisting of multiple choice instructions depending on the class or classes of object handled, and this code would have to be updated on each addition or deletion of classes. The advanced forms of polymorphism constitute probably the most powerful object-oriented programming tools which only exist when we have inheritance and dynamic binding.

2.4.10 Persistence

The time interval between the instant of creation and the instant of destruction of an object corresponds to the lifespan of an object. Various categories of objects can be determined according to their lifespan as follows (Booch, 1991):

- temporary objects used when evaluating an expression;
- objects local to a method being executed;
- objects local to a module (or to the description of a class) which are allocated statically;
- objects allocated globally for use by all of the software;
- objects allocated dynamically;
- objects which continue to exist from one execution of the software handling them to another;
- objects which continue to exist between various software versions.

Persistence may be defined as follows: 'Persistence is the property which allows an object to continue to exist after its creator has ceased to exist, (Booch, 1991). Objects whose lifespan exceeds the duration of an execution of software are called **persistent objects**. Persistence is not limited simply to the consideration of lifespan, but also concerns the problems of space allocation. In fact, an object created with an address in memory may be saved on disk (with its class and its state), and then restored from its image on disk to another memory address.

In addition to the immediate applications to DBMS (database management systems), simple CAD applications handle sets of objects in memory. These sets constitute models which we want to file on disk and then restore to memory in a simple manner. It would therefore be desirable to implement code portions of the style:

```
Filing      For the whole collection of objects
                    SAVE object in a file
            End for


Rereading   While Not end of file
            Read and instantiate the object read
            (depending on its class!)
            End while
```

These code extracts are intended to be highly reusable and extensible. A polymorphic SAVE method for all the classes of objects handled poses no problem, but rereading is more complicated because the class of the filed object must be recognized, memory space allocated for an instance and the object initialized with the filed state. Few implementations support persistence directly. Solutions proposed for the Objective-C language under NeXTStep release the developer completely from any intervention in the abstract parts of code, as mentioned above, in the event of adding one or several classes. Libraries have been developed to provide the notion of persistence for object languages which do not have it as standard (for example, the class library OOPS for the C++ language (Gorlen, 1987)).

2.4.11 Concurrency and actor models

Object-oriented modelling leads to decomposing the software into classes of objects. To distribute software, it is necessary to escape the conventional sequential architecture of the majority of computers. An object-oriented model of a concurrent system may therefore be viewed as a system of objects, which may be active simultaneously and communicating with each other by means of messages. In fact, it appears that concurrency is a natural consequence of the concept of object. Concurrency rests on the potential of parallel execution of parts of calculations. The components of a program may be executed sequentially or in parallel, on a single processor or on several processors. Competition makes it possible to abstract one part of the details of the execution. There are several modes of concurrency for solving problems (Agha, 1990):

- Use concurrency in pipeline mode. The stages leading to the constitution of elements of solutions usable by other stages must be listed. It is then necessary to bring about the evolution in parallel of these various stages to arrive at final solutions.
- Divide and conquer. This implies the concurrent preparation of different sub-problems and the bringing together of solutions to obtain the overall solution to the problem. There is no interaction between various procedures dealing with sub-problems.
- Resolve the problem by cooperation. This implies a network of complex connections between different cooperating objects. Each object has its calculation process and may communicate with the other objects, in order, for example, to share the intermediate results as the calculation progresses (by sending messages). With a process approach, this method of concurrency adapts well to simulation (Bezivin, 1988a) (simulation by a network of actors where each message is stamped with a virtual time or by a decomposition into clients (active) and servers (passive)).
- Simultaneous cooperation by blackboard. The principle consists of considering a 'blackboard' as being a structure containing a solution under-going incremental construction. Several modules, considered as sources of knowledge, specialize in different operations which they may carry out on the blackboard. Control is ensured by a 'strategy' module which analyses the state of progress with regard to the solving of the problem and decides on the operations to be carried out (Caromel, 1990).

The method of communication by messages proposed in Smalltalk by Alan Kay may support the parallel operation of several communicating processes (Bezivin, 1988b). It was in Simula that classes were first used to represent tasks. Simula processes are designed so that they can all be executed on the same sequential processor; we talk of quasi-parallelism with the notion of **co-routines** (Dahl and Nygaard, 1966; Birtwistle *et al.*, 1973). This is the simplest mechanism there is to simulate concurrency with a single processor (Figure 2.24). Each co-routine shares the central processor in turn, data is shared and communications are not limited. This technique is very simple to implement and only requires a few functions in assembly language to carry out the context changes efficiently. Co-routines are especially suitable for the production of simulation models which have to share a set of common data. With this technique, exclusion constraints on simultaneous accesses do not have to be verified because they cannot physically occur.

The concepts of object modelling are also extremely suitable for highly parallel systems implemented on several independent processors which share the same data. An object model is in fact adapted to distributed systems because it implicitly defines the distributed components and the way in which they communicate. Cox (1986) gives an example of an automated assembly plant, where

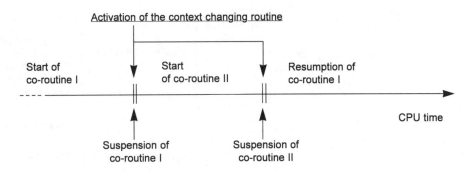

Figure 2.24 Co-routine mechanism.

a large number of microcomputers supervise a localized part of the plant in real time, while communicating with other computers having different responsibilities.

Amongst the other attempts at managing the problems posed by concurrency, we can mention **actor models** which are very similar to class-based object models. The actor models presented by HEWITT at MIT in the 1960s came from the techniques of representing knowledge (Hewitt, 1973) and then from parallelism (Liberman, 1987). Several models were proposed and implemented in the form of prototype languages, the best known of which are PLASMA, ACT 1 and 2, and ABCL 1. Interested readers should consult Gul Agha (1990). We shall try to present the common characteristics of these models.

An actor model uses only one type of object: actors. The notion of an actor is akin to the notion of independent active objects because it groups together the protected data (called **acquaintances**) and a set of procedures (called a **script**) defining the behaviour of the actor. The script determines the type to which an actor belongs. An actor's list of acquaintances may develop over time (addition of new knowledge). Actor models are therefore completely dynamic. The concept of class does not exist; actors are simply independent entities which may be duplicated. Actors are independent and interactive components that send unidirectional and asynchronous messages (certain implementations also propose synchronous communications).

The instantiations are effected by **differential copying**. This is a duplication of an actor, and the script of the actor produced is identical to that of the actor which is reproduced. The contacts may have different values and it is even possible to add new contacts (which did not exist in the original actor).

The sharing of information is effected by **delegation**: an actor who cannot handle a message delegates it to another actor, its **proxy** (Figure 2.25). In a way the delegation mechanism replaces inheritance. The proxy gives access to an actor that plays the role of a superclass in the inheritance hierarchy. A message that cannot be understood by the receiving actor is transmitted to its proxy which is 'delegated' to deal with the message. This technique, when it is repeated, makes it

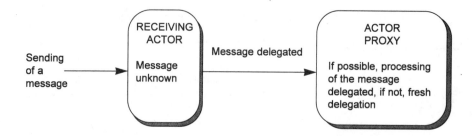

Figure 2.25 Delegation mechanism in an actor model.

possible to cover the equivalent of an inheritance tree dynamically. This type of operation can be achieved because it is possible to change the proxy of an actor dynamically. The model produced gains in flexibility because inheritance becomes a special case of message sending. With this model, it is possible to implement dynamic classification and inheritance simply.

With an actor model, the response to a message is not necessarily returned to the sender. This reply may be transmitted to a third party following the concept of continuation. The recipient of the result is specified as the contact for the message. The potential of the continuation and delegation techniques still has to be studied in detail.

We prefer not to detail notions such as change of behaviour or non-serialized and serialized actors which depend on the implementations, since the concepts associated with them have not yet been unified. Any reader interested in greater detail and references concerning the actor models may refer to the article by Roche and Laurent (1989) and the article by Agha (1990).

2.4.12 Memory management

When producing large software, objects may 'die' (when there is no longer any reference to them), which may involve a waste of memory. When software makes abundant use of dynamic memory allocation, an allocation request may fail because the space required is being used by dead objects which have not been recycled. Good programming should not leave dead objects lying around. What is more, some programs only create very few objects compared with the size of memory available. However, experience shows that a garbage collector remains very useful for offsetting human weaknesses. Bertrand Meyer proposes that garbage collectors should come within the sphere of language implementation. It is then necessary to manage the detection of dead objects, as well as the recovery of the space they occupy. The solution recommended by Meyer is garbage collection by a co-routine which may be activated or deactivated at will. Other solutions are possible for languages which do not support this mechanism, and any reader interested in this may refer to Meyer (1988).

◁2.5 Conclusion

We have emphasized the concepts of the class-based object model and given very few details of actor models. Moreover, the frames or schemes allowing an object-oriented approach to representing knowledge have not been described. The concepts which have been presented will allow us to tackle development life cycles and object-oriented analysis and design methods. Indeed, if we wish to preserve the analogy raised between the object-oriented development of software and the production of simulation models, we would have to study not only the concepts and techniques from object-oriented programming, but also object-oriented analysis and design methods. Our next chapter will therefore present a sample of the more important of these methods.

◁KEY POINTS

- The majority of software applications are complex, involving prohibitive development and maintenance costs.
- Software engineering techniques attempt to propose a set of solutions allowing control of development costs.
- Reusability provides solutions for reuse of the code, design or analysis.
- The notion of an object is only a development of the abstraction concept used by computer scientists.
- A class of objects is an abstract data type describing the actual attributes and methods common to all the instances (or objects) of this type.
- An object encapsulates a state which is defined by the value of its attributes, as well as by services defined by its methods. Encapsulation also protects access to attributes, because any consultation or modification of the value of an attribute peculiar to an object can only be effected by methods of that object.
- Message sending is the only method of communication between objects.
- Static typing associates types with identifiers and allows useful checking of software validity. Dynamic typing associates a type with the content of an instance of a variable, thereby contributing interesting flexibility even if it may turn out to be dangerous in terms of software validity.
- The classification of a set of classes uses the notion of inheritance which implements the generalization/specialization relationships explicitly sharing common attributes and services by means of a class hierarchy.
- The composition (or aggregation) relationships are as fundamental as inheritance for classification within an object model.
- The notion of a polymorphic method, exploited by inheritance, constitutes one of the most powerful characteristics of the object model.

- Objects whose lifespan exceeds that of one execution of the software which created them are described as persistent.
- Actor models are largely akin to class-based models and make use of the notion of active objects (already present in SIMULA) which possess their own control flow described by a script (describing the role of the actor).

◁ Exercises

2.1 Explain the class/instance relation.

2.2 Try to give one difference between data abstraction and encapsulation.

2.3 Is an abstract class always an abstract superclass?

2.4 May polymorphism be used without inheritance and without dynamic binding?

2.5 Give the principal advantages and disadvantages of dynamic typing.

2.6 Why must the implementation of a virtual function always have the same arguments signature?

2.7 Explain the techniques which make it possible to use dynamic binding; what are the advantages and disadvantages?

2.8 Give an example of multiple inheritance. State the problems that such inheritance poses and give one or more solutions.

2.9 Give an example of selective inheritance.

2.10 Does the relationship between a metaclass and a class correspond to an inheritance relation or an instantiation relation?

3

Software development life cycles and object-oriented analysis and design methods

◁ OBJECTIVES

This chapter describes the principal software life cycles and examines the consistency between the various stages of a development cycle. We then give a sample of the principal analysis methods by examining first of all various categories of methods. The need for such methods is discussed before giving a general description of major methods which marked the end of the 1980s and the beginning of the 1990s. Finally, we finish this presentation with a discussion of the graphic and textual notations used to support analysis and design results. The intention of the whole study of this chapter is to determine whether the existing techniques and methods are sufficient to satisfy the needs of the simulation community mentioned in Chapter 1.

◁ 3.1 Studies of software development life cycles

3.1.1 Description of a few cycles

The development of software requires a number of tasks which constitute the software's life cycle. The traditional software development life cycle is known as the 'Waterfall Software Development Life Cycle' (Booch, 1991; Wasserman, 1991). It has been used as the basis for the development of the V model (V model, Figure 3.1 (b)) and its variants (VP, VR).

The waterfall image is suggested because the software progresses successively from an analysis phase to a design phase, then to coding and finally testing. The stream of results from the various phases descend the waterfall with no

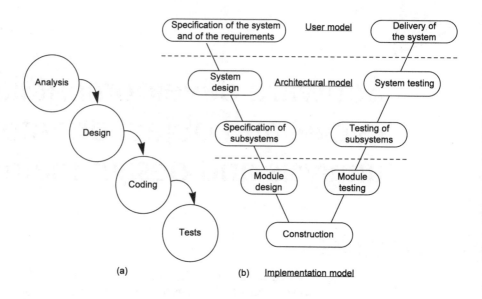

Figure 3.1 (a) Waterfall software development life cycle. (b) V model.

hope of return (Figure 3.1(a)). This rigid life cycle was criticized by Boehm (1988) who highlighted the following main faults:

- This development life cycle assumes a relatively uniform progression through the various software preparation phases.
- This development process does not allow the production of families of programs, nor the organization of software with a view to facilitating the inevitable modifications and new developments.
- This model cannot take into account the development of methods that use rapid prototyping which are offered by object-oriented languages. Likewise, the possibilities of automatic programming, of program transformation and development being assisted by knowledge bases, cannot be understood with this cycle, which is too rigid.

Boehm proposed a spiral life cycle in accordance with Figure 3.2.

Another development life cycle corresponding to an X model was proposed by Hodgson (1991). Many authors agree with Boehm in specifying that the stages of analysis and design follow neither bottom-up nor top-down procedures. On the contrary, they recognize that object analysis and design follow an incremental and iterative process where each stage is capable of providing information which involves the modification of results at other stages, including previous completed stages.

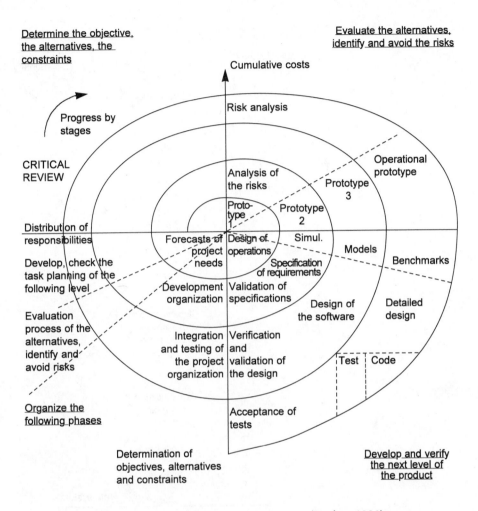

Determine the objective,
the alternatives, the
constraints

Evaluate the alternatives,
identify and avoid the risks

Cumulative costs

Progress by
stages

Risk analysis

CRITICAL
REVIEW

Analysis of
the risks

Operational
prototype

Prototype
3

Proto-
type

Prototype
2

Distribution of
responsibilities

Forecasts of
project
needs

Design of
operations

Simul.

Models

Benchmarks

Develop, check the
task planning of the
following level

Specification
of requirements

Development
organization

Validation of
specifications

Design of
the software

Detailed
design

Evaluation
process of the
alternatives,
identify and
avoid risks

Integration
and testing of
the project
organization

Verification
and
validation of
the design

Test   Code

Organize the
following phases

Acceptance of
tests

Determination of
objectives, alternatives
and constraints

Develop and verify
the next level of
the product

Figure 3.2 The spiral development process (Boehm, 1986).

A life cycle for the development of object-oriented software systems was also presented by Edwards and Henderson-Sellers (1990) who see the life cycle of a piece of software as a fountain model (Figure 3.3).

The beginning of the development of a software system is situated at the base of Figure 3.3. Each activity is represented by a circle. The circles which overlap represent closely linked activities. The arrows which return to the base of the figure indicate the iterative points of the procedure and give the illustration the appearance of a fountain. The fact that with such an approach maintenance is diminished is represented by a small circle for this type of activity.

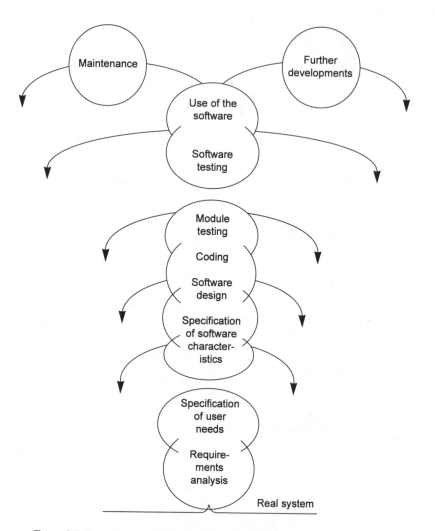

Figure 3.3 Fountain model for the life cycle of software (Edwards, 1990).

3.1.2 Consistency between the various stages of a development life cycle

To achieve an effective approach throughout the development process, it is preferable to think 'object' from the moment a project is started. Indeed, it is important to maintain an object-oriented approach for the stages of analysis, design and implementation so as to preserve a seamless consistency between various stages. It is, however, possible to use analysis methods which are not object-oriented upstream of an object-oriented design method. Structured analysis methods (Yourdon, 1989; DeMarco, 1979; Nijssen, 1986; IGL Technology, 1989 (SADT)) and information modelling methods (Chen, 1976; Mellor and Shlaer, 1988) may be quite suitable. The essential factor is that analysis results provide a sufficiently complete model of the problem for which software is to be produced. In fact, object-oriented development methods do not assume the abandonment of all the techniques acquired, by experience, throughout the past few decades; on the contrary, they supplement those techniques.

Indeed, object-oriented software development tends towards techniques which have turned out to be more effective for the development of large-scale software.

3.2 Studies of analysis and design methods

3.2.1 General presentation

Amongst the various phases of the development process of a software system, we are only interested here in the analysis and design stages. There is so far no universal method for either analysis or design. Many methods take these two phases of the software life cycle into account, while others are concerned only with analysis or with design. New methods are introduced each year to supplement or overcome the deficiences of former methods. It is only recently that methods capable of using the full power of the object-oriented approach concepts have appeared.

3.2.2 Various categories of methods

We briefly present three important categories of analysis and design methods selected by Coad and Yourdon (1991), which preceded and inspired object-oriented analysis and design methods:

- Methods based on functional decomposition: These concentrate on the processing which the system to be designed is intended to effect. This processing is decomposed hierarchically.
- Methods based on data flow: These are often called 'structured analysis techniques'. Edward Yourdon deals in detail with these types of methods in his book on modern structured analysis (Yourdon, 1989). The SADT method (Structured Analysis and Design Technique, also known as IDEF) is another example of structured analysis methods adapted to the constraints of technical data processing (IGL Technology, 1989).
- Methods based on information modelling: This approach has developed considerably since the appearance of Chen's (1976) Entity/Relationship (E/R) diagrams, ending up with semantic data models which are very close to diagrams describing static relationships between objects.

Later, we shall only consider methods which use an object-oriented approach and which attempt to incorporate the best ideas proposed by the three categories of methods just discussed. To characterize and recognize an object-oriented approach, we adopt the criteria of Bézivin and Cointe (1991).

A method using an object-oriented approach must: possess the principle of code and data encapsulation, separate classes from instances, use inheritance, and communicate by messages.

3.2.3 The need for object-oriented analysis and design methods

We may wonder why it is only now that we talk of object-oriented analysis and design methods when concepts of the object model have existed since the appearance of Simula at the end of the 1960s. Three replies are given by Coad and Yourdon (1991):

(1) The concepts of the object-oriented approach require time to be assimilated.

(2) Experience in programming is often at the base of analysis and design techniques. Concepts of procedural abstraction were a prerequisite for functional analysis methods, and structured languages led to structured analysis. Likewise, the massive adoption of object-oriented languages in recent years has led to the development of object-oriented analysis and design methods.

(3) The object-oriented approach is interesting in view of large-scale software which has appeared in the past two decades.

Furthermore, it is always difficult to change habits and many people are reluctant to make the effort involved. When some people have still not assimilated the techniques of structured analysis, how can we expect them to migrate towards object methods? Moreover, it is recognized in the industrial world that good analysts were initially good developers. Many analysts, however, have sometimes not written codes for several decades, and object programming is in our opinion an essential prerequisite for a good assimilation of the object model concepts. It is not uncommon for a great many people to fail to understand the advantages to be gained from object-oriented analysis methods and their application. This stage is all the more essential as an apprenticeship in an object-oriented language is not simply learning 'another language'. It implies a change of state of mind which, with the effort involved, is not always trivial. As regards the development of large projects, requirements specifications produced using a classic functional approach are in our opinion satisfactory and this may be why the concepts of the Objectory method (presented later) are so much appreciated.

3.2.4 Some object-oriented analysis and design methods

THE OOA
(OBJECT-
ORIENTED
ANALYSIS)
METHOD
ACCORDING
TO COAD
AND
YOURDON
(1991)
The technique of object-oriented analysis proposed by Coad and Yourdon (OOA) is an attempt to incorporate the best ideas proposed by the three categories of methods which have just been described. In fact, analysts must be ready to accept all the assistance they can get, which is why all the techniques and analysis tools which have proven themselves in a domain must be taken into consideration. If this analysis method is based on the concepts of object classes, inheritance and composition, it is also based on essential classic approaches developed during these past three decades.

OOA explicitly uses inheritance for sharing attributes and services. It is also possible to reuse analysis results which remain robust with regard to the system studied. This option of adapting to any changes in analysis results stems from the fact that analysts base their work on the most stable elements (the data). The OOA analysis method may therefore be presented as a merging of methods, taking into account certain principles of information modelling techniques, object-oriented programming and knowledge representation systems (Figure 3.4 illustrates this merging). Object-oriented analysis remains very close to the problem to be dealt with, for the model which results from it is composed of the objects and processes peculiar to the real system being studied.

The procedure to obtain an OOA model has five principal activities:

(1) Find classes and objects.
(2) Identify structures.
(3) Identify subjects.
(4) Define attributes.
(5) Define services.

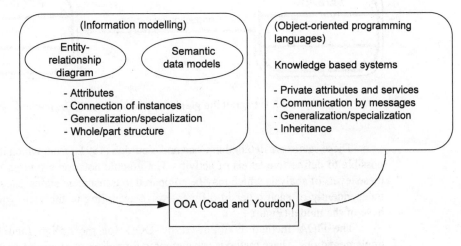

Figure 3.4 Merging of disciplines (Coad and Yourdon, 1991).

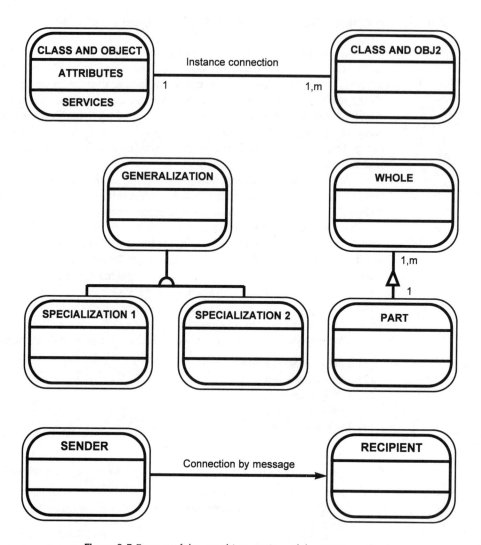

Figure 3.5 Extract of the graphic notation of the OOA method.

These stages are detailed in Coad and Yourdon (1991), from which it becomes possible to define five levels of activity. The graphic notation proposed highlights these levels of analysis which may be compared to transparent slides, superimposed independently of each other in different ways according to the view you wish to have of the model (Figure 3.5).

The OOA method is followed by OOD for the design (and OOP for implementation). These methods use a graphic formalism to represent exchanges of messages between classes. The internal behaviour of the classes is specified with finite state automata. The advantages we find in this pair of methods are principally:

- the consistency and ease of transferring the results between the two stages of analysis and design;
- the use of separate views, used like slides, to present graphically various types of relationships between classes;
- the relative simplicity of the graphic notation.

THE OOD
AND OOA
METHOD
ACCORDING
TO GRADY
BOOCH

In 1987, Grady Booch proposed a design method described as object-oriented (Booch, 1987). In fact, this method was largely dedicated to the Ada language and did not take account of inheritance and polymorphism. Simple graphic notation was used to represent packages, their interfaces, tasks and subroutines. This method made use of a five-stage procedure to design a system:

- Identify objects.
- Identify operations.
- Establish the visibility.
- Establish the interface.
- Implement the objects.

A second version of this method was presented at the end of 1990 (Booch, 1991) and other improvements have since followed (Booch, 1994a). Aware of the impact of object-oriented languages such as Smalltalk (Goldberg and Robson, 1983), C++ (Stroustrup, 1986) and Eiffel (Meyer, 1988), Grady Booch proposes a method independent of Ada, using the concepts of class, inheritance and message sending, as well as all sorts of relationships between classes. There are four new principal stages.

- Identify classes and objects at a given level of abstraction. The design process starts with the search for classes and objects peculiar to the vocabulary of the domain, while restricting itself to the problem to be solved.
- Identify the semantics of these classes and objects. The developer must give details of the internal representation of classes so as to understand their operation and their precise role. This makes it possible to determine the interfaces of each class.
- Identify the relationships which exist between classes and objects.
- Implement these classes and objects. If the level of abstraction used previously is too high, it may be necessary to repeat certain stages in order to obtain an adequate level of detail for programming.

The graphic symbolism which is used by this method is based on four types of basic diagrams and two types of supplementary diagrams. The first four types of diagrams concern classes, objects, modules and processes (they are inspired by the first OOD version in Figures 3.6 and 3.7). The last two types of diagrams are state transition diagrams of objects and temporary diagrams (used as chronograms for processes of real-time applications). New, more complete diagrams have appeared

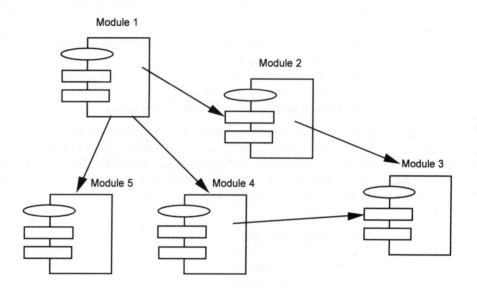

Figure 3.6 The first OOD module diagrams.

in Booch (1994b), and in 1995 the Booch Method and the transition diagrams are very like those of the OMT method (presented hereafter). Furthermore, the Booch method now covers analysis and design.

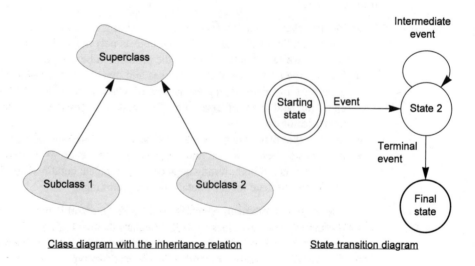

Figure 3.7 Extract of the OOA method notation (after Booch, 1994a).

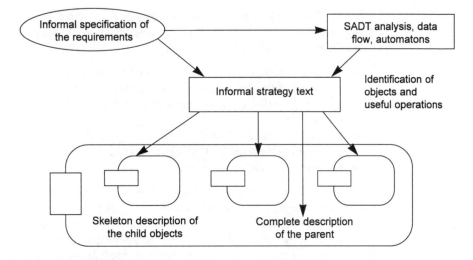

Figure 3.8 HOOD stage in a development cycle (Heitz, 1987).

THE HOOD
(HIERARCHICAL
OBJECT-
ORIENTED
DESIGN)
METHOD

HOOD is a hierarchical object-oriented design method which was designed for the development of large-scale technical and real-time software (Heitz, 1987). This method was proposed by Cisi Ingénierie and CRI (a Danish company), and was retained by the European Space Agency for European developments concerning the COLOMBUS space station and Hermes space aircraft projects. Heitz describes HOOD as an object-oriented top-down design method, supported by a form of notation close to the Ada language, which comes in after the analysis work has been done (Figure 3.8).

HOOD is based on the approach proposed by Grady Booch's first version of OOD. This approach is extended by adding the static and dynamic structuring criteria of the system. The criteria chosen are as follows:

- Use of the principles of abstraction, masking of information and encapsulation.
- Use of a hierarchy using composition as the classification criterion. With HOOD, a parent object is broken down into a certain number of child objects. The objects may also make use of operations (Ada methods) proposed by other objects within a hierarchy. We are then talking of senior objects which use the services of junior objects.
- Expression of the control flow or any kind of flow: real-time systems are either asynchronous systems operating by interruption, or parallel systems. For these reasons, several control flows may use different operations of a single object at a given moment (in virtual time if the machine is sequential). The HOOD method explicitly distinguishes active objects from passive objects as in Booch's OOD method.

HOOD proposes its own graphic formalism inspired by that proposed by Grady Booch's first version of OOD. The main advantages of this method, compiled by Heitz, are as follows:

- The use of HOOD leads to an object-structured architecture recognized as a guarantee of flexibility and maintainability.
- HOOD is a sufficiently flexible design method to adapt to different analysis methods.
- HOOD supports the formalization of designed system by means of graphics and control structures for the objects (textual formalism, ...).
- Support for validation is integrated throughout the HOOD design process.

The use of languages other than Ada is now accepted, but the essential vocation of this method is to define real-time systems which will be implemented in Ada. Being linked to Ada features, the HOOD method proposed neither generalization/specialization structures corresponding to inheritance nor support for the sending of messages which might implement polymorphism. In addition, a large part of the specifications (data structures and operation structures) are provided in a language close to Ada. This method may therefore be accused of a lack of generality. However, the arrival of Ada 95 embedding classic object-oriented concepts might change things.

THE OMT ANALYSIS AND DESIGN METHOD

The OMT (Object Modelling Technique) method proposed by James Rumbaugh *et al.* applies to all the software development processes, from analysis to implementation (Blaha *et al.*, 1991). This method uses three different views, each capturing important aspects of the software, with all of the views being necessary for a complete description. These three views are:

- The object model which represents the static aspects of software (the definition of classes, of inheritance relations, of aggregation, ...).
- The dynamic model presenting the behaviour of the software over time.
- The functional model which takes account of the software information transformation processes.

Each of these models contains references to entities of the other models: they are not therefore completely independent. The set of models proposed is independent of programming languages and uses uniform graphic notation for all the phases of software development. This notation is derived from Chen's E/R diagrams for the static part, from finite state automata for the dynamic part and from data flow diagrams for the functional part.

The three kinds of models separate a system into a set of views which are manipulated and which develop throughout the development cycle (analysis, design and implementation for OMT). The purpose of the construction of the OMT object model is to provide the essential working framework in which the dynamic and functional models will be placed. The objects are considered as basic components which are intended to capture the elements of reality which the analyst considers to

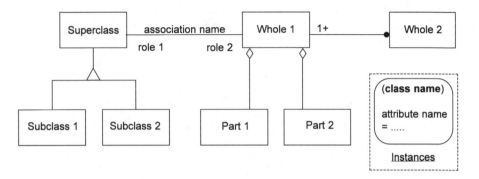

Figure 3.9 Extract from the notation for the OMT object model.

be important for an application. The OMT object model uses diagrams containing the classic relationships of inheritance, composition, association, and so on (Figure 3.9).

The dynamic model describes the temporary aspects, the sequences of operations and the events which involve changes in state within a class. The role of the dynamic model is therefore to present various control aspects of the system. This takes the form, at the level of graphic notation, of state diagrams and sequences of events (Figure 3.10). The state transition diagrams are sophisticated, with notions of concurrency, macro-states, guards and actions on transitions, and so on.

The functional model describes the transformations contributed by the system and the functions offered, without worrying about how this is effected or when it occurs. The functional model is represented by data flow diagrams showing the interdependencies of input and output data of the processes responsible for carrying out the precise functions of the software (Figure 3.11). The functional model currently in use is an evolution of the one presented in the first OMT version (Rumbaugh, 1995).

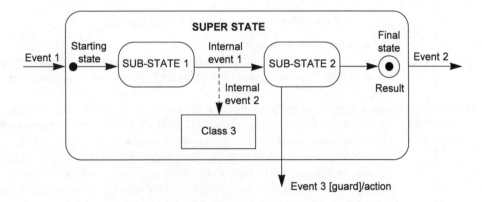

Figure 3.10 Extract from the notation for the OMT dynamic model.

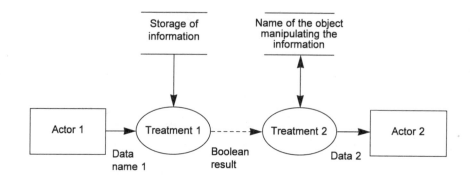

Figure 3.11 Extract from the first notation for the OMT1 functional model.

The OMT method seems sufficiently complete to tackle a wide category of problems. In our opinion it has the backing of the considerable experience of its authors and has merited its success. I personally have chosen this method for my teaching in a number of schools for French software engineers as well as at university. The only complaints we could make relate to the complexity of the formalism in the case of the object model diagrams (involving poor readability for complex systems); also, it seemed to us that the functional diagrams proposed in the first version of OMT moved away from the concepts of the object-oriented approach by separating the notion of processing from objects and by preventing a strong expression of the polymorphism (Figure 3.11). Recently, Rumbaugh proposed a new graphic formalism which takes account of the various comments made and instances of lack of understanding encountered with this model (Rumbaugh, 1995). New OMT features for operation specifications, object-oriented data flow diagrams and interaction diagrams (whether concurrent or not) satisfy many criticisms.

The trump cards of this method are principally:

- a very complete static model;
- use of the same graphic notation throughout the phases of analysis and design;
- a powerful description of the internal behaviour of the objects.

THE OBJECTORY METHOD OF IVAR JACOBSON

Objectory is a Swedish method proposing a procedure for tackling both the analysis and design of large systems (Jacobson, 1987). The Objectory method must be perceived as an extensible system which may be developed into several versions (extensions for real-time and distributed database systems have been designed (Jacobson *et al.*, 1992)). It covers the whole software development life cycle and its aim is classically to produce reliable software which is of good quality and can be cheaply maintained. The name used for the Objectory method (in the latest book by Jacobson (Jacobson *et al.*, 1992)) is OOSE, which stands for 'Object-Oriented

Software Engineering'. OOSE proposes a development process which produces five models:

- The requirements model
- The analysis model
- The design model
- The implementation model
- The test model.

These models are homogeneous so as to obtain good traceability of the objects. This means that it is possible to follow an object and its development from one model to another during the development process. As the models proposed by OOSE are closely coupled, this traceability becomes implicit. Another solution for traceability is proposed by the OSM model (Béjiven, 1995). OOSE assumes that the requirements specification is available in some (any) form. This allows a development process in three phases: analysis, construction and testing, providing the five aforementioned models (Figure 3.12). The requirements model must capture the functional requirements, the analysis model must supply a robust and modifiable structure of objects, the design model must refine and adapt this structure of objects to the target environment for implementation, and the test model must be capable of verifying the correct operation of the system.

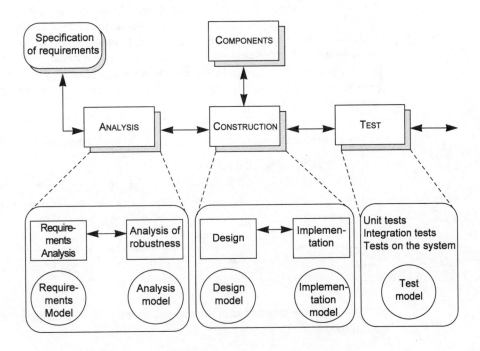

Figure 3.12 OOSE development process and associated models.

The analysis process produces two models on the basis of the requirements specification. It is first necessary to create a model in which it is possible to specify the functions required for the system (requirements model). In this model everything the system must be capable of doing must be specified. With OOSE this is principally done by means of scenarios called **'use cases'** in a 'use case model' which is a sub-part of the requirements model. This model is also used as the basis for the construction and test process. The requirements model is reused to create the analysis model which forms the basis of the structure of the system, by specifying all the objects which must be included in the software and by showing how they are linked together.

The construction process has the task of designing and implementing the computer system; it uses the requirements model and the analysis model as inputs. Design is given the task of producing a detailed specification of all objects and must take account of constraints imposed by the implementation environment. The implementation model corresponds to the source code which has to be tested in terms of requirements and of design. The test process requires as input the requirements model, the design model and the implementation model in order to provide a test model.

The design is based on the 'use case' model extracted from the requirements model. The 'use case' model uses **actors** and **'use cases'** (Figure 3.13). The actors are entities which exist outside the software system. An actor instance may, for example, be a user who carries out various operations with the system. These operations are organized into sequences of transactions which establish dialogues with the software system. These sequences of transactions are cases of utilization or 'use cases' which determine what the software system has to do. Each 'use case' is a particular way of using the system and each execution of a 'use case' may be considered as an instance of a 'use case' class. The 'use cases' are awaiting stimuli from an actor.

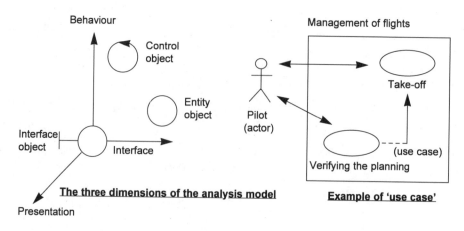

Figure 3.13 Dimensions of the analysis and 'use case' model.

The OOSE graphic notation proposes a distinction between three types of object: entity objects, control objects and interface objects.

These three categories are distributed in at least two of the three following dimensions: the information dimension, the behaviour dimension and the presentation dimension (Figure 3.13). The information dimension specifies the information generated by the software in the long and short term and also describes the internal state of the software system. The behaviour dimension describes the behaviour which the software must adopt by specifying how the software system changes state. The presentation dimension generates the interface and presentation details of the software in its dialogues with the external world. The OOSE state diagrams are specified with organization charts which we think are complex with regard to the number of symbols used (if you compare them with the OOD diagrams according to Booch or OMT) (Figure 3.14). The representation of the information part may also be complex.

In conclusion concerning this method, it is of course necessary to emphasize that analysis and design in OOSE is directed by the 'use cases' which are considered as classes with instances (on execution). The authors recognize (Jacobson *et al.*, 1992, p.130) that this view does not seem natural to people familiar with object-oriented programming.

It does seem that Objectory corresponds to an 'encapsulated' functional approach for the specification of requirements. This point of view is in our opinion very interesting for large projects. The consistency of the method and the taking into account of the requirements analysis and tests in the development life cycle, give a uniform technique. Moreover, the experience of the author with regard to this 'use case' approach, while keeping close to the object model, is worthy of interest.

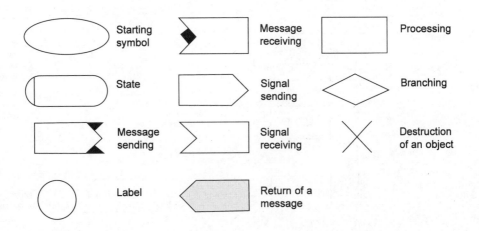

Figure 3.14 OOSE notation for state transition graphs.

A NUMBER OF   Within the domain of manufacturing systems and industrial engineering, there is
OTHER OBJECT-   also an object-oriented methodology for analysis and design. This is the MOOD
ORIENTED   (methodology for object-oriented design) method presented at the second Tools
METHODS   conference (Jochem *et al.*, 1989). Various classic methods for manufacturing
systems analysis are, moreover, compiled in Pierreval (1990).

Other references may be consulted regarding methods which only deal with object-oriented design, and the following list is not exhaustive: Bailin (1989), Dean (1991), Dixneuf and Aubert (1990), Wiener *et al.* (1990). Also, a certain number of methods, dealing only with object-oriented analysis, may be studied in Buchanan *et al.* (1991) and Sangbum and Carver (1991).

Certain methods are based mainly on events which control models of independent and cooperating objects (Martin *et al.*, 1991). These methods may be considered as deriving from the REMORA (Rolland *et al.*, 1988) method. Examples of the use of an object version of the REMORA method are given in Barbier and Jaulent (1992). There are also object-oriented design methods which are derived from E/R models (Mellor and Shlaer, 1988; Desfray 1989, 1990, 1994; Shlaer and Mellor, 1992) (Figure 3.15). In fact, it now seems trivial to associate the operations of an entity with the classic list of its attributes. Furthermore, an enrichment of graphic notation makes it possible, via relationships, to implement message sending, inheritance structures and composition (this was previously only possible through associations). Analysts and designers already trained in the E/R model (used for the Conceptual Data Model of the Merise method (Tardieu *et al.*, 1985)) are liable to adopt a method derived from the E/R model. It was with a view to this that the MOO method (an object variant of Merise) was created (Rochfeld, 1991, 1992). This method possesses interesting validation techniques, in particular for

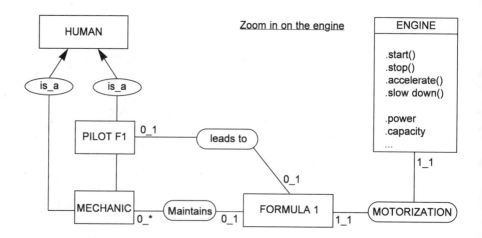

Figure 3.15 Extract from the graphic notation of the Desfray (1990) class/relation method.

dynamic aspects, by using entity life cycles and objects supported by Petri nets.

Some methods are described as being of the second generation, such as Syntropy by Cook and Daniels (1994), because they are based on existing works which have proved themselves. Syntropy is said to be more like a set of techniques and notations than a method. It presents special features, especially for the integration of special specifications in a graphic notation or for the incorporation of a concurrent architecture. Some of the techniques used by Syntropy come from work done on the Esprit project DRAGOON (Gilb, 1988). Another method deriving from work on the Esprit II project is the BON (Business Object Notation) method presented in Nerson (1992, 1995). It may also be considered as a second generation method in so far as it is based on the work done by Booch, Rumbaugh, Coad, Yourdon, Shlaer and Mellor.

It is a method which takes into account the point of view of the company and which proposes a continuity in development. Notions of view and of scale factors make it possible to tackle large projects while the logic of predicates guarantees constraint specification. The Eiffel Case tool supports the BON method even if this method remains independent of any programming language (Walden and Nerson, 1995). Another hybrid method of the second generation is proposed by Hewlett Packard from a synthesis of the most popular methods. This is the Fusion method which is aimed at simplifying certain aspects (notation, deletion of the state automaton describing the internal behaviour of objects, ...) (Coleman *et al.*, 1994).

Each method proposes its own graphic notation. The graphic notations supply excellent supports for representing the static and dynamic aspects of software. Likewise, textual notations are proposed to capture the various less visual aspects. As regards the static part of software, numerous authors propose diagrams to represent classes and their relations (Blaha *et al.*, 1991; Booch, 1991; Coad and Yourdon, 1991; Meyer, 1990; Rochfeld, 1992, ...). Descriptive sheets of classes describing their attributes and their methods are also used. These forms or sheets are known as CRC ('Class Responsibility Collaboration' forms (Beck and Cunningham, 1989)). The dynamic part of software is also represented by means of graphic notations. Thus we find state transition diagrams or execution diagrams giving the sequencing of the messages between the objects of the different classes. Some of these diagrams were presented in the figures illustrating notations of various methods. In most cases notations are often complex and may put people off using the methods. OOSD (Object-Oriented Structured Design) is a notation designed to assist the representation of object design work. This notation is independent of the various approaches used by object-oriented design methods. It was proposed in 1990 by Wasserman, Pircher and Muller (1990). Their authors wish to generalize this notation as a standard notation to represent design work in the same way as standard diagrams for representing electronic circuits (Figure 3.16).

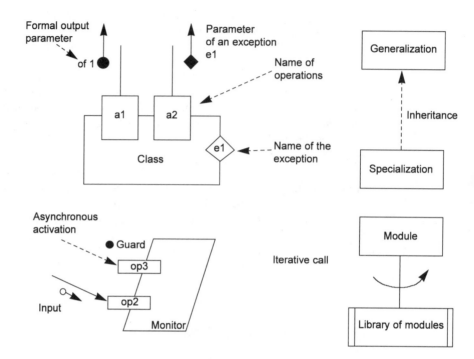

Figure 3.16 Extract from the OOSD graphic notation.

◁3.3 Conclusion

The concepts of the object model studied in the previous chapter have enabled us to tackle development life cycles and object-oriented analysis and design methods. An excellent study of analysis and design methods is given by Ian Graham (1994) and should usefully supplement this rapid tour of the methods. We have studied these methods because the analogy between software systems and models of real systems must allow us to find a set of tasks adapted to simulation modelling. We have announced that we are looking for an object-oriented analysis and design method adapted to both the modelling of real systems and the design of the corresponding simulation software. We are also seeking to separate the static aspects of a real system (structure of classes and description of the characteristics) from the dynamic aspects (making it possible to understand the operation of the system).

Amongst the methods presented, we did not find a modelling process which includes a domain analysis phase. We also wish to take this phase into account as well as decomposition into three subsystems (physical, logical and decisional) when this is necessary to establish simulation models.

This decomposition seems to us fundamental in order, on the one hand, to establish a clear and concise knowledge model and, on the other, to facilitate the generation of simulation code. This code generation will be based on the transaction flow of a system (defined by the logical subsystem), while being based on the two other subsystems. The experience of specialists in simulation also makes it possible to understand better the modelling of the dynamic aspects of systems. It is therefore necessary to profit from the contribution of the two communities by including results put forward by the static and dynamic modelling of software systems as well as the experience acquired by the simulation community in the dynamic aspects of complex systems (details of transactions in the systems modelled, modelling of complex object behaviour and interactions between these objects, the taking into account of dynamic classification, ...).

We will therefore identify the basic tasks of the principal methods of object-oriented analysis and design so as then to supplement them in terms of the objectives set down in Chapter 1. This work leads to the constitution of a software development life cycle adapted to the modelling of systems with a view to evaluating their performance by simulation. This will allow us to propose an object modelling method.

◁ KEY POINTS

- The traditional V or waterfall development process is too rigid to take account of the evolution of development methods using rapid prototyping which are offered by the object-oriented languages.
- The stages of object-oriented analysis and design are neither bottom-up nor top-down.
- Object analysis and design follow an incremental and iterative process where each stage is liable to supply information involving the modification of results of other stages, including previous stages which have already been completed.
- To obtain an effective procedure throughout the development process, it is preferable to think 'object' from the start of a project.
- It seems important to maintain an object-oriented approach for the analysis, design and implementation phases so as to obtain a seamless process and preserve consistency between the various stages. This consistency brings about an improvement in the traceability of objects.
- Four important categories of analysis and design methods may be distinguished: functional decomposition methods, methods based on data flow, information modelling methods and object-oriented methods.

◁ Exercise

3.1 We are trying to generate pieces of music on a computer. Each piece of music uses several channels (one channel being dedicated to one instrument, itself characterized by one particular sound). On each channel, we define a set of notes to be played by an instrument. The notes are defined by their frequency, their amplitude and their duration. The sounds associated with the instruments are defined, either by an envelope or by samples. A sample corresponds to the digitization of an analogue sound and therefore gives a set of values. The sounds and the pieces of music are stored in files. Use successively OOA, Objectory and OMT to carry out an analysis with a view to obtaining a prototype of a piece of musical sequencing software for a microcomputer. Refer to the works by Coad and Yourdon (1991), Blaha *et al.* (1991) and Jacobson *et al.* (1992) for details of the stages of these various methods.

4

Proposal of an object modelling method

◁ OBJECTIVES

This chapter first tries to describe the basic tasks of the various object-oriented analysis and design methods. The result of this will make it possible to propose a modelling process and an object modelling method (M2PO) adapted to discrete event simulation. It is not a matter of imposing another fresh method but rather of making an effort to bridge the gap between software engineers and simulationists. Again with the same concern in mind, we prefer not to introduce fresh graphic notation but stick to the most commonly used forms. The purpose is not, however, to bring together within one method as many composite elements as possible but to propose a reasonable degree of complexity, taking account of some of the concerns of the simulation community.

◁ 4.1 Introduction

Software designed using object-oriented concepts may be considered as a system of objects communicating by messages, each object being responsible for the accomplishment of certain actions which depend on its state and on its behaviour. This view of software is similar to that used with discrete event simulation, to model the various entities of a real system and to describe their interactions during simulation. Since the introduction of Simula there is a great analogy between the object-oriented development of software and the production of a simulation model. The idea of considering the object-oriented design of a software system as coming within the sphere of modelling is not new.

We must moreover quote Bertrand Meyer: 'in reality, whether physical or abstract, objects are present! ... it is not by accident that since Simula-67, simulation has been a preferred domain of object-oriented techniques. To model the real world with a view to simulating it, what better than describing the objects to be simulated.' (Meyer, 1990).

Preserving this analogy, it is first appropriate to identify the principal stages of object-oriented analysis and design methods. The contribution of certain adaptations specific to the simulation of complex systems allows us to create a modelling method which can also be used for software engineering. Following the study carried out in the first chapters, we shall summarize again here the principal objectives we set in 1992 for the development of a non-commercial object-oriented analysis and design method:

- To use the principal concepts of the object-oriented approach.
- To be able to carry out domain analyses.
- To take account of decomposition into three subsystems (physical, logical and decisional).
- To highlight the dynamic aspects.
- To detail transactions in the systems modelled.
- To take into account the validation and verification of the various models which the method will manipulate.

◁ 4.2 The work required for an object-oriented analysis and design method

4.2.1 Introduction

Design methods, whether presented or quoted, all propose a certain number of stages accompanied by a procedure peculiar to each author. We have tried to identify and classify the basic tasks in the methods we have studied. We have done this because, if the majority of methods have a great number of basic tasks in common, each possesses interesting special features which could be desirable to include in a fresh second generation object-oriented analysis and design method. We present a summary of the basic tasks which a designer is liable to undertake, and which are not intended to be carried out sequentially because the process of object-oriented design remains incremental and iterative. For each task, it is necessary to verify whether it is possible to reuse the existing results of analysis or design. The basic tasks we have selected from the methods studied (and in particular, Booch (1991)) are given below:

- Identification of the classes relating to the software system being designed.
- Classification by means of inheritance and aggregation.
- Establishment of communication relationships which exist between the various classes.
- Definition of structures permitting the objects to collaborate to achieve the objectives set down.

- Choice of the interface of classes with their internal representation.
- Evaluation of the quality of the results obtained.
- Improvement of the results until the desired level of detail is obtained.

The result of these tasks must lead to obtaining an object model which has a static and a dynamic part. The static part describes the structure of classes in terms of classification by inheritance and composition and of relationships between classes but also in terms of methods and attributes (whether for instances or classes). The basic dynamic part makes it possible to specify, on the one hand, interactions which exist between various objects and, on the other, the individual behaviour of objects. We shall take up each of these basic tasks in detail below.

Graphic and textual notations are generally used to document these various tasks. The graphic notations supply excellent support for representing static and dynamic aspects of a software system. The possibilities of graphic representations assist designers in concentrating on the structure of the system they are producing, before tackling the programming phase. The textual notations are also essential to capture various less visual aspects. The usefulness of descriptive forms for the characteristics of classes together with their attributes and methods need no longer be demonstrated (these forms are known as CRC (Class Responsibility Collaboration forms) (Beck and Cunningham, 1989). Figure 4.1 presents the template of a CRC form which comprises the name of the class concerned and the responsibilities assigned to it as well as references to other 'collaborating' objects which are necessary for the accomplishment of the services of this class. The individual behaviour of objects of a software system is usually represented by means of state transition diagrams (finite state automata, Petri nets, ...). Interactions between objects are specified by means of execution diagrams which give the sequencing of messages between objects of various classes and of chronograms for methods that also take real-time applications into account.

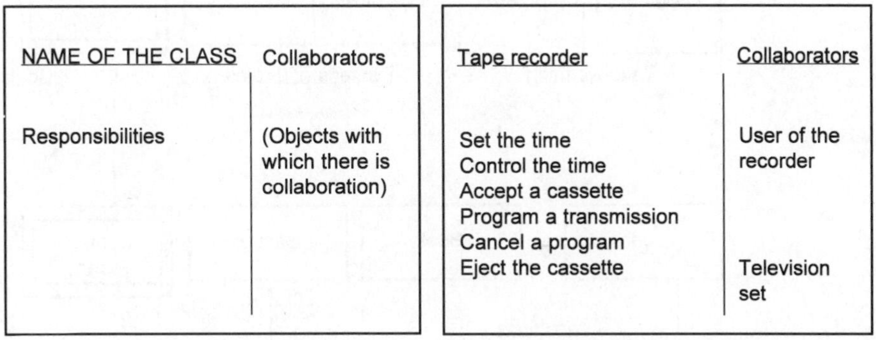

NAME OF THE CLASS	Collaborators	Tape recorder	Collaborators
Responsibilities	(Objects with which there is collaboration)	Set the time Control the time Accept a cassette Program a transmission Cancel a program Eject the cassette	User of the recorder Television set

Template of the CRC form   Example of the CRC form

Figure 4.1 Example of the CRC form for a video recorder.

4.2.2 Identification of classes

There is no deterministic procedure for identifying classes. This is a very difficult intellectual job which requires a huge amount of experience. Initially, it is a matter of recognizing abstractions and objects used by the experts in the field: it is a discovery phase. The choice of class names must reflect their meaning very precisely. It is necessary to verify whether we can reuse the results obtained for other designs or analyses already completed to solve similar problems. To facilitate the search for classes, there are non-exhaustive lists of various candidate objects as well as heuristic objects proposed by certain authors (Coad and Yourdon, 1991; Booch, 1991; Gamma *et al.*, 1994; Figure 4.2). It is also desirable, when studying large-scale complex software, to introduce the notion of object subsystems. These subsystems combine, for example, objects peculiar to a specific subject, carrying out a high-level function for the system to be modelled.

4.2.3 Establishing the relationships between classes

The collaboration of all the objects is essential to bring a system of objects to life. There are numerous types of relationships between objects which may indicate these forms of collaboration. We will present three types of relationship: two are

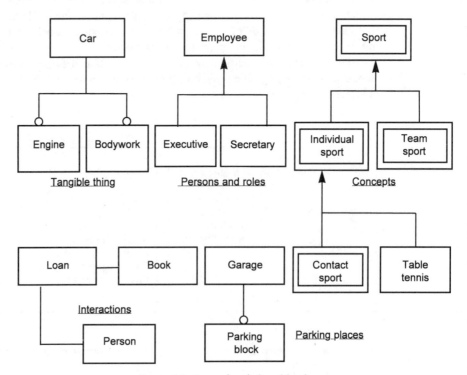

Figure 4.2 Example of plausible classes.

widely used during classification (inheritance and composition), and the third type deals with communications (interactions between objects). This distinction into three types of relations comes from ACE (Avoir (have), se Comporter (behave), Etre (be)), making it possible to specify a system of objects on three planes: structuring, inheritance and behaviour (Flory, 1991; Ayache and Ou-Halima, 1992). The three principal types of relation are as follows:

- **Inheritance relationship** ('is of type', 'is a') which is also known as the generalization/specialization relationship. This type of relationship is required to authorize multiple and selective inheritance (inheritance fault, violation of constraints, ...).

- **Aggregation relationship** or composition ('is composed of', 'comprises'). Aggregation is a strong form of association and not an independent concept. If two objects are closely linked by a Whole/Part relationship, the relation is an aggregation. If the other two objects are considered as separate, although they are frequently linked, this is a simple association. The distinction between the two concepts is often based on empiricism.

- **Communication relationship** or utilization. These relationships specify the type of interactions between two objects which communicate by messages. This type of relationship describes a part of the dynamic behaviour of the system to be modelled.

Numerous authors attach great importance to certain other relationships which are sometimes special cases of the three types presented. It seems to us important to present the following two other categories of relationship:

(1) **Instantiation relationship**. In addition to the classic instantiation relationship between a class and its objects, frequent use is made of parametrized classes (which implements genericity). Let us give an example: we have an abstract class to manipulate Binary Trees; if we wish to manipulate Binary Trees of People (People being a class of object), there will be an instantiation relation between the new class Binary Trees of People and the class Binary Trees (the generic parameter being the class People). The last use of the instantiation relationship concerns **metaclasses**. There is an instantiation relationship between the classes (considered as objects) and their descriptions called metaclasses.

(2) **Dynamic classification relationships**. These may be considered as a sub-category of the inheritance, communication and aggregation relationships. We distinguish two notions, the first closely linked to the notion of composition and the second to the notion of inheritance. The first notion appears when an object of a class is destroyed to transform into one or more objects of another class following a process or the occurrence of a special event; or when several objects are assembled to create a single entity (Figure 4.3). This type of relationship may take the form of several elementary communication and aggregation relationships. For example, when a sawn tree trunk generates several planks, there is an aggregation relationship between the trunk and the planks as well as a communication relationship between the machine

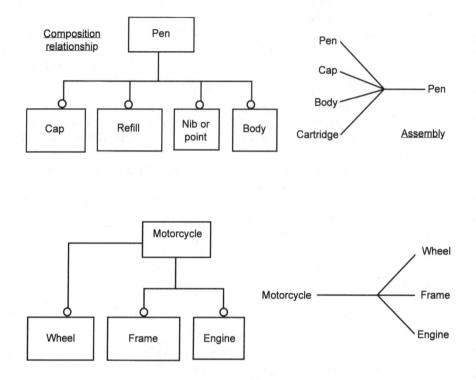

Figure 4.3 Creation and destruction of objects linked to composition relationships.

triggering the sawing operation and the trunk. The second notion appears when one and the same object may be attached to different classes during its life. This notion implements inheritance and communication. These are objects which follow linear transformations from an initial state to a final state. For example, in a factory the parts undergo various machining phases depending on their progress in a flexible workshop. The phenomenon is identical if we follow the evolution of a person entering a hospital and undergoing several treatments involving state changes. This notion is closely linked to the notion of inheritance, in practice, with all the classes to which an object may belong during its life possessing a common superclass. For example, bachelors and married persons are persons, and a bachelor will move to the 'married' class after a marriage ceremony (the two subclasses 'bachelor' and 'married' being legally exclusive). In order to avoid a proliferation of subclasses, this type of classification is elegantly dealt with by the typing links in Flory and Ayache (1993) and Figure 4.4.

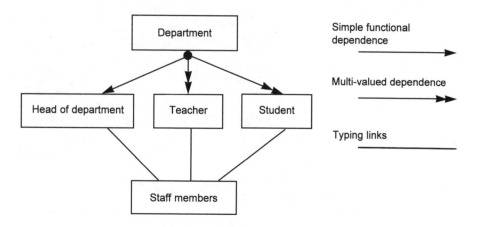

Figure 4.4 Use of typing links.

4.2.4 Classification

Classification is a tedious task. The classic analogy with biology gives an idea of the volume of work and amount of time necessary to find general and reusable models. The appropriate classification is complex to produce and it frequently happens that a class structure is proposed very early on, only for it to be revised as time passes. When classifying abstractions which have already been compiled, a great deal of creativity is needed to come up with abstract classes to simplify analysis and design. It is possible to state without exaggerating that there are as many classifications as there are scientists capable of carrying out the task. The discovery of pertinent general abstractions (abstract superclasses) requires a tremendous amount of creativity and experience.

The technique of classification by distribution into **categories** is the one most frequently used. We recognize the classes according to the knowledge we have of their properties and their behaviour. The properties and behaviour selected must be such that all the classes which possess a set of common properties and forms of behaviour together form a category which in itself constitutes a class (in the most frequent case, this is an abstract superclass). As regards classification, Booch (1991) mentions a technique of Marvin Minsky which suggests that the most useful sets of properties for the identification of objects are those where members do not interact too much. He gives the example of the combination of the following properties: colour, size, shape and substance. Since these attributes hardly interact, it is possible to use any combination to create a small or large object, red or green, spherical or cubic, in wood or in glass (Figure 4.5).

It is important to stress that the quality of the classification work is bound up with the knowledge we have of the domain in which the model is to be produced. Inheritance and aggregation techniques assist in controlling the complexity of a

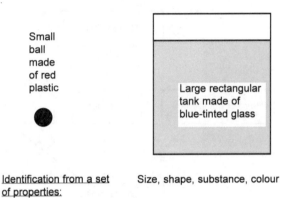

Small
ball
made
of red
plastic

Large rectangular
tank made of
blue-tinted glass

<u>Identification from a set
of properties:</u>   Size, shape, substance, colour

Figure 4.5 Example of a set of properties with few interactions for the
identification of objects.

problem. However, they may be a fresh source of complexity if we obtain
classification levels which are too large (an inheritance graph which is too deep,
nomenclature which is too detailed). It is, moreover, very difficult to set a limit on
these levels of abstraction; perhaps it is necessary to set the limit at the famous figure
of 7 plus or minus 2.

If the design of classes and structure of classes is laborious and tricky, it is
necessary to recognize that apart from the most trivial cases, it is impossible to
propose good abstractions as well as a good classification right from the first
iteration. This is why criteria for the evaluation of the quality of an object-oriented
design have been proposed (Wiener *et al.*, 1990; Booch, 1991; Blaha *et al.*,
1991).

4.2.5 Organization of the tasks of objects

With analysis, a description and a specification are established, and classes and class
structures peculiar to the problem for which a model is to be produced are
identified. At the design stage, it is necessary to invent new classes which constitute
substantial structures and which make it possible to provide the expected behaviour
of the future software. The term used by Booch (1991) to designate these structures
is mechanism. The invention of mechanisms represents a design decision
concerning the way in which objects cooperate (the structure of a synchronizing
kernel for a simulator or algorithms of a window manager are examples of
mechanisms). Mechanisms are objects capable of making great use of reusable
component classes (data structures, user interface objects, ...).

The control of a fairly complete library of components may, moreover,
constitute a new form of complexity. It is appropriate not to ignore this complexity

by supplying software tools adapted to the management of such libraries, for example Digital Librarian under NeXTstep (or more recently OpenStep).

4.2.6 The choice of attributes and methods

This means selecting attributes and methods for instances and classes. In certain cases, it is necessary to choose between storing a state (in an attribute) or calculating its value by a method. The choice of one solution rather than another is tricky and depends on the problem concerned as well as the efficiency sought (in time or in space). It also happens that a state is implemented by a procedure when, for example, an attribute is a function of time. Thus the fuel level of an F1 engine is a function of engine load, speed, and so on. This is a state variable of a Formula 1 object which will be implemented by a method (Figure 4.6).

When the level of detail begins to become refined, the precise choice of attributes and methods comes within the sphere of the design of a solution. Apart from making a distinction between private (or internal) methods, not visible through the objects of other classes, and public methods (always accessible), the following categories are frequently encountered:

- Calculating and processing methods which, for passive objects, correspond to procedures activated by external events (requirement for service by another object). Certain calculation or processing methods may be internal methods.
- Modification methods (object states). The state of an object takes account of all attributes of an object and in particular those where values evolve continuously.
- Consultation methods. These methods stem from the principle of encapsulation and allow access to the attributes of an object without modifying them.

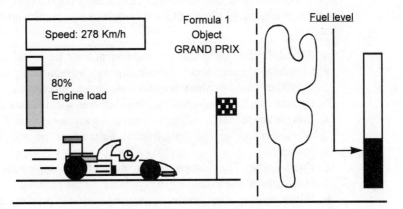

Figure 4.6 Fuel level attribute.

Amongst other categories of methods a little less frequently encountered, we find:

- Scripts which determine for active objects what their behaviour is going to be over time. They correspond to control flows and an actor (active object) may possibly change script (equivalent to a dynamic classification).
- Methods described as 'iterations'. They allow access to all the parts of an object in a properly defined order, for example covering a table object to effect certain operations on the elements of the table.
- Construction and/or initialization methods of objects. These are methods which create objects and/or which initialize their states. Pure construction methods must be considered as class methods.
- Object destruction methods. These specify details of the operations to be carried out when an object is deleted (whether its allocation was static or dynamic). Systems which propose a garbage collector need not consider these methods.

All of the public methods of a class (which are directly accessible by objects of other classes) define the interface (or the protocol) of the objects of this class. The establishment of an interface is a complex job. The classic technique consists of proposing an interface template with the standard knowledge; then, when other potential needs arise, it is necessary to modify and refine this interface. It even happens that groups of methods lead to inventing new abstract classes or to reorganizing the relationships between existing classes. This confirms the incremental and iterative approach of the analysis and design process. Other questions arise; should an interface propose a lot of elementary methods (the interface becoming perhaps too large) or a few powerful methods (the methods proposed then being complex)? The choices which are made often depend on past experience and require both an excellent knowledge of the field of application and a good understanding of the object development mechanism (Coad and Yourdon, 1991). Criteria retained for the design of interfaces are reusability and applicability, coupling, consistency, complexity and completeness, primitiveness, and sufficiency (Booch, 1991).

- Reusability. Assume that the component may be useful in another context.
- Coupling. The complexity of software may be reduced by constructing classes with the least coupling possible. However, inheritance, which is desired, introduces a high degree of coupling between superclasses and subclasses.
- Completeness. This suggests that a class has to take into account all characteristics and all significant behaviours of the abstraction being studied.
- Complexity. The component is difficult to implement and understand (difficulty of understanding the operation of the methods).
- Primitiveness. The classes must provide the primary methods in their interfaces, that is, those which may be effectively implemented and have a simple behaviour.

- Consistency. This measures the degree of connection between the elements (attributes, methods) of one and the same class (elements should not be grouped together within one and the same class by pure coincidence).
- Sufficiency. This means that the class has sufficient characteristics to allow effective interactions with other classes.

It is impossible to satisfy all these criteria at the same time and the complexity criterion should be avoided. In fact, while sufficiency suggests the establishment of a minimum interface, a complete class has to provide a fairly general interface if it is to be usable by any other client class. For a good design, a compromise must be made between these criteria by taking account of the problem to be dealt with.

4.3 Definition of an object modelling process

4.3.1 Introduction

The object modelling process we propose is derived from the main software development cycles presented and was introduced in 1992. It includes the concepts of the modelling process, which was summarized in Chapter 1 (Figure 1.2). This makes it possible to take up a position in a more general modelling framework than that of the creation of software, while taking into account the point of view of simulation experts (Hill, 1993). It seems to us that it is now recognized that the specification of models embraces the specification of software. The creation of object models intended to simulate or drive complex systems thus uses the advanced techniques of software engineering, associated with concepts used in simulation. Considering the contributions of simulation to software production techniques (Simula, 1967), it seems natural that modelling and simulation of complex systems should benefit in return from the progress in software engineering. It is with this in mind that we have effected a comparative synthesis of the principal life cycles of object-oriented development, as well as of the main object-oriented analysis and design methods (Hill, 1992).

4.3.2 Proposal for an object modelling cycle

OBJECT-
ORIENTED
DOMAIN
ANALYSIS

The general view of the modelling life cycle we propose takes account successively of a domain analysis, object-oriented analysis, object-oriented design and finally implementation. By analogy with software, maintenance constitutes the main part of the model life in view of evolutions and the correction of errors. The cycle we propose is incremental and iterative, each stage being capable of feeding the others. The cycle is stopped as soon as the level of information reached is judged sufficient by the modelling expert. Figure 4.7 is a diagram of the modelling process

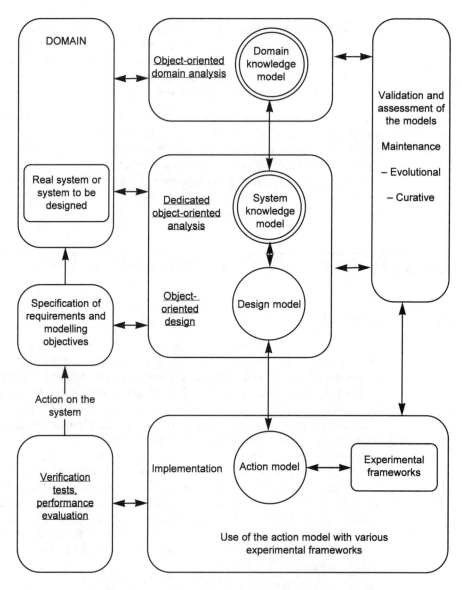

Figure 4.7 General view of the object modelling process.

we propose. Let it be noted that as regards the object-oriented analysis phase, we assume that the specification of requirements is done and available in some form or other. The preparation of test plans for the verification and validation of the software implemented is also required.

The identification of classes (in the sense of 'object') common to all the applications of a particular domain still remains one of the most tedious tasks of analysis and the quality of abstractions obtained still remains closely linked to the

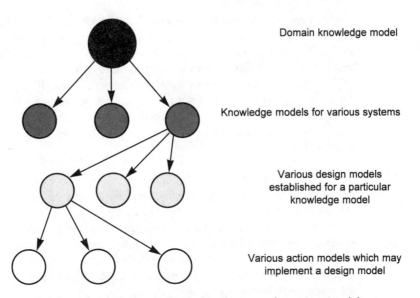

Domain knowledge model

Knowledge models for various systems

Various design models
established for a particular
knowledge model

Various action models which may
implement a design model

Figure 4.8 Hierarchical relationships between the various models.

experience of modelling specialists. Objects, relationships and behaviour discovered and retained must be those which are perceived as being important by experts in the domain. The result of this work constitutes a domain knowledge model, which also comprises a glossary giving the experts' vocabulary. With the recommended procedure, it is possible to reuse the results of a domain analysis, in order to initialize object-oriented analyses for other systems in the same domain. The hierarchical relationships between various models are given in Figure 4.8. The terminology problems linked to specific domains must not be ignored.

The construction of glossaries and their integration within the domain knowledge model has turned out to be essential.

**OBJECT-
ORIENTED
ANALYSIS OF
A PARTICULAR
SYSTEM**

In the modelling cycle we propose, we consider that object-oriented analysis is used for a single system in a particular domain. In fact, an object-oriented analysis method requires concentration on one problem at a time; an effort is made to model the system concerned by identifying only classes of the real world necessary for the establishment of a system knowledge model. This knowledge model must provide a complete description of the system which can be validated in relation to reality, is consistent, legible and can be revised by the various parties involved (in particular the experts of the system in question).

The terminology used must always be that of domain experts. Object-oriented analysis can correspond to an extraction of a set of classes and relationships of the previously established domain knowledge model (in accordance with a filter adapted to the system to be modelled). The system knowledge model still constitutes a sub-set of the domain knowledge model. If this is not the case, that is, the system to be modelled has classes and/or relationships which are not in the domain knowledge model, then we must update this knowledge model so that gradually it becomes complete. On the other hand, no attempt at solving the problem posed need be undertaken at the object-oriented analysis phase. The search for a solution is reserved for the design phase and constitutes, in a way, the boundary between the 'What' (analysis) and the 'How' (design). Concerning specification of needs which must be achieved in the analysis phase, we recommend the building of a requirements model such as the one developed in Objectory (Jacobson, 1992). Establishing good requirements models is complex and falls outside this general presentation.

OBJECT-
ORIENTED
DESIGN

The design phase must allow the computer scientist to express the structure and operation of the software system which will implement the action model, and to do this by using software-engineering terminology.

The object-oriented design phase therefore leads to the construction of a system of objects, which constitute a 'design model' of the action model to be produced. The design phase determines the level of simplification and/or detail used for modelling in terms of objectives set for the design of the system (the questions the model must answer).

This design model must consist of (1) the classes and relationships from the real world peculiar to the system dealt with (consisting of domain analysis results followed by an object-oriented analysis) and (2) the classes reflecting the internal structure of the software system to be designed (Figure 4.9). Classes which describe the internal structure of the software belong to one of three categories.

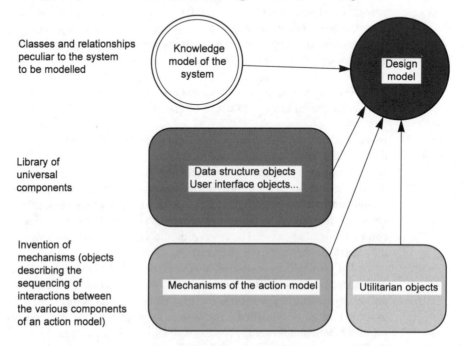

Classes and relationships peculiar to the system to be modelled

Knowledge model of the system

Design model

Library of universal components

Data structure objects
User interface objects...

Invention of mechanisms (objects describing the sequencing of interactions between the various components of an action model)

Mechanisms of the action model

Utilitarian objects

Figure 4.9 Construction of a design model.

The first category comprises classes of universal components (for example, managing data structures, user interface objects, and so on). The second category contains classes invented and introduced to solve the problem at hand, which govern interactions between objects of the design model (the synchronizing kernel of a simulator, event dispatcher for a user interface, ...), or those which reflect design optimization choices and which are linked to the algorithms used. These objects are the mechanisms of a design model; they govern interactions between and with the other objects of the system. The third category of objects is used to combine the utility functions which provide general services (mathematical objects for the mathematical functions, numerical algorithms, ...). With this last category we encounter the limits of the object-oriented approach, for the cohesion of methods grouped together in these classes of objects is slight (we are as liable to find a fast Fourier transformation as a simplex algorithm).

IMPLEMENT-
ATION

The implementation phase comprises the coding of an action model on a target platform, followed by various stages of tests, then validation of the action model when it is used 'for real'. There may be several action models for one and the same design model (different target machines, tools for evaluating performance or different simulation languages, ...). Separation of the model and its experimental frameworks is based on the theoretic concepts of Zeigler (1976). The action model of a system implements the static and dynamic characteristics of a system. The experimentation framework defines the conditions under which an action model is executed. It is thereby possible to effect a great many analyses of the action model, modifying only the value of certain parameters. As we have already stated, we shall not tackle the preparations for the validation and verification tests on models, since these would require an entire book to themselves (see Chapter 1).

The maintenance phase, whether curative or evolutionary, may involve questions being raised and modifications to results obtained with other phases. In fact, certain changes in the specification (the addition of knowledge or functions or corrections of errors) may throw the design or analysis off track. No work may be considered as perfect or complete. The rejection of certain changes is compared to the strategy of the Maginot line by Cox and Novobilski (1986). Meyer, who links up the design and implementation work to a high degree (Eiffel being an example of an object-oriented language including numerous design elements), also recommends that modifications be made if they are likely to improve the solution to the problem concerned. One of the reasons why a great many desirable modifications cannot be effected is the problem of compatibility with previous work (Meyer, 1988).

Even if we no longer consider the programming techniques in detail, it is impossible to talk of object-oriented implementation without slipping in a word for NeXTStep. This is not just because NeXT GUI is the easiest to use on the market, but also a matter of the best development environment at present available. The excellence and constant progress in the quality of object development tools proposed under NeXTStep cannot be compared with any other environment. This is so obvious that it becomes intellectually difficult ever to work with more primitive tools again. The dynamism of NeXT developers shows the path to be followed by other companies which have been inspired by it for several years.

◁4.4 Proposal for an object modelling method

4.4.1 General presentation

The M2PO (Méthode de Modelisation par Objets – Object Modelling Method) we propose follows the modelling process shown in Figure 4.7 and was presented in France in 1992. M2PO may be considered as a second generation hybrid method, for it is based both on a synthesis of various basic trends of the main object-oriented analysis and design methods, and on a set of criteria judged essential for the production of object models to simulate and control complex discrete flow systems (Hill, 1993). The viewpoint of a simulation specialist must allow the modelling of complex systems generally without being limited to software systems.

The M2PO method comprises the following phases, which arise out of the object modelling process proposed previously (Figure 4.10):

Phase 1: An object-oriented domain analysis

Phase 2: An object-oriented analysis for the system to be modelled

Phase 3: An object-oriented design providing a solution to the modelling problem posed.

The phases involved in specifying requirements, implementation and tests do not depart from the M2PO method proposals and can be tackled by other

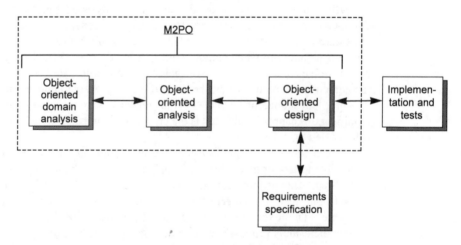

Figure 4.10 The M2PO method phases.

methods. Implementation with object-oriented programming providing an action model must follow phase 3. However, we do not give details about this phase, nor about the test preparation phase. Various existing methods or solutions suffice without us having to add new techniques of our own. In addition, the requirements specification is now handled successfully (Jacobson *et al.*, 1992; Graham, 1994; Rumbaugh, 1994) and we see no use in proposing other techniques when those that already exist (for example, 'use case'-based specifications) are powerful and meet with increasing success (Jacobson, 1995).

We now specify the basic objectives laid down for M2PO:

- Use all the major concepts of the object-oriented approach, recommending the use of abstract classes everywhere this is possible. Preserve this approach for all the phases of the modelling process, from domain analysis to implementation, in order to have consistent models.
- Separate the static and dynamic aspects of the systems to be modelled.
- Use a simple and unified textual and graphic notation for all the phases of the modelling process. This notation must be independent of any object-oriented programming language, and must be capable of supporting the majority of the object model concepts. These characteristics must make the notation easily adaptable to other object-oriented analysis and design methods.
- Promote reusability, not only at the level of the codes of objects produced, but also at the analysis and design level. There is no doubt that the effectiveness of reusability at the analysis level benefits the construction of domain knowledge models.

Other objectives are intended to include in the M2PO method the aspects specific to the modelling of complex discrete flow systems, with a view to their simulation:

- Taking into account decomposition into three subsystems (physical, logical and decisional), previously introduced.
- Detailing transactions, in the systems modelled, by separating the active and passive resources.
- Highlighting the dynamic aspects of the systems modelled as well as their reaction potential, controlled by the decisional subsystem.
- Taking into account the model separation and its experimental frameworks, following the M2PO modelling process.
- Validation and verification of various models with a view to effecting consistent simulations and animations. This type of validation supplements the advanced verification techniques coming from the software engineering community.
- Construction of technical glossaries peculiar to the terminology of domains concerned. These glossaries constitute the generalization of data dictionaries.

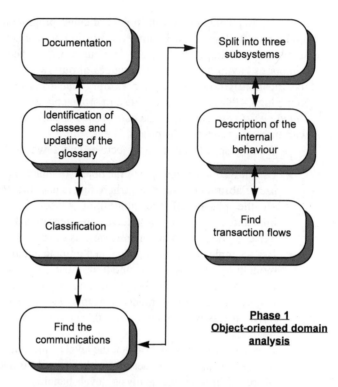

Figure 4.11 M2PO domain analysis phase.

4.4.2 Stages of main M2PO phases

PHASE 1:
OBJECT-
ORIENTED
DOMAIN
ANALYSIS

A list of the actual stages of the domain analysis phase is given in Figure 4.11. *These stages need not be considered as sequential and some of them may be optional, depending on the applications encountered:*

(1) Obtain all possible documentation concerning the relevant domain. Instigate close collaboration with experts in the domain, involving them as much as possible in the modelling projects.

(2) Identify the classes of objects which are essential to experts, isolating the characteristic attributes and methods of each class. Use data analysis techniques to determine reliably the attributes linked to the stochastic behaviour of certain classes of objects. This work is fundamental in obtaining consistent simulation results. Update the domain glossary for each class.

(3) Establish the static structure of classes using various relationships (inheritance, composition, instantiation, and so on). Discover the abstract classes which allow simplification of the knowledge model.

(4) Identify the communication (or utilization) relationships between objects of the various classes. Initially, the abstraction level remains high; it is sufficient to know the classes that have objects which communicate, without needing to

know the type and the quantity of messages. Secondly, it is appropriate to determine gradually the detail of the information exchanged, using a top-down hierarchical approach. At this stage, it is possible to identify the specific classes likely to use delegation, dynamic classification or dynamic inheritance.

(5) In the case of a simulation study, check the opportunity to distribute the classes obtained into the physical, logical and decisional subsystems as defined in Chapter 1. For each subsystem and if the size of the model requires it, effect hierarchical decompositions again into object subsystems, each dealing with a particular subject. Establish the communications which exist between the various subsystems.

(6) Determine the internal behaviour for classes of objects which have significant dynamic behaviour (an object life cycle is established in this way). This stage comprises the search for all events occurring significantly in an object's life, and makes it possible to establish scenarios (or traces of events) which are useful for the phases of testing and validating the models obtained.

(7) Find the transactions and discrete flows of the system. In a simulation case study, this phase has the effect of supplementing the information of classes belonging to the logical subsystem, while establishing in detail the transactions of this subsystem which make use of objects of the physical subsystem. This is a matter of taking into account discrete flow classes which pass through the system, the list of operation sequences applied to them, and the specification of demands and yields of passive resources as well as the various routing rules connected with them. The overall operating rules are peculiar to the decisional subsystem.

PHASE 2: OBJECT-ORIENTED ANALYSIS

The stages to be carried out for the object-oriented analysis of a system, in accordance with M2PO, are given below:

(1) If a domain analysis was carried out then extract from the domain knowledge model everything relating to the system to be modelled, in order to constitute the knowledge model of the system.

(2) If no domain analysis was carried out, then start the domain knowledge model using an initial analysis peculiar to the system studied. The knowledge of the system to be modelled will then constitute the inital domain knowledge model that will be augmented with future analysis.

PHASE 3: OBJECT-ORIENTED DESIGN

The stages involved in object-oriented design for M2PO are as follows (Figure 4.12):

(1) If necessary, invent mechanism objects which will govern the operation of the action model and allow objects of the system to collaborate in an organized way. This will permit the system to be capable of replying effectively to questions put to the action model. This stage includes the search for attributes and principal methods of mechanism objects.

(2) Identify and choose all the utility objects, as well as universal component objects which the mechanism objects require.

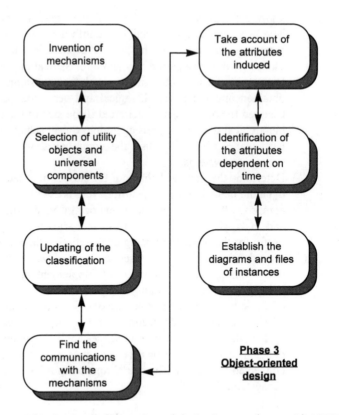

Figure 4.12 Stages of object-oriented design in accordance with M2PO.

(3) Update the classification established by the analysis phase in order to integrate, if necessary, the objects introduced at stages 1 and 2.

(4) Establish the communication (or utilization) relationships between mechanism objects and all the other object classes (objects of the system, universal component objects, utility objects, ...). Refine to the level of detail required by using a hierarchical decomposition. Determine the internal behaviour of mechanism objects.

(5) For all classes, take account of all attributes induced by certain relationships between classes introduced into the analysis phase. These attributes are essentially references to other objects (aggregation relationships for macro-objects, reference attributes for classes possessing common connections, reference attributes for agents of delegation relationships, ...).

(6) In the case of a simulation study, identify the attributes of instances which depend on time, and/or which frequently vary during the simulation time. For reasons of the effectiveness of the action model, it is often desirable that these attributes be implemented with functions. On the other hand, if these attributes are intended to be saved and restored (there is a need for

persistence), it is a good idea to consider an implementation by means of a variable, of access initialization and/or modification methods necessary to guarantee the principle of encapsulation. If choosing an implementation by variable, give the default values to be assigned when the variable is initialized.

(7) When adapted, count all the instances of classes corresponding to objects of the real system modelled and if necessary establish an instance diagram which can augment the knowledge model of the system. Establish an instance-card file for each instance by compiling the known values of its attributes, including the references to other instances (implementation of relationships).

After the completion of the stages recommended by these three phases, the implementation of an action model in an object-oriented language for discrete event simulation must be carried out. If there are problems in translating the design model into an action model, it will be necessary to modify the model and to refine the level of detail of the results provided by the various stages.

Let us remember that the stages presented in each phase are not necessarily carried out sequentially, for the modelling process remains incremental and iterative. Furthermore, certain stages may be optional, depending on the applications encountered. For each stage it is always advisable to check whether it is possible to reuse earlier results prepared for other studies.

4.4.3   Results provided by the application of M2PO

For the object-oriented analysis and design results, we retain only two dimensions (certain methods use three, such as OOM or OMT). The first dimension concerns the static aspects (descriptive) of the system, and the second concerns the dynamic aspects. This split is found again in the various models (domain knowledge model, system knowledge model and design model), as well as in results which we wish to obtain gradually, by completing the aforementioned basic tasks. The possible categories of results we propose are:

For the static part:

- Classification diagrams with class structures.
- A textual description of classes with CAC forms.
- A description of instances with specific forms.
- Instance diagrams.
- A glossary (one for each domain).

For the dynamic part:

- Interactions between objects and between subsystems with message flow diagrams.
- Internal behaviours of objects specified with extended Petri nets.
- Sequences of operations associated with the flow circulation diagrams.

- Scenarios (and traces of events).
- Dynamic classification relationships.

Scenarios or traces of events may be associated with message flow diagrams, with specifications of internal behaviours and with the transactions effected by system flows.

Thanks to the qualities of unification provided by the object-oriented approach, it is possible to keep the same categories of results throughout the phases of analysis and design; this is now called the seamlessness of the modelling process. Only the number of classes and the level of detail will change. For the remainder of our presentation, we have chosen to present our method in relation to the two dimensions (static and dynamic) and to the categories of results which we propose (Figure 4.13). The notation used will present the various phases (domain analysis, system analysis, design, ...), since the notation which we will introduce to present the results is the same for all the phases of the modelling cycle (enforcing the seamless process). The phases of domain analysis and object-oriented analysis provide the

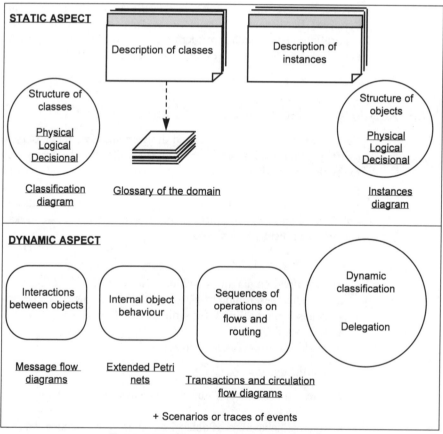

Figure 4.13 The various categories of results.

same categories of results, with object-oriented analysis supplying a subset of the results obtained by domain analysis.

As regards the elementary stages of the various phases presented, the identification of classes and objects (the classes may be objects with their methods and attributes) must provide a summary description of their characteristics and interfaces. This description is presented in a textual notation and feeds the object dictionary (glossary). The establishment of relationships between classes makes it possible to constitute classification diagrams (static and dynamic) as well as message flow diagrams (utilization relationships). We also find the notion of concurrency, affecting the dynamic aspect of a system of objects. Concurrency may occur at the level of internal object behaviour (several control flows within one and the same object) and at the overall level of object interactions (message flow between active objects each having one or several control flows of their own). These choices are highlighted, on the one hand, by the use of extended Petri nets to specify the internal behaviour of objects, and on the other, by the use of hierarchized message flow diagrams for communications at different levels of abstraction. Processing undergone by system flows are studied with diagrams which highlight various possible paths.

4.4.4 The choice of a graphic and textual notation

We have already mentioned the advantages of using graphic and textual notations for various categories of results. The choice of one notation rather than another still remains a question of personal preference (just like the choice of word processor, or a car). That is why, while waiting for a hypothetical standard, it is necessary either to make a choice from the existing notations (Wasserman *et al.*, 1990; Coad and Yourdon, 1991; Booch, 1991; Blaha *et al.*, 1991), or to propose a form of notation. The use of CASE tools adapted to the proposed methods and notations is a safe means of concentrating the knowledge of a great many experts on complex systems in a single location. However, these types of tools, although essential for large projects, must not slow down the small rapid vocational developments whose schemes and diagrams must be easy to trace in pencil on the corner of a table.

So far we have found no simple graphic notation which allows the majority of the concepts to be supported simply (which is easy to understand since the more you wish to add concepts the more you multiply the graphic symbols). To model complex systems, we chose to design a new notation, rather than extend or modify an existing form of notation. We preferred to stick to a very small number of symbols, which were widely used just before the explosion of methods and notations. Working with students has shown us that if you wish to make them use a method it must be based on only a few symbols. The graphic and textual notation we use must be just as easy to use with paper and ink as with a CASE tool. This notation proposes various layers, which may be considered as slides (as in OOA according to Coad and Yourdon), and it supports the various categories of results presented. We believe that this notation is sufficiently flexible to be used continuously throughout the proposed modelling process.

4.4.5 Taking static aspects into account with M2PO

GENERAL
PRESENTATION

The static aspect deals with most standard relationships between classes using a graphic notation. The graphic notation used does not give details of class interfaces, still less a description of their attributes. Our teaching experience makes us strongly reject any graphic notation taking account of these details on classification diagrams. In fact, it becomes relatively difficult to understand the semantics of a diagram if we are looking at diagrams including more than about ten methods and attributes for each class (which is far from being rare ...). What is more, no one may reasonably state that such diagrams are legible when you are studying systems which have over ten classes. That is the reason why we propose to use a textual notation, separate from graphic classification diagrams, to describe interfaces in detail (as well as the private parts of the classes). This procedure stems from the CRC (Class Responsibility Collaboration) charts of Beck and Cunningham (1989), where, on the visible face of a chart, we find the name of the class concerned and its interface, and on the hidden face (the other side of the chart), the private parts. The suppression of attributes and methods in classification diagrams greatly helps in keeping our minds at the high abstraction level necessary for analysis and design reusability.

THE GRAPHIC
NOTATION
FOR THE
STATIC ASPECT

In our graphic notation a classification diagram consists of several layers, which may be considered as slides to be displayed separately or combined if this is consistent. To describe the static aspect, we believe that eight layers are sufficient for the complex systems we have encountered. Not all the layers are necessarily present in each model! A substantial number of systems may be represented by using only the first four layers. A descriptive list of the layers is as follows:

A: The class layer concerns the graphic representation of classes.
B: The inheritance layer deals with simple and multiple generalization/ specialization relationships.
C: The composition layer manages Whole/Parts, aggregation and have relationships.
D: The association layer takes account of the connections between objects which make use of the utilization relationships (for example: acts on, requires, works for ...) or relationships which are not Whole/Parts relationships (for example: knows, is linked).
E: The genericity layer deals with instantiation relationships.
F: The subsystem layer introduces the notion of subsystems of objects in order to understand hierarchically a part of the complexity. Decomposition into three subsystems (physical, logical and decisional), proposed in the SIGMA methods, is taken up again for simulation models. Other subsystems are frequently necessary for large-scale systems.
G: The constraints layer is concerned with constraints (functional relationships between the various elements of a system of objects).
H: The instance layer makes it possible to display the static structure *of the objects* (and not of the classes) which make up the system if this is necessary.

The class layer — The graphic notation uses classic rectangles to represent classes. A visual distinction is made between an abstract class and concrete classes which possess instances.

The inheritance layer — To deal with simple and multiple generalization/specialization relationships we will adopt a very widely used graphic notation, namely an arrow pointing from subclasses to superclasses.

As regards inheritance, we believe that construction inheritances are analysis errors due to bad practice in object-oriented programming. When the splitting up or bringing together of functions seems interesting and there is no specialization notion, then it is appropriate to use the concept of delegation. It may be considered that a horizontal type relationship should be used, rather than a vertical type relationship such as inheritance. The graphic notation proposed for inheritance and for abstract and specific classes is given in Figure 4.14. The constraints on inheritance are specified with the textual notation in order not to overload diagrams.

Aggregation or composition — We propose a graphic notation for the Whole/Parts relation, classically using a link and cardinal numbers as a primitive form of constraint. *When a cardinal number is not specified, it is equal to one.* (Some people do, however, wish to display the cardinal number 1; no constraint is imposed at this level). Visually a Part is attached to a Whole by a bonding point (small empty circle) and the cardinal number is specified at the side of the Whole. This relation may involve a certain number of questions such as: When a Whole is destroyed, are the parts destroyed? In reply to this question we produce two notions: the notion of an aggregate and the notion of a macro-object. A macro-object is destroyed without destroying its sub-parts, while an aggregate is destroyed along with its sub-parts.

There may also be another question: can an object outside a macro-object, or an aggregate, communicate directly with an object which is a sub-part of the macro-object or the aggregate? Here is our point of view on this matter: if the reply is yes and the Whole is an aggregate, then there is a violation of the principle of encapsulation (the extension of encapsulation to Whole/Parts relationships is called

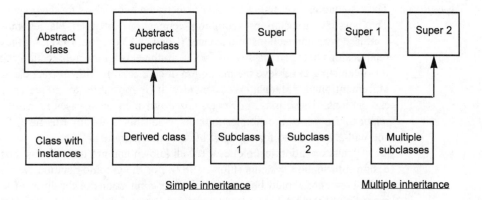

Figure 4.14 Graphic formalism adopted for inheritance and abstract classes.

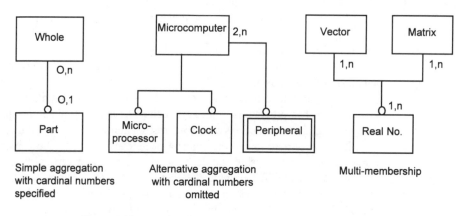

Figure 4.15 Graphic formalism for aggregation relationships.

lexical encapsulation). On the other hand, if the Whole is a macro-object, we consider objects which are sub-parts as being free (thus encapsulation is not violated), the macro-object being only a set of references to other objects. As regards the problem of multiple membership, we consider that it is possible for one Part of a macro-object to belong to several Wholes.

It is important, if possible, to use abstract classes to the maximum in composition relationships for this involves numerous simplifications of reasoning and considerably increases the legibility of diagrams, which are relieved of a great many relationships.

The first diagram of Figure 4.15 reads as follows: a whole consists of 0 to n parts and one part belongs or does not belong to a whole. The second diagram uses implicit cardinal numbers which may be omitted when they are equal to 1. The diagram is translated as follows: a computer has a single microprocessor and a single clock but at least two peripherals.

The association layer   The association layer uses a simple link between two classes for the graphic notation. The possible associations (common connection) between classes must not be confused with connections of instances (Coad and Yourdon, 1991), for these are also relationships between classes. In fact, as in the case of the aggregation relationship, it is interesting to achieve the maximum of connections with abstract classes, for the aforementioned reasons. We consider it is possible to conceive n-number associations. These may, however, come down in most cases to a set of binary relationships which are simpler to understand (this is already true for E/R diagrams and will always be so for any kind of derivate diagrams).

Transformation techniques are well known and are the same as those used to design information systems (Flory, 1987). For the graphic notation we recommend that a comment should be specified for the connections in the form of a verb. An example of Figure 4.16 uses the expression 'knows', which, in taking account of the cardinal numbers, gives the association the following meaning: a student knows one

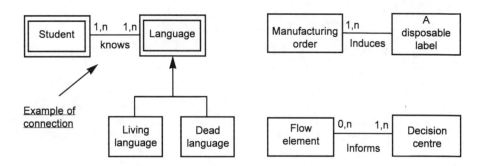

Figure 4.16 Example of connections between classes.

to n languages and one language is known by one to n students. If possible, the verb and link should be placed in such a way that the corresponding relationship can be easily read (from left to right if English is used). Roles may also be specified for each end of a connection (they are often necessary for associations between objects of the same class). As with aggregation, a cardinal number not specified implies that this is equal to 1,1; however, those who so wish may write 1,1 if that seems more legible to them. In the case of multiple cardinal numbers on each side of an association, implementation choices must be made when designing a solution in order to determine the reference attributes to be added. Multiple cardinal numbers show sometimes hidden aggregation relationships. Classically, a student who knows n languages has a reference to a list of languages, but where a language is known by n students, is it necessary to add a list of students for each language? These implementation choices depend on the requirements of the application.

The genericity layer
The graphic notation for the genericity layer uses a double arrow pointing from the instance class to the generic class. On this arrow in brackets is the name of the class or of the type which serves as a generic parameter (Figure 4.17). The instance class is then constrained by the type or class given in the parameter. In Figure 4.17, it is essential not to make a mistake by mixing inheritance and genericity; if this happens

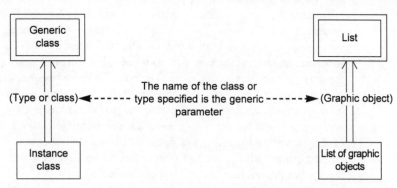

Figure 4.17 Representation of genericity.

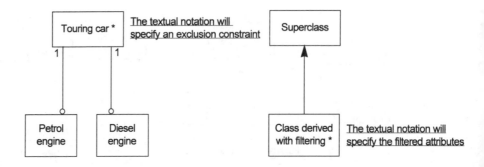

Figure 4.18 Marking classes which have constraints.

it is a good idea to refer to Meyer (1988). This type of error is equivalent to mixing inheritance and instantiation relationships and may reveal a lack of understanding of the object model and its concepts.

The constraint layer

Certain simple forms of constraint, as well as certain constraints between associations, could be accepted by the graphic notation. The most complex forms of constraint, however, would be difficult to represent graphically. We recommend that all constraints should be dealt with by means of textual notations so as not to burden diagrams. It is a good idea not to multiply graphic symbols if we want the notation to be easy to use and the diagrams to remain legible. However, in order not to lose sight of the fact that certain classes are subject to constraints, we propose to add an asterisk in the graphic rectangles which symbolize them (Figure 4.18).

The subsystem layer

A subsystem of objects combines a set of classes cooperating to the same end. The notion of a subsystem of objects can be represented graphically by surrounding all of these classes (any type of contour may be used: frame, circle, lassoo, and so on). It is not a notation peculiar to M2PO and the choice of representation is therefore left to the designer.

This layer is necessary to tackle large complex systems. In this way we study the various subsystems separately (with their associated graphic diagrams). Hierarchical decomposition of systems of objects is derived from earlier concepts presented in IDEF form (for manufacturing systems simulation). An example of a subsystem of objects may combine all user interface objects within the same software, another subsystem may combine all objects necessary for compilation or for desktop publishing, and so on. The compilation subsystem may be decomposed into several subsystems of objects (one subsystem which deals with the lexicographical analysis, another for the preprocessor, a third for the semantic analysis, a fourth for the coding and a last one for optimization). This allows a view of a system by abstracting the detail of classes and uses a Cartesian hierarchical decomposition which, even if it now has to be supplemented with the systemic theory, has proved itself for several centuries (Figure 4.19).

The subsystem graphic layer may also be combined with all the other layers to

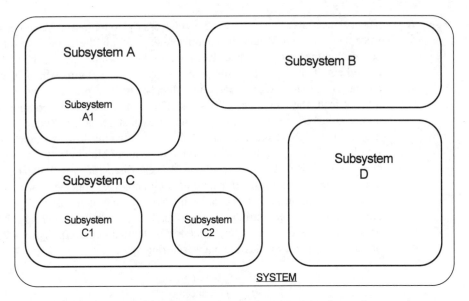

Figure 4.19 Hierarchical approach to assist mastering of complex systems.

give the internal detail (or zoom picture) of a subsystem. Figure 4.20 shows, for example, a combination of the inheritance layer with the subsystem layer. Interactions between subsystems are easily displayed in this way, for any relationship leaving one system and entering another intersects with the contour of the subsystems involved. These interactions will be examined in greater detail when we tackle the dynamic aspects of models.

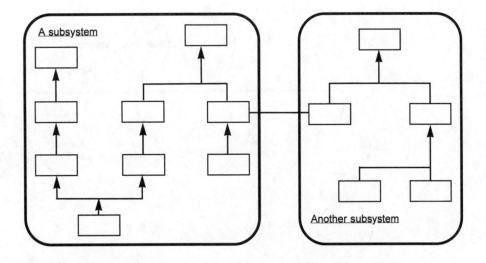

Figure 4.20 Example of the graphic representation of the notion of subsystems.

The instance
layer

The instance layer makes it possible, if necessary, to represent the composition of the system, as we no longer focus on classes but on the extensive set of objects composing the system studied. It is the only layer which may not be combined with the others. This layer presents a real view of the system, which is very useful, especially for simulation modelling. Objects can be represented here by circles as distinct from the rectangles of classes. This symbolism is not compulsory and the choice is left to the designer. In certain cases abstract objects (which do not exist!) may be necessary to represent a set of objects deriving from a single abstract class which we do not wish to detail. We then use a double circle (by analogy with the double rectangle of the abstract classes). These distinctions will also be found again in the notation used for the dynamic part which makes abundant use of objects. The necessary relationships (especially inheritance and composition) use the same graphic formalism as introduced for other layers. Details concerning the values of object attributes are given by instance forms (textual notation). Figure 4.21 shows an (instantiated) part of a flexible manufacturing system.

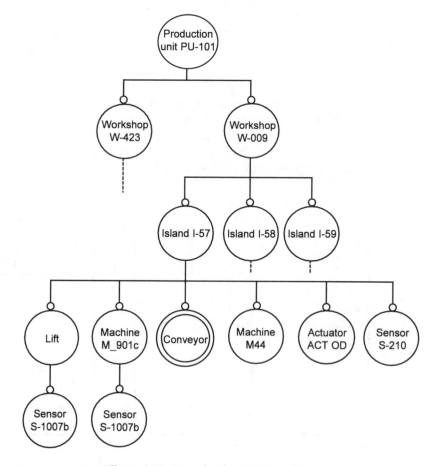

Figure 4.21 Example of an instance diagram.

Name of the class:
Reference to superclass:
Object identifier:
List of collaborating objects (class + identifier)

Value of inherited attributes:

Value of specific attributes:

Figure 4.22 Type headings for an M2PO instance form.

TEXTUAL
NOTATION Textual notation is used for the detailed description of classes and instances with forms of files. In the class forms we include classic information such as the name of the class, reference to superclass, class methods and variables, instance methods and variables, and a list of the collaborating classes. To this classic information we add information concerning the nature of objects generated by the class concerned: active or passive objects (whether or not they possess their own control flow), persistent objects, aggregate or macro-objects, and constraints. For the instance forms, it is mainly necessary to know the object identifier, its class, the value of its attributes and the list of references concerning collaborating objects (object identifier with its class).

Figure 4.22 gives the headings of an instance form and Figure 4.23 the headings of a class form. The textual notation of the static part is also used for the comments which are necessary to understand the connections between objects, especially the justification of all the cardinalities advanced. Information is also found in the textual part, such as the list of classes and instances of each subsystem. Identification of attributes and methods to supplement class forms remains a difficult task where experience still plays a great role (as it does for identifying classes). We recommend using a combination of the following approaches: the approach guided by responsibility, the approach guided by data and the procedural approach. It is a good idea not to limit oneself to a responsibility-guided approach, which is frequently used with an object model, for the two other approaches may greatly assist analysts in describing their classes.

It has been previously said that information necessary to take into account various constraints is given at the level of the textual class description, so as not to overload diagrams unnecessarily. An example of a constraint on a relationship may be as follows: a car has a diesel engine or a petrol engine (the possession of one excluding possession of the other). Amongst the possible constraints, we advise

Name of class:
Reference to superclass:
Persistent objects: Active objects:

Types of aggregation: Macro-objects   Aggregate
Class methods:

Class attributes:

Instance methods: It is sometimes also interesting to
                                             separate the specific methods and
                                             attributes from the inherited methods
                                             and attributes.
Instance attributes

Collaborating classes:

Constraints:
    on attributes
    on inheritance
    on genericity
    on common relationships

Figure 4.23 Headings of a class form with M2PO.

against inheritance constraints since a subclass instance is automatically an instance of the superclass and should not violate the protocol of this superclass. An example of an inheritance constraint is given by ostriches which are birds but do not fly. A technique consisting of filtering the flying method at the time of inheritance does not seem to us to be correct. It is preferable to create a subclass of birds which fly and another of birds which do not fly, which will give rise to classes like Kiwi, Ostrich, Penguin, and so on. The description of constraints and comments is drawn up in natural language. The major disadvantages of this choice are the lack of accuracy and the ambiguities which may result from using natural language.

This approach is, however, flexible and allows the greatest number to be expressed. We do not dismiss the formal specification languages which are capable of taking into account the constraints of an object model, such as Object-Z (Duke *et al.*, 1991). This type of tool remains reserved for specialists and it would be unreasonable to expect that experts who are not computer scientists might invest in such tools.

Just as for the design of databases, the integrity constraints (predicates on values of the attributes of a knowledge model) must allow us to make sure that the operation of the model and the state of objects are consistent by comparison with the real system. We separate the simple constraints relating to each instance of a class and the set constraints relating to several instances of a class (Flory, 1987). A simple constraint, for example, is the fact that the power of motorcycles must not develop more than 100 hp on the rear wheel. A set constraint may be the fact that imports of cars must not exceed 30% of national production. We extend simple constraints to abstract classes, which, if they do not directly have instances, allow us to specify constraints at a higher level of abstraction and therefore to reduce the number of constraints mentioned. Within the two categories mentioned, we can distinguish constraints relating to the static aspects from those relating to the dynamic aspects (where the time component intervenes).

The constraints may also be used as tools for verifying and validating simulation models. They are associated with the establishment of the contractual interfaces recommended by Meyer (linked to the preconditions, invariants and post-conditions for each method). The use of constraints as assertions allows us to verify whether an action model is functioning in accordance with the hypotheses made and the behaviour specified (for example: the temperature will always be less than 0°C, the speed of the shuttle must not exceed 25 km/h, the welding time must be between 30 and 45 seconds). What is more, the presence of assertions clearly documents the intentions of the model designer. Assertions are expensive in human time (reflection and implementation) and in machine time (calculation), but they have a considerable verification power.

4.4.6 The dynamic aspect

Controlling the dynamic aspect of systems is a very important task in the modelling process. The systems which we shall consider have a state which develops in time; the models of these systems are of course dynamic. Initially we will present the categories of results of the dynamic part, which are associated with layers developed in the static part. At a second stage, we shall explain the formalism retained (at the end of 1992) to represent the interactions between objects, internal behaviour of objects, and the routing of flow elements of systems to be modelled.

DYNAMIC INHERITANCE The terminology of dynamic inheritance is often used to identify an inheritance implementation technique. We also use this terminology to indicate the modifications of the inheritance graph which take place during the life of a system and therefore during the execution of an action model. From our point of view, the addition/deletion of new classes in an existing hierarchy comes within the sphere of the design and implementation facilities. At the design phase mechanisms are often provided which only manage an abstract superclass. The addition (dynamic loading) of a subclass hierarchy may occur during the life of a system of objects, without having too many effects on the number of operations to be effected to preserve consistency. By means of polymorphism and the mechanisms of dynamic binding, the 'grafted' subclasses make it possible to respond to a desired configuration for a system of objects at a moment 't'. It may then become possible to deal with another configuration by unloading the standard hierarchy and reloading new subclasses. This feature is offered on certain powerful development platforms (for example: NeXTStep with

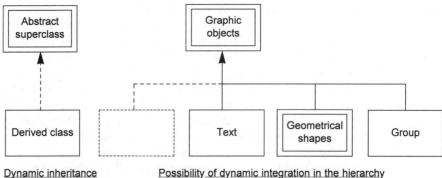

Figure 4.24 Example of dynamic inheritance.

Objective-C) and is carefully used by masterpieces of software such as InterfaceBuilder.

We are keen to point out that we do not take into account dynamic insertions/deletions of inheritance links at any point on an inheritance graph but only at terminal classes. The modifications which occur at any point on a graph involve operations intended to keep the system in a consistent state. In addition, these operations are important compared with the low frequency of this type of requirement. We have not studied dynamic multiple inheritance, even if it is possible to emulate it. We do not wish to impose a graphic formalism retained to show, if necessary, the possibilities of dynamic inheritance. Figure 4.24 only gives one example; the notation is not imposed in M2PO.

DYNAMIC
CLASSIFI-
CATION

The terminology of dynamic classification hides several concepts. We will examine the two aspects which we take into account. The first aspect (transformation or break-up) concerns the fact that an object of a class 'C' may become one or several objects from one or several classes, 'C1', 'C2', ... and correspond to a simple transformation or to a 'break-up'. A person, a single employee, may become an executive; a motorbike going for scrap may become a frame, an engine, two wheels, a steering wheel, and so on. The second aspect, which is very frequently found, corresponds to a transformation by assembly. Several objects of identical or different classes may be assembled, so as to constitute one or several objects of other classes, after processing. These types of dynamic classification are associated indirectly with the composition/aggregation relationships concerning the static aspect. There is no need for any special graphic notation for this type of transformation, for these events are taken into account by the management of interactions between objects. In addition, composition relationships also translate the possible assemblies and break-ups.

Still considering dynamic classification, we do not dismiss the possibility of modification and the addition/deletion of attributes or methods during the execution of an action model.

If the sharing of information is effected by delegation, any modification of the model is then possible by changing the delegate actor. This makes it possible, for example, to simulate (just as with the ROSS simulation language) combat aircraft which during one and the same day may be armed like fighters or light bombers, depending on the mission. Likewise, in an administrative system an invoice may be considered as a legal administrative paper object; in the case of a judicial inquiry, the invoice may then turn out to be a false invoice, considered as a confidential evidence object. Another example may be dynamic communication protocols which, having the same properties, may change transmission speed, size of blocks, error verification and correction techniques according to the quality of the line (Davis, 1992). With this type of dynamic classification, we shall use the textual notation to indicate instances which might change class. This is done by the addition of a dynamic classification heading on the instance form; this heading could indicate the future possible classes. Contrary to dynamic inheritance which concerns classes, the dynamic classification we presented concerns instances.

INTER-
ACTIONS
BETWEEN
OBJECTS

The object model only allows communication by messages: this authorizes the verification of interactions between objects. We organize these exchanges in the form of **message flow diagrams** (hereinafter called MFD), which designate a set of messages exchanged by various objects. We take up three categories of objects: the pure servers, the pure clients and the agents (possible client and server). The MFDs are dedicated and centred on the agents of the object system; these agents in fact govern the main activities of the system modelled. At the design level we find the MFDs again for mechanism objects (which are agents since they give and receive services). The results of the analysis and design, concerning interactions between objects, are therefore taken into account by a set of hierarchized diagrams which would use a graphic notation such as the one in Figure 4.25.

The MFDs use circles to represent objects as distinct from the rectangles of the classes of the static part. Double circles distinguish abstract objects corresponding to abstract classes; they allow simplification of diagrams by forcing the analyst to take up a position at a high level of abstraction. Likewise, rounded rectangles represent subsystems of objects which allow the use of a hierarchical approach to managing

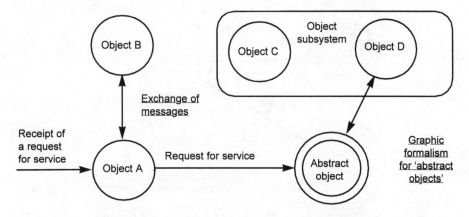

Figure 4.25 Notation used for message flow diagrams.

communications within very large systems. Message flows are symbolized by arrows between the various objects without specifying when these messages are transmitted. Scenarios are associated with the MFDs to describe the important treatments of the system studied and to specify the conditions which lead to the activation of these treatments, which involve changes in the state of objects and the creation or destruction of objects.

The use of MFDs consists in fact in taking up and adapting a part of the data flow approach of structured analysis methods (Yourdon, 1989; IGL Technology, 1989 (SADT)). This approach is very useful in communicating with experts and in validating the dynamic aspects of knowledge and design models. We propose to liken control and data flows to single message flows. These flows circulate between the objects of the system whether they are abstract or not. Abstract objects are associated with abstract superclasses, and symbolize a multitude of objects belonging to the subclasses which may be derived from these superclasses. We believe that the fact of being able to integrate abstract classes in this type of diagram simplifies the diagrams and their readability. This considerably increases the level of abstraction at which the analyst may and must take up position, and promotes the use of polymorphic messages.

In the example of Figure 4.26, it is possible to see how a simulator object controls an animator object which has the responsibility of restoring a graphic model, then of loading a set of icons, in order to be able to move sets of graphic objects. The use of an abstract object for the graphic objects simplifies and clarifies the diagram; to be convinced, it is sufficient to imagine the message flows which it would have

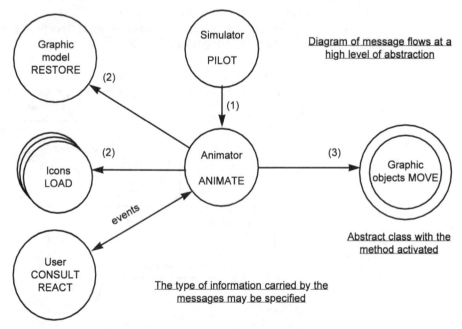

Figure 4.26 An example of a message flow diagram.

been necessary to draw if, for example, you had wished to represent 20 subclasses of different graphic objects! Each object specifies its class (here in lower case) and may specify its principal activity on the diagram by means of an action verb (here in upper case). The activities correspond in general to sequences of methods, or to methods when the level of abstraction is low. It is possible to detail each activity much more finely, by bringing in the details of communications. We then obtain a hierarchy of diagrams in accordance with the desired level of abstraction.

When the order in which messages are exchanged is important, it is possible to specify the sequence by numbering the message flows (numbers in brackets on the illustration). If two message flows occur in the same time window, they have an identical sequence number. The type of information carried may be specified by a comment on the message flow.

When the level of abstraction is low, it is interesting to supply scenarios which are sequences of activities indicating in natural language the methods to be activated and the objects concerned. The use of natural language, with the risks this involves, is now also advocated by the KISS method (Kristen, 1994).

We take these scenarios into account textually by indicating the conditions that trigger them. M2PO imposes no constraints on the way scenarios are formalized and it may be of interest to use the scenario management of Booch (1994a) or the 'use cases' of Jacobson *et al.* (1992). Figure 4.27 gives a scenario as well as the associated MFDs. It will be noted that at this level of abstraction, circles do indeed represent instances (the two input and output files may be of the same class). Since the MFDs are being centred on agents, several activity scenarios may be associated with a single diagram.

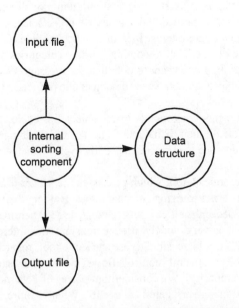

SCENARIO

A   Open the input file
B   Fill the data structure with the file elements
C   Close the input file
D   Sort the data structure
E   Create and open the output file
F   Empty the sorted data structure into the output file
G   Close the output file

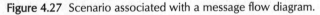

Figure 4.27 Scenario associated with a message flow diagram.

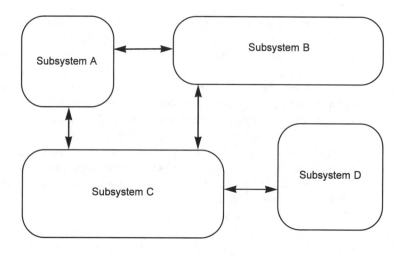

Figure 4.28 Interactions between subsystems.

It is of course possible to mix interactions between object subsystems and objects. Interactions between subsystems only are also taken into account by the graphic notation and correspond to the highest level of abstraction in the hierarchy of MFDs. At this level of abstraction, it is sufficient to know what the possible communications between the subsystems are (there cannot be any isolated subsystems). The details of interactions are given in the MFDs at a lower level of abstraction. Figure 4.28 gives the graphic formalism retained to display communications between different subsystems. For simulation modelling, stage 5 of the domain analysis will have separated the classes of objects identified in the physical, logical and decisional subsystems. It is of course possible to have other subsystems, especially at the design level to combine certain categories of universal components or utility objects. It is important to note that the message flows give the coupling both between the objects and between the object subsystems.

OBJECT LIFE CYCLES AND THEIR INTERNAL BEHAVIOUR
The internal behaviour of objects corresponds to an object life cycle. Not all the classes require representation of their behaviour. The scenarios prepared for the MFDs may be taken up and detailed to construct these life cycles which are generally specified by finite state automata.

Like other authors, we prefer a tool which possesses the power to express the important parallelism and synchronizing mechanisms. Rather than add new notations, our choice is focused on the Petri nets (Brams, 1983) (hereinafter called PN) and more especially on a very widely used extension: the interpreted and communicating PNs. With PNs, it is possible to use the same tool, regardless of the fact that we consider one or several control flows within the same object (depending on the desired granularity). We consider that places of PNs model a state of an object and that transitions are triggered by events. What is more, notions of macro-places and macro-transitions permit a hierarchical approach, allowing the use

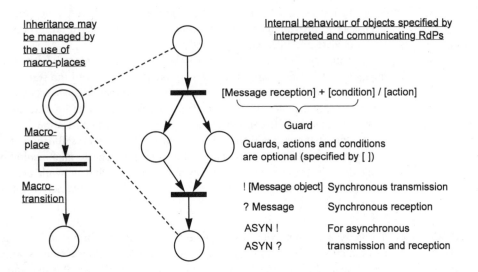

Figure 4.29 Notation used for interpreted and communicating Petri nets.

of several levels of abstraction to understand the complexity of certain behaviours. Each class which possesses a significant dynamic behaviour must provide a life cycle for its objects. We choose to represent this life cycle by means of an interpreted and communicating PN, which may be decomposed hierarchically into sub-networks by means of macro-places and macro-transitions.

The graphic notation which we use for interpreted and communicating PNs is given in Figure 4.29. Macro-places are macro-states and a token in a macro-place means that there is a token in at least one of the aggregated places. The hypotheses made for interpreted and communicating PNs are as follows:

- Each transition may be guarded by an event, a Boolean condition or both.
- The only method of communication between objects is message exchange; consequently the only type of event is the receipt of messages. Not using any global variable and having asynchronous messages makes it possible to specify concurrent object systems, without too many adaptations.
- We will consider that the sending of messages from the communicating PNs may be synchronous or asynchronous, and corresponds to the request for the activation of an object method. The graphic notation is given in Figure 4.29.
- Each transition may involve an action part allowing the transmission of a message or the interpretation of an instruction relating to variables of the interpreted PN (local to the object).
- The Boolean condition may relate to variables of the object modelled or may, for example, test whether a place of the PN has tokens or relate to the synchronous activation of a method corresponding to a Boolean function associated with an object.

To represent the life cycle of an aggregation using a Whole/Part relation, it is necessary to provide all of the PNs modelling the parts. All the PNs of the set may communicate and interact concurrently.

With regard to an inheritance relationship, a subclass inherits the PN of its superclass. It is necessary to try, when modelling the PN of the subclasses, to make them independent of those of the superclass. To do that, it is necessary to concentrate on the actual attributes of the subclasses inducing new states, and to consider places (states) of the PN of the superclass as macro-places which must be detailed.

One of the major difficulties is, however, still the establishment of effective dialogues between objects. It is a good idea in particular to take inspiration from the work done in the preparation of telecommunication and network protocols, which frequently use interpreted and communicating Petri networks (Ayache and Ou-Halima, 1985).

DESCRIPTION OF TRANS-ACTIONS

General presentation

To study a system with a view to evaluating its performance by simulation, we recommend a transaction approach. Transactions are flow elements which undergo one or several treatments by an active resource, with the possible assistance of one or several passive resources. Classes corresponding to these flow elements are identified by domain analysis and are compiled in the logical subsystem. With a transaction approach, the operation of the system is determined by the routing and processing undergone by flow elements. This approach was introduced with GPSS at the beginning of the 1960s (Gordon, 1962), and was then taken up again by other simulation tools such as SLAM (Pritsker, 1986) and SIMAN (Pegden and Sturrock, 1989).

We consider that flow elements must satisfy the following definition (which came out of the SIGMA project):

> A flow element is a physical or logical entity, not belonging to the physical subsystem and having at least one of these properties:
>
> - entering the system and leaving or not leaving the system,
> - created by the system (by a processing of one or more other flow elements) and leaving or not leaving the system.

With this definition it is possible to give as examples flows of persons, flows of documents, flows of material, data processing flows, telephone flows, and so on. Continuous flows can be taken into account after they have been made discrete. It may be noted that flow elements are completely separate objects. The identification of transactions may act as a reliable guide for the representation of the flow processor objects of other objects (Le Moigne, 1977). The aim is to provide **flow circulation diagrams** (called FCDs hereinafter). The FCDs present creations and destructions of flow elements which are themselves objects. These diagrams supplement the message flow diagrams (MFDs). The FCDs are essential for simulating a system with a transaction approach. Moreover, they make it possible to show up class changes. In an FCD, we separate two categories of objects. The first category corresponds to flow elements (belonging to the logical subsystem) and will be represented by arrows in the FCDs. The second category of objects (belonging to the physical or logical subsystem) manipulates these flows and will be represented by circles already used for the MFDs. The FCDs are data flow diagrams where the only data taken into account are flow elements, and where processing must be associated with objects.

The concepts used

To describe the operation of a system with a transaction approach, we use the notions of phase and path (Gourgand, 1984). A path is an itinerary followed by a flow element, from its input or its creation in the system up to its departure from the system or its destruction. The path taken by a flow element depends on the state of the system, and on the routing time. A path is defined as a string of phases, each phase grouping together a set of elementary operations. We will therefore speak of flow element treatment phases. For each class of flow, all possible paths must be defined for flow elements (instances of the class studied). The paths of different classes of flow elements may share the same FCD.

The treatment phases are associated with the objects manipulating the flows. This may mean activation of methods peculiar to the objects (or sets of methods) depending on the level of abstraction used. The MFDs make it possible to define several different scenarios; with the FCDs, a phase is associated with a single scenario specified in natural language. Scenarios make it possible, for example, to take account of the execution of an elementary operation on a flow element, the taking and returning of resources (modelled by objects or associated with objects), timings, and so on.

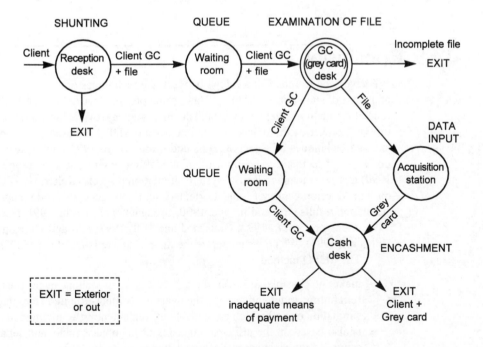

Figure 4.30 FCD to obtain a grey card.

Figure 4.30 gives an example of an FCD to obtain a grey card (identification certificate for motor vehicles in France) in a prefecture. It may be noted that it is possible to use the same object several times on one path (in this case 'waiting room'), and the treatment phases may be different. In this case the 'abstract' object 'GC desk' represents here the fact that one of the instances of the 'GC desk' class will be used without the need to specify which one (a common active resource). Arrows show the direction of flow element circulation which may be combined (example: 'client + file'). Phases are specified in capital letters and the identifications of the objects are in lower case. One phase such as DATA INPUT may be detailed by one scenario such as: Recover file, Seek a free terminal, Get the file, Start the printing of the grey card. It is possible to detail one flow element in the form of elementary flow elements (in this case 'file' which consists of a form, a passage order number and proof of domicile). This type of information is sometimes useless, for it is described on the static aspect. The notation 'EXT' means that you leave the FCD; a comment is generally associated with this.

It is also interesting for the modelling of certain complex systems (administrative systems, flexible manufacturing systems, ...) to have a schedule and data about the availability and capacity of resources (active or passive) during the simulation time. This notion partially corresponds to the 'SCHEDULES' element of the SIMAN simulation software (Pegden and Sturrock, 1989). This type of specification may be taken into account by the textual notation and be associated with each class which may be used as a resource.

◁4.5 Conclusion

We have tried to establish a bridge between the techniques of software engineering and those of simulation modelling. Basic principles put forward for the M2PO object modelling method attempt to establish this gangway by taking advantage of the unifying power of the object-oriented approach. M2PO is based on a synthesis of existing techniques of object analysis and design (Hill, 1992) and is also based on our experience in the development of modelling environments (Breugnot et al., 1990) in a great many industrial system simulation projects (Kellert, 1992), and also on our developments of object-oriented tools to generate code and animate simulation results (Hill and Junque, 1990; Breugnot et al., 1991a, 1991b; Caux et al., 1991; Gourgand et al., 1992; Gourgand and Hill, 1992; Hill and Gourgand, 1993; Hill et al., 1993). We now summarize the main characteristics of the M2PO method. The M2PO method:

- makes it possible to cover the whole object modelling cycle presented by remaining independent of the various object-oriented languages (for simulation or not) which are capable of implementing action models;
- is also based on the principal concepts of the object model and separates the static and dynamic aspects of a real system to be modelled;

- may be used at a high level of abstraction by taking account of the object-oriented domain analysis (and the reusability arising therefrom), but also by putting forward the abstract classes, both for the static and dynamic aspects;
- uses a simple graphic notation, referring to the textual notation the details which usually overload diagrams, for both the static and dynamic parts. This simplicity is also due to the deliberately limited number of symbols;
- takes into account principal dynamic aspects of the object model. These dynamic aspects are used to best represent the operation of real systems (from dynamic classification to taking into account concurrency within object internal behaviour). Interactions between objects are studied with the message flow diagrams which allow us to examine the coupling between objects and between object subsystems;
- specifies the object internal behaviour with interpreted and communicating Petri nets;
- uses decomposition into three subsystems (physical, logical and decisional). This decomposition is interesting for our simulation modelling approach;
- establishes paths and phases for the flow elements making it possible to understand the operation of complex systems with a view to effecting object simulations using a transaction approach;
- improves the traceability of objects through various models by making it possible to ascertain easily whether an object belongs to the problem domain or the solution domain.

In the chapters which follow, the M2PO method will be used to analyse and design software tools for simulation. The graphic notation of M2PO will be used to illustrate elements of results belonging to the various possible categories. Detailed analysis reports of the software tools which are to be presented are outside the framework of this book.

At present, M2PO remains sufficiently open to tackle fields of application other than that of simulation (it has been helping to specify biological systems for two years), and it must be possible to refine and add to it during future projects (in order to specify requirements, tests, real-time systems, ...).

◁ KEY POINTS

- Current object-oriented analysis and design methods make it possible to identify a set of basic tasks to which may be added a set of tasks peculiar to simulation modelling.
- Identification of classes remains a tedious task and is linked to empiricism despite some heuristics.
- The three principal relationships between classes are the relationships of inheritance, aggregation and communication.
- The M2PO modelling method takes account of domain analysis, object-oriented system analysis and object-oriented design.

- An M2PO design model combines classes from:
  - the knowledge model of a system,
  - the library of universal components and utility objects,
  - the mechanisms.

- The domain knowledge models, the system knowledge models and the design model (which distributes its classes as specified above) bring about an improvement in object traceability. It becomes easier, while using the same degree of formalism, to ascertain whether an object belongs to the problem domain or the solution domain.
- The M2PO method includes the breakdown of a system to be modelled into three subsystems: physical, logical and decisional.
- As regards the static aspect, the results provided by M2PO are: classification diagrams giving the structure of classes and their relationships, the description of the classes and instances using forms, domain glossaries and instance diagrams for the system modelled.
- As regards the dynamic aspect, the results provided by M2PO are: the message flow diagrams describing the interactions between objects or between subsystems, the PNs which specify internal behaviour of classes, the flow circulation diagrams which describe the sequences of operations on flows and the routing of scenarios (or traces of events), and the possibility of dynamic classification.
- M2PO uses a graphic formalism corresponding to the notations most frequently encountered.
- M2PO is an open method which, if it draws influence from discrete event simulation techniques, attempts a unification of modelling techniques and must be capable of tackling other domains.

◁EXERCISES

4.1 What classification techniques are listed?

4.2 What are the categories of methods frequently identified within objects? Does the choice of the visibility of a method have more to do with detailed design or implementation?

4.3 Describe the role of a mechanism object.

4.4 What are the different categories of objects with respect to communications relationships?

4.5 What distinction do you make between analysis and design? Discuss the differences between an object-oriented domain analysis and an object-oriented system analysis. What is the usefulness of domain analysis to a company dealing with simulation modelling problems?

4.6 Does a universal component object (a small unfolding component, for example) belong to the problem domain or the solution domain?

4.7 Repeat Exercise 3.1 with M2PO.

4.8 Give the PN specifying the internal behaviour of a video tape recorder (if necessary use macro-places). Let this be limited to the following functions: setting the date and time; programming the day, the time and the channel on which you wish to record a program (only one program); setting and cancelling a program.

4.9 Give a flow circulation diagram to send a letter with acknowledgement slip using a Post Office counter.

4.10 Students, teachers and researchers are members of the university; there are teachers-researchers and students-teachers-researchers. Find the classes and relationships which exist between these classes, give a static M2PO diagram, and discuss problems.

5

Analysis and design of a multi-domain toolbox for the animation of simulation results

◁ OBJECTIVES

This chapter describes the use of M2PO to design GIGA, a toolbox to assist in the construction of simulation animation environments. First of all we shall describe simulation results animation techniques, stating what these techniques contribute to a simulation project. We shall then turn our attention very specifically to visual interactive simulation techniques. We shall finally present the concepts and objectives of the GIGA toolbox by developing the key points such as the integration of simulation program debugging techniques within graphic objects.

◁ 5.1 Introduction

Graphic animation of simulation results often involves considerable programming. There are at present several simulation software products associated with an animator (SIMAN/CINEMA, SIMSCRIPT or MODSIM III with SIMGRAPHICS, GPSS with various tools, Proof animation, ...). There are also environments which include the animator and simulator (ARENA, based on SIMAN and CINEMA, SLAMSYSTEM, based on SLAM II, or other environments such as WITNESS, CADENCE, HOCUS, INSIGHT). In addition, there are animators which are independent of simulation packages. A study of all these tools and a certain number of others was carried out in the Computer Science Laboratory of Blaise Pascal University and a report was produced for a European project, Tempus (Hill *et al.*, 1992). We are interested more especially in the last category mentioned, animators capable of being adapted to various discrete event simulation tools. It is this category of tool which comes within the graphics and animation interface part of the modelling environments described in Chapter 1.

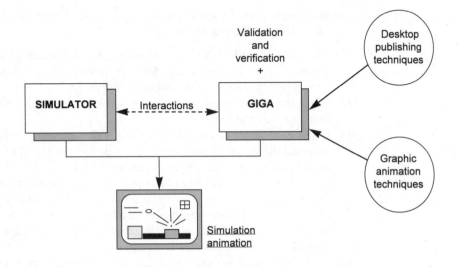

Figure 5.1   Composition of GIGA.

The objectives are to propose solutions to increase the potential assistance that object-oriented animation might provide for the validation and verification of simulation models.

In this chapter we describe a toolbox called GIGA (Generation d'Interface Graphiques Animées – Generator of Animated Graphics Interfaces) designed to construct object-oriented software for the animation of discrete event simulation results (Figure 5.1). This toolbox has a set of software components which may be reused and are independent of any simulation software. These components concern essentially:

- the construction of models consisting of graphic objects, and
- the animation of graphic objects according to their actual behaviours.

The main aim is to assist modelling specialists in producing software that allows the construction of valid animations. Each piece of software produced with GIGA is dedicated to a particular domain and allows the construction of consistent and realistic animations having a high level of validation and verification. Unlike existing tools, which include very little validation/verification potential in their animations (simple movements of icons on the screen), we choose to implement, in the code of domain objects, elements controlling their internal behaviour. Any inconsistency with the behaviours predefined in this domain may therefore be signalled immediately at the time of animation. This solution makes it possible to isolate both the reusable and independent components of problem domains, and the objects peculiar to the domains to be dealt with. This allows the production of hybrid tools which have features in common with general editing/animation software, while having the power of dedicated tools. Animation tools produced with GIGA mainly include validation and verification techniques. Even so, there are still powerful communications and decision support tools. The main objectives which we set for GIGA are the following:

(1) The tools created with GIGA must remain independent of the simulation software. This independence makes it possible to guarantee substantial composability with all open simulation software.

(2) Communications between simulation software and animation software are based on message sending.

(3) GIGA must allow a substantial increase in the analysis potential, and in the potential for validating and verifying simulation models, by comparison with existing animation tools. Object animation makes it possible to achieve a high level of abstraction for the verification and validation of simulation models. For example, it must be possible to debug at the abstraction level of graphic objects of the system which are monitored visually. This facilitates the understanding of parallel and transient phenomena which are impossible to apprehend at the source code level of a simulation model.

(4) The GIGA structure and its design must be based on a methodological framework allowing reusability not only of the code of GIGA standard components, but also of the results of analysis and design for the creation of other animation tools (use of the M2PO method).

(5) The standard GIGA components must be independent of the domain involved.

(6) The creation of libraries of objects to deal with different domains must follow the same methodological framework as used in point (4).

(7) The graphics associated with objects peculiar to one domain must have a sufficient degree of realism, while remaining symbolic.

(8) The visual behaviour of the objects of a domain must correspond to significant states of these objects.

The GIGA software components are written in C++ on a PC/PS compatible microcomputer and on a UNIX workstation. Some of the components are also written in Objective-C on a NeXT workstation. We give certain descriptions of classes and methods with C++ and Objective-C to illustrate the way in which these languages are used.

Following a presentation of simulation results animation techniques, the principal functions of GIGA are described in detail.

◁ 5.2 Graphic animation of simulation results

5.2.1 Background history

The availability of low-priced microcomputers and workstations with good graphics capacities has largely contributed to the general spread of graphics techniques which, before the 1980s, were only accessible on very large computers. We are interested more especially in the impact of graphics for modelling complex systems, using discrete event simulation as a technique for evaluating performance. The first uses of graphics, as a tool to assist in solving simulation problems, go back to the end of the 1960s (Bell, 1969). In 1976 a paper by Bazjanac, read to the ninth simulation symposium, presented a visual interactive study of the emergency evacuation of people in a skyscraper, by means of lifts (Bazjanac, 1976). This situation perfectly illustrates the contribution of animation, which makes it possible to analyse the transient behaviour of a system and which effectively supplements the overall statistical results. To our knowledge, one of the first attempts at object-oriented animation goes back to Palme (1977) who explained the advantages of having animation generated by models written with SIMULA. The work of Hurrion, presented in 1976 in his thesis, introduced the concepts of visual interactive simulation (Hurrion and Secker, 1978). The past decade has seen an explosion in the use of graphic simulation results animation techniques in a great many domains, and more especially in the domain of automated manufacturing systems. A review of various software products for graphic simulation results animation, as well as visual interactive simulation software, is given in Bell and O'Keefe (1987). Green and Sun (1988) present various methods used to implement a visual interactive simulation.

The animation of models now constitutes a considerable part of a simulation project, indeed an essential part, in order to undertake certain studies involving numerous transient phenomena. The advantages of simulation results animation cannot be denied. Shannon (1986) and Gipps (1986) present the various trump cards of animation as regards the validation of models. Smith and Platt (1987) give some of the contributions of animation to the modelling of assembly systems. We develop the various contributions of graphic techniques and animation in the following section.

Two different approaches to the use of graphic techniques for simulation are developed, one mainly supported by researchers working in the USA and the other by researchers in Great Britain (Figure 5.2). The technique recommended in the

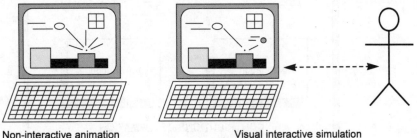

Non-interactive animation   Visual interactive simulation

Figure 5.2 Two approaches to simulation results animation.

USA consisted of animating the simulation results, without allowing the user to interact with the model during execution. The technique used in Great Britain allowed interactions between the user and the animated model. These are the visual interactive simulation techniques introduced by Hurrion. These two approaches are in conflict on particular points which we detail in Section 5.2.5 which discusses visual interactive simulation. We must state immediately that we do not tackle real-time visual interactive simulations, which offer impressive possibilities, combining simulation techniques, virtual reality and the real-time display of high definition images (Vince, 1992). The finances required for such productions are closer to the military research budget than to that of a small or medium-sized company. If minimum production is necessary for many simulation projects, excessive graphics may be counter-productive. In fact it remains to be demonstrated that advanced CAD techniques and image synthesis are really necessary for the majority of common simulation applications.

5.2.2 The contributions of graphics and animation in a simulation project

GENERAL
ASPECTS

Following a review of the bibliography, it may be considered that the principal parts of a simulation project where animation offers assistance are the following (Figure 5.3):

- the development and verification of action models;
- the validation of knowledge and action models;
- the analysis and design of experiments;
- the communication and presentation of results.

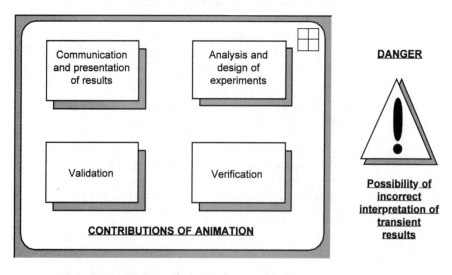

Figure 5.3   Contributions and dangers of simulation results animation.

We will describe the contributions of animation to each of these parts after having set forth the principal categories of errors which animation might make it possible to discover. These categories may be easily referred to the four parts mentioned above.

(1) Errors in the action model code (coding errors, which are common to all human programming approaches). The identification of this type of error takes place in the developed part and in the verification of an action model.

(2) Errors in the knowledge model. The action model is correct at the programming level; it does in fact correspond to the knowledge model, but is incapable of reproducing the expected behaviour of the system, and consequently provides only useless results. Detection of this type of error relates both to the validation part of the knowledge model and to the validation part of the action model.

(3) Errors occurring in the form of abnormal behaviour which the modelling specialist did not intentionally include in the model, but which has not been explicitly excluded (forms of behaviour not envisaged). This type of error involves the validation part of the knowledge model.

In fact, animation uses the capacities of the human mind to visually recognize forms of behaviour and complex spatial relationships and so makes it possible to detect possible deviations compared with the expected operation of the model. The detection of an unknown number of indeterminate errors in a simulation program by reading the overall statistical results, or by browsing in an intermediate trace list, may be likened to seeking four-leaf clovers. On average, the loss of time involved in this type of exercise is considerable. What is more, the detection of the third category of errors would assume that the modelling specialist has no errors to begin with in the model he or she has produced (the probability of the occurrence of such an event is very slight). Graphic animation techniques offer various solutions which make it possible to assist analysts to carry out their simulation projects. Hereinafter we will use the term analyst or modelling specialist indiscriminately, but we must be precise about who the user of a model will be. In fact, the user of a model may be the analyst who constructed the model, an expert in the system modelled or a manager who has the final say in the future of the system (without being a specialist in the system modelled). To designate this last category of users, we will use the term decision-makers (this choice does not mean that system experts do not have the power to take decisions).

DEBUGGING AND VERIFICATION

From the point of view of an analyst, animation is a powerful tool to assist in the development of action models. Animation supplies in a user-friendly way a set of information concerning the sequence of events generated by a model. This visual trace allows an approach which is quite superior to that of the classic debugging tools because it allows us to follow simultaneously several entities navigating in the system. Animation is very useful for understanding the various interactions between concurrent entities. Complex interactions between several entities of a model are often difficult to understand, especially if we are limited to a paper trace. Most authors agree in saying that the suppression of a certain number of coding errors is facilitated by a graphic tool which is capable of representing the transient behaviour of a system.

As regards verification of the control logic of an action model, it is appropriate to show some reservation. If the model is not strictly animated, that is, a substantial part of the events that a trace might supply are not animated, then correct animation does not under any circumstances mean that the model is correct and fully debugged and even less that it has been verified. We consider that a high degree of consistency between animation and the action model is fundamental in order to be able to consider animation as one tool (amongst others) that allows verification of the operation of a model.

ASSISTANCE IN VALIDATING KNOWLEDGE MODELS
Animation makes it possible to contribute to the validation of action and knowledge models. The validation of a knowledge model consists of making sure that the knowledge that we have of the system (from the inputs of the system to its operating logic) is correctly represented, and has a level of accuracy and abstraction in relation to the objectives set.

It is not sufficient for a model to be validated; it must also depend only to a very small degree on the modelling hypotheses which were made (level of detail, hypotheses concerning the laws of inputs, ...). This is then described as the robustness of the model. A robust model allows relative confidence even when the conditions under which the results are obtained are quite different from those used for validation (success in the tests for extreme conditions and degeneration).

The task of validating a model is extremely complex, and it is often impossible to validate a model completely, especially when carrying out a priori modelling. Considering that in most cases the modelling specialist (analyst) is not an expert in the system concerned, animation may provide a vital link between the analyst and the expert in the system who is not familiar with simulation tools and languages. Graphic communication is very effective and provides a starting point for discussions and constructive criticism of a model (comparison tests of the action and knowledge models). Bearing in mind that the expert knows the system in detail, animation using a sufficient level of detail may suffice for the expert to completely recognize the system (whether it exists or not). This representation of the dynamic operation of systems must, from our point of view, provide assistance with the validation of the hypotheses and choices present in the knowledge model and also with structural validation. This remains the case if the graphic animation was designed to reflect the mechanisms peculiar to the internal operating structure of the model. These mechanisms must correspond to the real mechanisms. It is important to obtain this structural validation, since a structurally valid model may give more precise results, or even results concerning submodels (due to taking into account the physical structure of the real system) (Leroudier, 1980).

	Verification	Validation
		Action model and knowledge model
ANIMATION	Informal analysis Static analysis Dynamic analysis Analysis of constraints	Comparison tests Validity of events Extreme condition tests Sensitive analysis Traces Predictive validity Structural validity

Figure 5.4   Table of verification and validation techniques for which graphic animation provides assistance (see Chapter 1).

In the case of a posteriori modelling, repetitive validation is greatly facilitated since the expert may visually understand the behaviour of the model and compare it with his or her knowledge of the real system. Figure 5.4 lists the various verification and validation techniques described in Chapter 1, for which the techniques of animating simulation results provide assistance.

ASSISTANCE IN ANALYSING MODELS   The animation of simulation results gives an opportunity to observe the interactions of numerous simultaneous and interlinked events, thereby providing information which is not available in the statistical measurements of performance calculated by a simulator. In certain cases, the values of performance measurements indicate a problem but cannot identify its source. With analysis, an attempt is also made to use the predictive nature of a model in order to test certain hypotheses; this means using animation to the best possible advantage to understand the results provided by prediction. An example is the effect caused in a manufacturing system by simultaneous micro-breakdowns on assembly processes synchronized in series. Looking at the animations may inspire alternatives to the solutions implemented. Tests of complex management rules, intended to get rid of bottlenecks and making use of a great number of the system's entities, may reasonably be evaluated visually, as we can use the human faculty for understanding spatial relationships. Animation may also assist in analysing the system when it is coupled interactively with the simulation model. In this way it is possible to end up with interactive scheduling systems (Hurrion and Secker, 1978). We shall return in detail to the advantages and disadvantages of interactive visual simulation. It is essential that the animation model is structurally consistent with the action model, otherwise it is impossible for animation to provide any assistance.

ANIMATION
AS A
COMMUNI-
CATIONS
AND
PRESENTATION
TOOL

The animation of simulation models is undoubtedly a considerable asset when presenting results. In this respect we may quote Smith and Platt (1987): 'Animation makes lively and accessible what would otherwise be a dry and somewhat obscure presentation of tables and figures'. It is essential to be able to communicate the results of simulation to the decision-makers for it is they who authorize the modifications of an existing system or who validate the design decisions of systems to be produced. In fact, the objective of any modelling effort is to furnish information to the people who take the decisions, and therefore it is important for the information to be passed on and above all to be credible. Now, if the statistical results with their intervals of confidence are useful elements in the hands of an analyst, animation considerably increases the credibility of the model. This credibility is not always proven and is often exploited. It is in fact easier to develop an animated drawing than a graphic animation model having sufficient qualities to be able to validate action and knowledge models.

Animation is also an effective tool for training, authorizing the presentation of complex cases visually, using numerous entities simultaneously. If interactive visual simulation is used, trainee systems analysts or operators can learn by understanding how their actions affect models and consequently real systems.

A study of the advantages felt by users of graphic animations of simulation results was carried out by Hollocks (1984). It presented three principal gains in the form of a dialogue between a decision-maker, an analyst and an expert. The gains perceived today are still the same:

- A gain in confidence by the user who can see the model and link it to his or her knowledge of the system and the problem to be dealt with. The justified suspicion of a simulation user towards a black box (the action model), manipulated by a specialist, disappears since the information generated by the graphic model is closer to the user's reality and makes it possible to follow the development of the process modelled.
- A gain in the understanding of the system. Experience has shown that the similarity of the graphic model to the real system has a great effect on the user's understanding. We believe that this similarity need not be based solely on the degree of detail of the graphic images displayed, but principally on the consistency of the behaviour of the graphic objects animated.
- An increase in the involvement of the system experts. Graphic animation increases the enthusiasm of these experts for simulation. This takes the form of a greater consideration for the results provided by the model and an awareness of the possibilities of the tool, which brings about the identification of other possible applications and the recommendation of the tool to other people. This involvement of experts is even greater if they have the possibility of interacting with the model.

As regards the understanding of the operation of a system, Johnson and Poorte defined a factor of recognition as being the degree of ease with which a person knowing neither the system nor modelling is capable of recognizing and

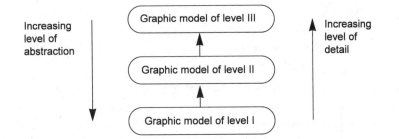

Figure 5.5   Hierarchical approach with three levels by Poorte and Johnson.

understanding what is described by the animation (Johnson and Poorte, 1988). Johnson and Poorte describe a hierarchical approach at three levels for animation models (Figure 5.5). The first level that they define is intended to be used by the analyst during the initial model development phase. This level possesses a very low factor of recognition (display of variables, gauges, changing of colours, little movement, no icon ...). A second level possesses a moderate factor of recognition. The animation may be recognized by people familiar with the system modelled, or with a number of explanations if the person does not know the system.

This level is intended to be used by the analyst for verification and by the system experts for validation and communication (2D animation, icons representing their physical counterparts, movement of icons, ...). The third level is characterized by three-dimensional graphic models incorporating all the significant movement of the system. The factor of recognition is high, for the graphic model is recognized by all with few explanations. It is intended for the decision-makers and constitutes a powerful tool which may be used for sales and training.

We believe that the cost of developing third-level graphic models is not justified on most projects. It is a matter more of commercial weapons than tools for use by professionals. In addition, the aesthetic appearance of a graphic model has often been given precedence, neglecting the consistency of its operation in relation to the simulation model and requiring very long graphic design time.

5.2.3 Various techniques for animating simulation results

Graphic animation of discrete event simulation results is now recognized as an essential tool for undertaking a simulation project. The past decade was very rich in the production of simulation animation software. In most cases, these items of software are linked to special simulation tools or to a special simulation language. The best known are SIMAN/CINEMA (Miles *et al.*,1988), SEEWHY/WITNESS (Gilman and Billingham, 1989), SLAM/TESS (Pritsker, 1986) or SLAMSYSTEM on microcomputers (O'Reilly and Nordlund, 1989), SIMSCRIPT and MODSIM

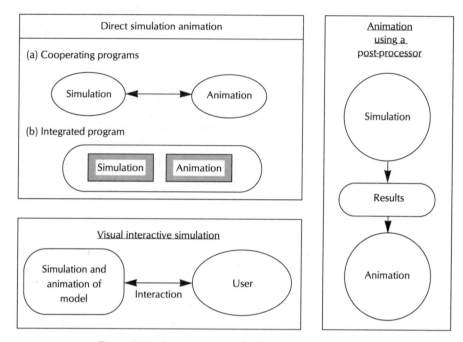

Figure 5.6   Various categories of simulation animation.

with SIMGRAPHICS (Brian, 1989). Certain tools are independent of the simulator, such as that developed at Wolverine (Brunner and Henriksen, 1989), and also wish to be independent of the modelling domain. Independence from simulation packages is good but we believe that the independence of an animation tool from modelling domains might be harmful in that a fairly large part of the validation potential is lost.

Amongst existing software we can identify three types of technique (Figure 5.6). The first technique deals with simulation results using an animation post-processor. The second, which we call direct simulation animation, offers the possibility of effecting simulation and animation at the same time, without having the possibility of interacting with the model. The third technique, called interactive visual simulation, allows modifications of the model during execution, in order to display immediately the effects caused by these changes. We give details of these three techniques below:

- The use of a post-processor is very simple from the moment an external file can receive data which comes from simulation software. The processing of the file by the animator guarantees independence from the simulation software. Having a file of animation-triggering events allows the implementation of interesting functions such as a flashback during the simulation time, in order, for example, to display again a sequence which poses a problem.

■ 'Direct' simulation animation may be implemented in two ways. The first consists of constructing a program which includes the animation software and the simulation software, allowing it to be executed on a microcomputer with a single-tasking operating system. The second method uses two communicating programs (the animator and the simulator) on the same machine in a multitasking environment, or on a network of workstations (the animator being on a host specializing in graphics, and the simulator on a host specializing in calculation).

■ Visual interactive simulation allows interactions during the execution of a model. This technique is sufficiently important for us to devote a section to it, in which we shall develop the advantages and disadvantages of visual interactive simulation as well as possible solutions for overcoming these disadvantages.

5.2.4 Technical problems of simulation animation

PROBLEMS WITH TIME MANAGEMENT IN ANIMATION For all the simulation animation techniques which have been described, there are different ways of managing the ratio between the virtual time of the simulation and the virtual time of the animation. For discrete event simulation, either the time flow mechanisms are directed by a clock, or they are directed by events. The majority of recent tools use simulation directed by events which consists of jumping from one date of occurrence of an event to another. The events are arranged in a time schedule and two events which have the same date of occurrence are described as simultaneous (Figure 5.7).

Animation must, however, give the illusion of a continuous process. In fact, the time of a real system is a continuous variable (it is said that the space of the time

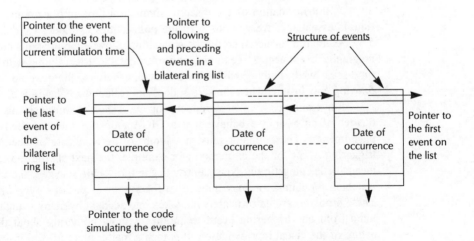

Figure 5.7 Time schedule in the form of a bilateral ring list.

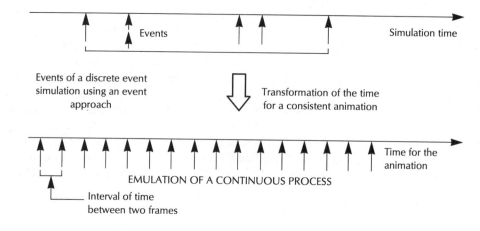

Figure 5.8   Transformation of time for the animation.

is continuous). It is therefore appropriate to emulate a continuous process by means of a clock which will synchronize all the displays at a frequency acceptable to the human eye. The animation threshold for human sight is around 10–15 images per second (Thalmann and Magnenat, 1985); films typically use 24 images per second. We propose that the time interval separating frames of an animation be set, but still allow a user to modulate it, so as to accelerate or slow down the 'film'. On the other hand, the ratio between this unit of animation time and a unit of simulation time depends on the knowledge model of the system. It is necessary to take as the basis the entity of the system having the fastest event generation frequency (the simulation model must only contain a single time scale).

A transformation of the discrete simulation time into a pseudo-continuous time is essential if we wish to keep the possibilities of model validation (Figure 5.8). As the time scale taken for the simulation allows time intervals during which no graphic event occurs, we think it is fundamental to effect timing with the current time scale when nothing has to be animated, otherwise there would be a risk of drawing conclusions when the screen does not reflect the behaviour of the system.

For example, if in a manufacturing workshop a shuttle is inactive for a quarter of an hour, we believe that a GIGA animator must correctly time this phenomenon. The animator must not jump to the next date of occurrence of a triggering event for the animation (for example, the next shuttle movement). By means of keeping timing consistent with the time scale selected, the user who is watching the animation may notice that the system is perhaps over-dimensioned. These problems are unfortunately not taken into account by many animators, which jump from one triggering event to another without bothering about the realistic nature of the visual representation. It is then a matter more of demonstration tools than model verification and validation tools.

PROBLEMS
INVOLVED IN
ANIMATING
MULTITASKING
SYSTEMS
Since animation has to be continuous, there is a problem on multitasking systems using multiprogramming, such as UNIX (microcomputer or workstation). With such systems, an application is suspended (either periodically or not) to release execution time for other processes. When the movement of real objects is simulated, it is necessary to design a sophisticated technique to offset these periodic process suspensions. Without this, the position of the objects, in terms of the real time perceived by a user, will not be correct. However, from the point of view of the animation process, the position of these objects is consistent in relation to the animation time variable, because the suspension of the animation process has stopped the incrementation of this variable. This problem is very important; with software for animating discrete flow systems on workstations using UNIX (or any other system using multiprogramming), the perception the user has of the graphic model depends on the operating system load. In fact, the user perceives stoppages in the movements of objects (Figure 5.9) which are not real at the level of the system simulated. If these stoppages are small, it is felt that the animation is jerky and not smooth. On the other hand, if the stoppages are large (there is a substantial load on the operating system), they completely falsify the vision of the user and consequently his or her perception of the model, thereby harming the validation potential of the animation tool.

In the event of the pseudo-parallel operation of an animator and a simulator, another problem may be added to that described above. In fact, the animator must not run short of animation events provided by the simulation. The simulator must therefore always be ahead of the 'real' time of the operating system. The use of a buffer and the time delay in starting the animator compared with the simulator (so that the buffers filled by the simulator have reached an adequate size) make it possible to maintain this advance. This does not, however, in any way solve the problem of animation stoppages, when the simulator monopolizes the main processor.

There is a technique used for the animation of continuous processes on multiprogramming systems which makes it possible to partly offset suspensions during the animation process. This technique consists of calculating the state and position of moving objects in relation to the absolute time supplied by the operating system. Therefore after a suspension, it is necessary to calculate the position the objects should be in and adjust the movements for the display. By taking into account the constraints of discrete event simulation, it is necessary that when the animator recovers control of the main processor after a suspension, it advances the processing of the events, by updating its internal data structures, without any display and until it has made up the simulation/animation time corresponding to the absolute time of the system on which it may finally display.

This solution causes visual jerks but has the merit of situating the entities in the positions (on the screen) where they should be, in terms of the real time perceived by the user and not solely in relation to a time variable local to the simulation and animation processes. The only solution which seems to us to be

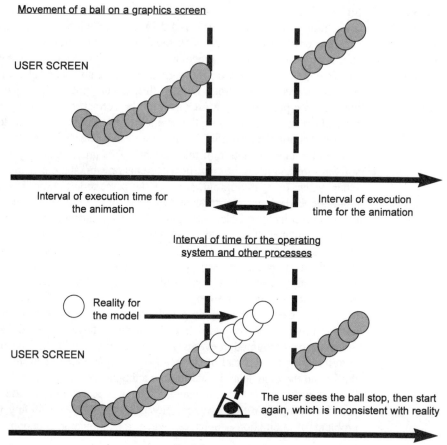

Movement of a ball on a graphics screen

USER SCREEN

Interval of execution time for the animation

Interval of execution time for the animation

Interval of time for the operating system and other processes

Reality for the model

USER SCREEN

The user sees the ball stop, then start again, which is inconsistent with reality

Real time perceived by the user

Figure 5.9   Perception of the user during a suspension of the animation process.

really acceptable for this type of operating system is the use of a specialized processor, which guarantees that no visual suspension will occur at animation level.

5.2.5 Visual interactive simulation

ADVANTAGES AND DIS-ADVANTAGES   We have already described the basic principle of this technique, which has the merit of substantially lowering the barriers which exist between simulationists and real experts. These experts are then capable of interacting with the models in order to explore various strategies (Figure 5.10). This technique, which comes from Great Britain, is criticized on the grounds that disorganized use of interactions with

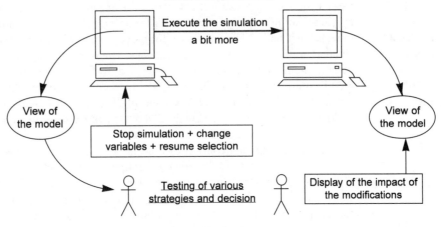

Figure 5.10   Interaction sequence.

models seriously harms the validity of simulation results. Interacting with a model during its execution may completely falsify the calculations of statistics, which may be based on samples which are far too small.

The problem of small samples also occurs again at another level. When a model is animated, the speed at which the events are examined is considerably slowed down compared with the possible speed of a simulation without animation. This slowing down is necessary to allow a human user to understand the animated model. Now, due to this low speed, the user displaying the animation may unfortunately draw conclusions on the basis of samples of an insignificant size. In fact, ten minutes of animation must not cause anyone to forget that what they are looking at constitutes only a small sample of a stochastic process. With the possibility of direct interaction during execution, modifications of the model by a user who has not been warned may lead to abnormal situations which can never be found in the real system.

Despite these drawbacks, it should be pointed out that the involvement of users who are experts in the system modelled is, as we have already mentioned, far greater if they can use the 'commands' of the model themselves. This approach is far more preferable than that which excludes the expert from the project analysis phase. Because of their knowledge of the system, experts contribute tremendous skill at the model validation level. What is more, when it comes to the analysis and experimentation of new strategies, the experts themselves can make proposals directly and so take over the new modified model which in a way becomes their model. Visual interactive simulation therefore brings about a greater involvement of experts in the simulation project.

DEVELOP-
MENTS OF
VISUAL
INTERACTIVE
SIMULATION
(HURRION,
1989)

The various
types of
interaction

The possibility of interaction seems to provide a richer approach compared with passive animation, because it authorizes the experts to contribute their experience by participating actively in the search for acceptable solutions. However, in order to preserve a statistical significance for the results, it may be interesting to examine an alternative, namely limiting interactions. The original visual interaction method with a model during simulation proposed by Hurrion (1976) authorizes the modification of all the attributes of all the entities of the model. This powerful approach, situated at a fairly low level of abstraction (individual entities of the model), assumes that only the analyst who has written the original model is capable of making consistent and valid modifications.

Another approach consists of limiting interactions by means of menus, thus avoiding the possibility of incorrectly modifying certain entities. It is then a matter of developing an interaction menu for each model, in exactly the same way as an animation relates specifically to one model. This technique seems restrictive but has the advantage of only authorizing valid changes in a model, so that the expert cannot inadvertently corrupt the model.

The possible
links with
artificial
intelligence

Hurrion (1989) points out that in the classic technique of visual interactive simulation, there is no means of retaining the expertise of a user who happens to improve a situation through a sequence of interactions. Only the user decides when to interact, what actions to take and when to accept the results as valid; not all of this knowledge is retained by the software.

The concept of adding expert software components, using logic programming, with a visual interactive simulation tool is described by Flitman and Hurrion (1987). This means adding a PROLOG component which acts as a monitor supervising the development of models. A simulation specialist is capable of providing a set of rules determining whether a model has reached a stationary state, and whether it is possible to assume that the statistical results are valid. There are numerous rules which may be used; they are described by Law and Carson (1979). The PROLOG module contains a set of rules capable of determining whether the system has reached the steady state. When the user interacts with the model, all the methods of recovering information for the calculation of statistics are stopped until this PROLOG module determines that the model is again in a valid state for recording this information and incorporating it in the calculation of final results.

The proposed PROLOG module also possesses the ability to learn; it manages the state of the model, the type of interactions carried out by a user and their dates of occurrence. The experiments carried out by Flitman and Hurrion have made it possible, after the learning cycle, to allow the PROLOG module to take over control of the model by using the combined knowledge of the users who participated in the learning cycle. The work by Taylor and Hurrion (1988) uses a PROLOG module as a counsellor for the user, which proposes various analyses, supervises their scheduling and assists in interpreting the results. This approach also has interesting possibilities for training the users of a system.

◁ 5.3 Description of the GIGA toolbox

5.3.1 Presentation of the general concepts

OBJECT
ANIMATION

The choice of an object-oriented approach for the design of interactive graphic systems is now accepted as being one of the best possible choices, if not currently the very best (Blaha *et al.* 1991; Booch, 1991; Bezivin and Cointe, 1991). The principal contributions of this approach, in the matter of animating discrete event simulation results, will be made at the level of the support for validation and verification techniques. It is now possible to integrate, within the graphic animation objects, the fundamental forms of behaviour which might reveal possible inconsistencies. If current animation software has contributed to popularizing simulation techniques, they do on the other hand require very substantial human resources to give fairly poor gains as regards analysis, validation and verification of models. What is more, animation may force an analyst to model a system with a view which, while appropriate for animation, may not suit the application at all. Detailed graphic animations, with backgrounds in three dimensions, are a waste of time at graphic acquisition level. In addition, analysts may, in the design of complex simulation models, wish to detail too many things solely to obtain visual information, which may lead to models being too large or too slow to be operated reasonably. A great many software products therefore only move icons on a flat background, following the orders of the simulator, without even trying to verify whether what is requested by the simulator is consistent with the current state.

On the other hand, symbolic animations often have a worthy degree of realism and are more appropriate to representing the dynamic operation of complex systems. Furthermore, they are executed much more quickly. This type of symbolic animation must be based on the objects present in the real system. These objects have a visual behaviour which may contribute information concerning the dynamic transient operation of a system, and must therefore possess a graphic model including visual reactions which are related to the significant states of objects of the real world. Having regard for the desired independence between animator and animation software, we consider that object animation corresponds to a communication by messages between both a simulation model (if possible consisting of simulation objects modelling the real system) and an animation model consisting of graphic objects. Each graphic object, knowing its current state (linked to the model of its behaviour), is capable of determining the consistency of the messages it receives.

THE
COMPOSITION
OF GIGA AND
THE CHOICES
MADE

GIGA proposes a library of basic software components which can be reused; it contains a graphic object editor, an object animation kernel, elementary user interface objects, standard graphic animation objects (gauges, curves, variables, icons, ...) and drawings (circles, lines, rectangles, texts, ...). The objective set for GIGA is that it should be able to rapidly produce graphic animation construction

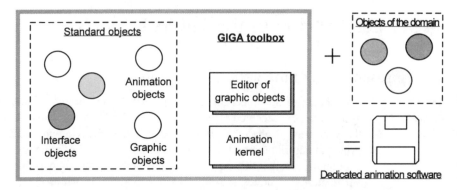

Figure 5.11   Construction of animation software dedicated to a domain.

software, dedicated to a precise domain, from an assembly of basic components and components peculiar to the domain concerned. For the moment, whenever we wish to produce animation software for a particular domain, it is necessary to provide a library of objects specific to the domain concerned. These objects come from a domain analysis followed by the analysis and design phases recommended by M2PO. Objects identified must be implemented by taking into account specifications of the abstract superclasses defined, for animation and object editing, by the GIGA components. This work authorizes the construction of a library of objects specific to each domain tackled. A library peculiar to one domain is intended to be associated with the library of standard components by binding. The result of this binding has the power of a dedicated tool (Figure 5.11), while keeping the same functions as all the tools produced with GIGA (the habits of potential users are preserved). The development of such a family of tools is largely facilitated by the separation effected between the objects of the domain and the objects of the standard library. In fact, not only is there reuse of the analysis, the design and the code of the standard components (mainly the editor and the object animator) but any development of the code of these components may be immediately reflected in all the tools of the family.

Each software item created with GIGA for a particular domain includes a graphic object editor and an object animator. The editor is, in a way, a graphic model construction tool which manipulates the standard animation and drawing objects, as well as the objects specific to a particular domain. The animation of a graphic model is based on the reception of events which trigger animation. These triggering events can be sent, in the form of messages, to graphic objects by any kind of simulation software. Each animation object is capable of interpreting a message intended for it and of visually displaying the behaviour associated with this message according to its class.

To continue the description of GIGA, we will use the graphic notation of the M2PO object modelling method, which may be applied with the same formalism from domain analysis to detailed design.

THE
CHOICE OF
AN OBJECT-
ORIENTED
LANGUAGE

To implement this toolbox, we need an effective industrial language with the following qualities: facilities for abstraction, encapsulation, inheritance and polymorphism, static typing and good modularity. We believe that the C++ language (Stroustrup, 1986; Ellis and Stroustrup, 1990) provides developers with the main object-oriented programming facilities that they may need to construct complex graphic software.

With the same criteria, we could have chosen the Eiffel language (Meyer, 1988) which would add excellent legibility to the list of qualities given above. However, the Eiffel ISE environment was not available on PC/PS microcomputers, which were the target machines when the project started in 1989. As regards our requirements, the C++ language has provided us with the efficiency of the C language and the powerful concepts introduced in Simula. Developments were also carried out on NeXt workstations where the Objective-C language is available; its contribution is the flexibility of its dynamic typing combined with secure static typing.

5.3.2 Analysis and design

THE
GIGA OBJECT
SUBSYSTEMS

The software components to be produced do not correspond to simulation models, as they do not possess, properly speaking, a decisional subsystem. We present logical and physical subsystems which are broken down into two sub-assemblies. The first sub-assembly corresponds to the library of standard GIGA components, and the second to libraries dedicated to various domains. These specific libraries contain all the objects of one domain which are capable of providing information concerning the dynamic behaviour of the systems of the domain concerned.

The library of standard GIGA components possesses the following object subsystems (themselves forming part of the physical subsystem):

- a subsystem for the user interfaces;
- a subsystem of graphic objects broken down into static objects and dynamic objects for animation;
- a subsystem for the editing of icons;
- a subsystem for the editing of models;
- a subsystem for animating models.

The subsystem of user interfaces was created for microcomputers when there was still no C++ tool for constructing interfaces on PCs (1988). The classes identified in this subsystem are the classic scrolling menus, dialog boxes with filtering, buttons and other objects in relief which can make the life of a user armed with a mouse much easier. The number of user interface objects which have been implemented is sufficient for prototyping. Their use is only justified in so far as there is no other more powerful alternative. It would be out of place to implement this group of objects under openNeXT or NeXTStep, when we have a monument such as InterfaceBuilder. Figure 5.12 gives the classes identified, as well as the

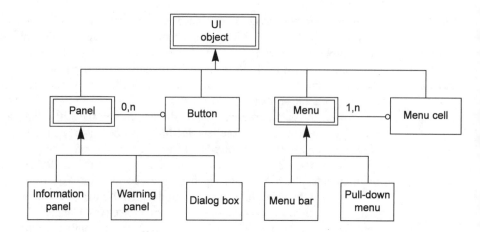

Figure 5.12 Class layer/inheritance layer/composition of object subsystems for user interfaces.

static structure of these classes.

The subsystem of graphic objects proposes two abstract superclasses, one corresponding to the objects described as 'static' and the other to 'dynamic' objects. The static objects are the graphic objects which do not move and which do not change state during an animation. These objects include commentary texts, lines, arrows, circles, boxes and icons used for the captions and to make the flat background of a graphic model agreeable. The dynamic objects, which change state during animation and are animated on receipt of messages from a simulator, are again split into two groups.

The first group corresponds to graphic objects specific to the domain, and the second to the independent objects of the domain. The first group of objects results from a domain analysis followed by an analysis and a design with a view to producing simulation animations. These objects could be, for example, machines, conveyors, stocks and wire-guided automated vehicles (AGVs) for the domain of flexible manufacturing systems, or places, transitions and arcs for the domain of Petri nets. The second group consists of graphic objects: curves, gauges, variables and animated icons, capable of moving on the screen if ordered to do so by an animation message (Figure 5.13). Figure 5.14 gives an example of a class index card for variables.

The logical subsystem takes transactions into account. To represent the transactions (dynamic entities, clients, and so on) which will transit graphically through a discrete flow model during an animation, we have chosen coloured icons. Each class of transaction is associated with an icon defined by an object-oriented colour icon editor, which also manages the library of icons. A transaction will, for example, be represented by a part or a finished product in a manufacturing system, by a token in a Petri net, or by people who are clients of an administrative system.

All the objects necessary for the manipulation of icons are grouped together

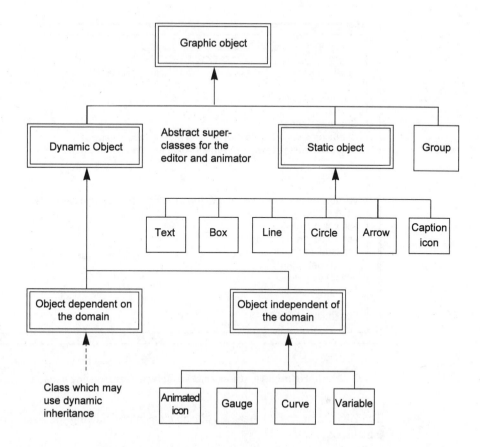

Figure 5.13   Inheritance graph of GIGA graphic objects.

in the icon editing subsystem. The advantage of object-oriented icon editing lies in the fact that a user no longer manages pixels on a bitmap, but has a basic drawing object toolbox which facilitates input, capture and modifications. The user therefore has the possibility of carrying out operations such as capturing, selecting, moving, grouping together, and cutting/copying/pasting objects such as circles, boxes and lines, no longer at the pixel level, but at the level of a grid of graphic squares, representing enlarged pixels. The scale of the editor grid varies and the size of the icons also varies (2×2 up to 64×64 rectangular icons being authorized). This technique, which is very flexible for the user, required the reprogramming of the basic drawing algorithms (Bresenham, 1965; Burger and Gillies, 1989) at the level of the editing grid squares. This work represents a substantial effort solely for the comfort of the user.

The editing and animation subsystems are mainly mechanism objects which include the features of graphic model manipulation and elementary graphic objects.

Name of the class: VARIABLE
Reference to superclass: STATIC OBJECT
Persistent object: YES   Active objects: NO

Instance attributes:

Character string
Character strings (which may contain real or integer values)
Character strings (twice the current value to safeguard main memory)

Instance method:

variable (string (name), string (wording), integer (x 4 coordinates), integer
short (colour))
set_value (string)
set_value_phmc (string)
set_label (string)
(string) get_label
(string) get_value
(string) get_value_phmc

Constraints: NONE

Figure 5.14   Class card for objects manipulating variables.

The GIGA object editor behaves like an elementary drawing software, controlled by a mouse.

The main objective of this editor is not to produce a pseudo-3D background but it should allow the construction and rapid and easy updating of models consisting of static and dynamic objects.

The subsystems for object animation and editing use an abstract superclass common to static and dynamic objects. This superclass allows the definition of polymorphic methods for the editing and animation kernels. Implementation mainly uses C++ members which are pointers to virtual functions. Objects specific to one domain are also organized in a hierarchy, and in the subclasses of such objects virtual methods inherited may be redefined. For all classes, the important attributes are associated with access and modification methods. The persistence of graphic objects is implemented by associating with each class a static C++ member (class method) responsible for its creation and initialization by calling up the C++ constructor of the class, as well as a virtual function (instance method) responsible for disk writing. It is also essential to store a class indicator as an instance attribute. The need for information concerning classes at runtime seems to plead in favour of dynamic typing models, which have this information. However, the fact that a not insignificant number of possible execution errors are detected by

Name of the class: graphic_obj
Reference to superclass:
Persistent objects: YES   Active objects: NO

Instance attributes:
Name   Character string
xig,yig   Unsigned integer: coordinates bottom left-hand
xsd,ysd   side and top right-hand side of the box
                                        containing the graphic objects
colour   Integer
type_object   Integer (stored to manage persistence)

Instance methods:
graphic_obj   Constructor and destructor (C++)
virtual void display(int)   Display the graphic object
virtual void save(FILE*)   Save it on disk
virtual void mcolour(int)   Change its colour
virtual void msize(int)   or its size
virtual int contains   Test whether an object is at the coordinates of
(unsigned,unsigned)   the mouse
virtual void affanim   Display the object for animation
char *getname()   Access to the name
int   gettype()   and to the type

Instance methods (continued)
  void getcoord(unsigned&,   Access to the object coordinates
    unsigned&, unsigned&, unsigned&)
  void erase(int)   Erase the graphic object
  void move(unsigned, unsigned)   Move it

Class method
  static int unarchive(FILE*)   Extraction from a file for persistence

Figure 5.15   Card for the abstract class of graphic objects.

the compiler swung the balance over to the side of static typing when the first development on a microcomputer was undertaken at the end of 1989.

The cards for the abstract classes of the graphic and dynamic objects are given in Figures 5.15 and 5.16.

```
Name of the class: dynamic-obj
Reference to superclass: graphic_obj
Persistence objects: YES                    Active objects: NO

Instance attributes:

animation_step                Integer (no variable animation)
hypergraph                    String (for hypergraphics link)

Instance methods:

dynamic_obj                   Constructor and destructor (C ++)
virtual void animinit()       Initialized animation parameters
virtual void saveshot(FILE *) Save and load an animation state
virtual void chargeshot(char *) to file
virtual void affstruct()      Display the clients contained in the object
virtual void savephmc()       Save and load a state of
virtual void loadphmc()       animation from main memory
virtual void listobj(FILE *fp) List the characteristics of the
                              object on a file
virtual void load(CLIENT *)   Load a client
virtual void unload()         Unload a client
void fnameobj(FILE*)          List the name of the dynamic object on the file
int get_anim_step()           Access to the variable animation step
```

Figure 5.16   Card for the abstract class of dynamic objects.

FUNCTIONS
COMMON TO
SOFTWARE
CREATED
WITH GIGA

Software created with GIGA is articulated around a graphic editing menu and a model construction plan. The editor menu gives access to the animator menu. The editor proposes an 'object' menu combining all classes specific to the domain dealt with, as well as independent dynamic animation objects of the domain. A background menu presents a list of static drawing objects. Once a model has been constructed, the animation menu makes it possible to choose the support for communication with the simulator. Animation of dynamic objects is activated on receipt of messages distributed by the GIGA object animation kernel.

Amongst the various techniques for exchanging messages, we mainly use the animator as a messages file post-processor. We also use 'direct' animation of simulations on a UNIX workstation using IPC (InterProcess Communication running under UNIX) to generate communications between the simulator and animator. Concurrent execution of simulation and animation may be effected on a network of workstations, the simulator being at a specialized calculation node, and the animator at a specialized graphics node. The visual interactive simulation technique which allows a user to modify the process during simulation has not been implemented for GIGA. It is in fact necessary to have simulation software items that are sufficiently open so that they can be interrupted in response to a user event, in order to modify certain simulation object characteristics of the model undergoing execution. The most critical thing is that it is still necessary for the

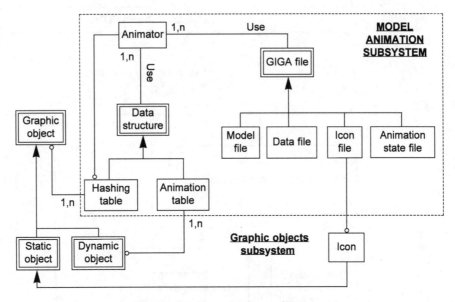

Figure 5.17   The animation subsystem.

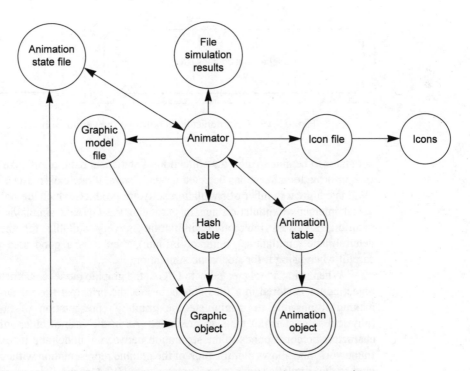

Figure 5.18   M2PO MFD centred on the animator object.

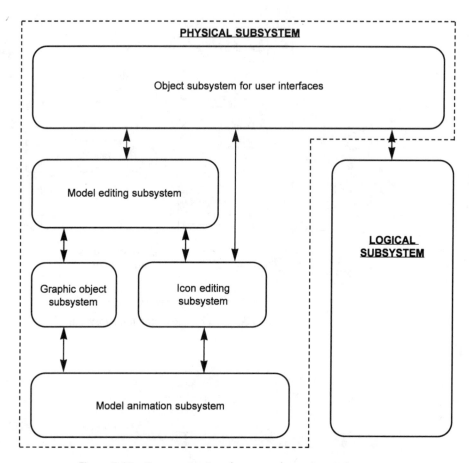

Figure 5.19   Communications between the various subsystems.

simulator to be able to stop the collection of statistical data, reinitialize it and only give information after it has detected a steady state, if one exists. These constraints eliminate a great number of simulation software products which are not adapted to visual interactive simulation and in particular the QNAP2 simulator we use. In addition, if visual interactive simulation is very suitable for the study of deterministic simulations (finite or infinite), then it is a good idea to be very careful when using it for stochastic simulation.

When using a tool created with GIGA, the graphic model constructed with the object editor is stored in a file. This is in fact the principal file for an animation, making it possible to manipulate the graphic representation of the topology (physical subsystem) of the system studied. As in the case of other software, this characteristic corresponds to the separation between a model and its experimental framework, and allows modification of the graphic representation without having to modify the simulation code. A tool created with GIGA manipulates other categories of files, principally the icon files and animation state files. The other categories of files are of a documentary nature (the list of transactions for a model (clients, active entities), list of instances specific to the domain for a model, ...). Icon files store information about coloured bitmaps and animation state files store the complete state of all the dynamic objects at a particular simulation time. Figure 5.17 illustrates the relationships between the animator, the various files, and the data structures manipulated within the model animation subsystem. Figure 5.18 gives the corresponding M2PO MFD. The links with the graphic objects subsystem will be noted. Communications between the various systems are given in Figure 5.19.

THE CHOICES FOR ANIMATION   To animate a simulation model it is necessary to include message transmissions in the source code of the simulation model. It is preferable to use an object-oriented simulation language such as Simula, ModSim, ROSS or QNAP2v8 but any general simulation language such as GPSS/H, SIMAN IV, SLAM II or SIMSCRIPT may be suitable. The most important fact remains that the simulation software must be completely verified, without which no serious study is possible.

In parallel with the development of the simulation model, the user may graphically construct the topology of the system using the GIGA editor. When the graphic model and simulation model are ready, simulation still has to be started and it is still necessary to indicate to the animator the support chosen for the simulation messages. Figure 5.20 illustrates the animation process proposed for the various possible approaches.

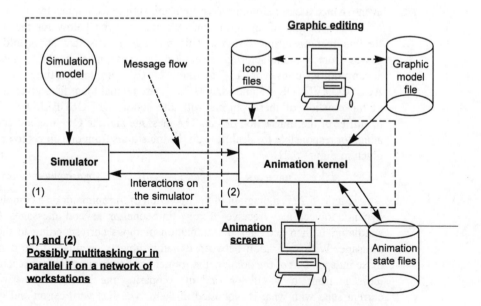

Figure 5.20 The animation process.

```
//──────────────────────────────────────────────────//
//transit   A client transits from one object to another    //
//At the input: p1, p2 and p3 are identifiers in textual     //
//              form of dynamic animation objects            //
//──────────────────────────────────────────────────//
void anim::transit (char *p1, char *p2, char *p3)
{
  dynamic_object *po1, *po2, *po3;

  po1 = hashtable->search (p1); //Test whether the object exists
  if (*po1) {U_gwarning (strcat (p1, objinex)); return;}
  po2 = hashtable->search (p2); //Test whether object 2 exists
  if (*po2) {U_gwarning (strcat (p2, objinex)); return; }
  po3 = hashtable->search (p3); //Test whether the client class exists
  if (*po3  po3->gettype () != CLIENT)) {
     U_gwarning (strcat (p3) classeinex));
     return:
     }
  po1->unload ();        //Dynamic change of client class
  po2->load (po3);       //possible on a transition
}
```

Figure 5.21   C++ Code of the animator method dealing with the passage of clients (transactions) from one object to another.

Each animation message concerns a set of objects, each of them knowing the animation method to be applied according to their class and state. The synchronizing kernel of the animator endeavours to smooth out the animation between two events which are not simultaneous, by using simple techniques from video games.

An example of an animation message is given below for the domain of flexible manufacturing systems. This message means that an unsoldered part passes from a manufacturing object (in this case machine 1) to another (the accumulating conveyor 15) at the 'TIME' simulation time. The names ACC_CONVEYOR_15 and MACHINE_1 are textual identifiers given at the time of the creation of these objects with the editor; UNSOLDERED_PART is an identifier of the transaction object. The message and the C++ method code of the animator responsible for dealing with the transitions from one object to another are given in Figure 5.21.

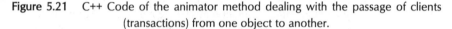

TIME   MACHINE_1   ACC_CONVEYOR_15   UNSOLDERED_PART

Figure 5.22 is a diagram of the operation of the animator on a computer. Each dynamic object may receive at any time one or several messages from the simulator. It then activates the animation methods corresponding to the current message. With separation between dynamic objects peculiar to the domain and those independent of the domain, the former have the opportunity of reacting to the message from the simulator, and of comparing the consistency between their current state with what is requested of them. The fine verification and validation techniques of knowledge models are therefore taken back to the code of the objects dependent on the domain.

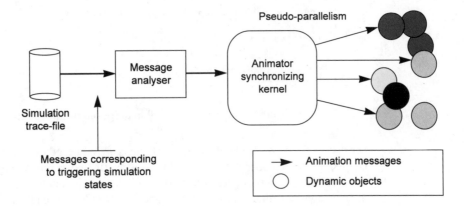

Figure 5.22   Internal animation process.

Dynamic objects to be animated are stored in an animation table which contains the references to dynamic objects which have to be moved, as well as the times at which these movements are to occur (a function of the variable animation step of each object). The code of the 'moveall' method of the animator object called up in the synchronizing kernel is given in Figure 5.23.

```
//─────────────────────────────────────────────//
//A_moveall     Moving of dynamic objects                        //
//─────────────────────────────────────────────//
void anim::moveall()
{
  register          i;
  struct obj_amim   *po:

  for(i=0 ; i < nbeltanim ;i++){          //walk through the
    po = (tab_anim + i);                  //animation table with
    if (T >= po->nexttime) {              //testing of objects
        ((dynamic_obj *) po->pobjet)->anim();   //which have to
        po->nexttime+=po->pobjet->get_anim_step(); //be animated
        }                                 //and MAJ variable
  }
}
//──────────────────────────────────────//animation step.
```

Figure 5.23   C++ code of the 'moveall' method.

THE STRUCTURES USED   The link between the graphic objects and the simulation model is achieved by the name of the object (which remains unique). A dynamic hashing table is used to obtain reasonable performance as regards access to dynamic objects (Lewis, 1988). All of the graphic objects (dynamic and static) are stored in this table. The key

```
unsigned int hash::Stroustrup (char *s, int modulo)
{
    unsigned i = 0;
    while (*s) i = i<<1  * s++;
    i = i & (modulo-1);
    return i;
}
```

Figure 5.24   Hashing algorithm proposed by Stroustrup.

consists of the name of the object; the collisions are managed by linking. This table is used as a container for the graphic objects (in the sense of object-oriented programming), and particularly to find the objects again rapidly when interpreting the messages contained in a simulation trace file. We have used the simple and fast hashing algorithm proposed by Stroustrup (1986) (Figure 5.24).

When the dynamic objects to which a simulator is addressed are found in memory again, by means of the hashing table, they are capable of receiving virtual method calls, requesting them to activate one of their methods. In the event of using the table as a container for dynamic objects, we have used C++ pointers to virtual member functions to implement the scanning with virtual method call-up in the most flexible way possible. Figure 5.25 gives an example of a hashing table class method accepting parametrized virtual methods.

```
// ——————————————————————————————————————— //
// scanV Access to all the table elements to activate a virtual method   //
// At the input: the virtual function to be applied to each element.     //
// ——————————————————————————————————————— //
void hash::scanV (void (dynamic_object::*ptrfnv) ())
{
    struct elthash *pcrt;
    register      i;

    for ( i = 0; i < MAXHASH ; i++) {
        if (!*(tab_hash + i)) continue;    // input empty
        pcrt = * (tab_hash + i);           // head of list
        while (pcrt) {
          (pcrt -> pobjet -> *ptrfnv) (); // virtual fn active
          pcrt = pcrt -> psuiv;            // on the current object
          }
        }
}
```

Figure 5.25   Scanning of the table with activation of a virtual method parametrized for all the objects.

FUNCTIONS OF THE ANIMATOR   The basic functions of the animator include the ability to slow down or accelerate the speed of animation, to stop animation for a moment and to trace all the simulation events triggering animation step by step.

Software constructed with GIGA allows an animation state to be saved at any

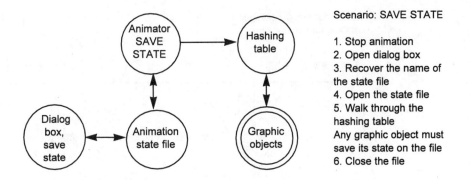

Figure 5.26   MFD and scenario for archiving an animation state.

moment 'T' of the simulation. This very useful technique for the presentation of results then allows the animation to be started at simulation time 'T', after the loading of the animation state file. In the event of using the animator as a post-processor, it is sufficient for the animator to find the position at time T, using direct access, in an animation messages trace file. In the case of direct animation, it is also necessary to safeguard the state of the simulator in order to be able to load it again subsequently. Figure 5.26 gives a message flow diagram and a general scenario for saving a state.

Another function of the animator makes it possible to prevent any graphic displays occurring until the user has reached a simulation time which he or she specifies. The animator receives messages and distributes them to objects which update their states without displaying anything. This function may be used to avoid certain transient phases of a system which are not of any interest, or to save time in manipulating large, complex models.

This technique, moreover, allows acceleration of the animator kernel (three times faster than when the displays are effected). This type of technique can be easily implemented, for the codes of the objects created respect a separation between the graphics part and the part which updates data structures.

When communication between animator and simulator is supported by a file (the animator operating as a post-processor), it is possible to effect flashbacks in the simulation time. For instance, if a user lacks the details of a sequence of events, he or she may revise this sequence by effecting a flashback in the simulation time (it is then possible to slow animation down or to effect it step by step). This technique requires each dynamic object to have a copy of all its state attributes in memory. This copy is updated every 'dT' (where 'dT' is an interval of simulation time specified by the user) (Figure 5.27). By means of dynamic polymorphic state saving and restoration methods, it is relatively simple and extremely fast to keep a previous state and reload it.

Figure 5.28 summarizes the general operation of the animator object by presenting its communicating Petri net with macro-places (in accordance with

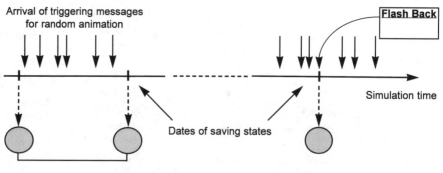

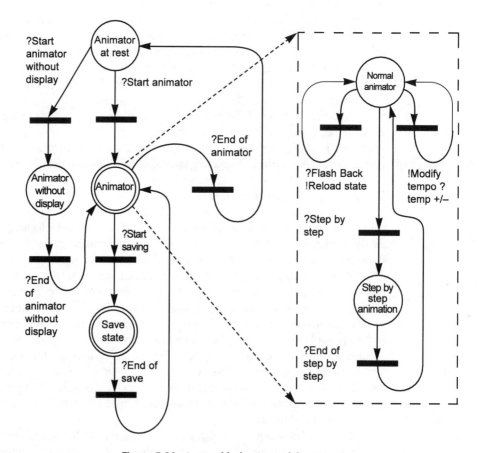

Figure 5.27   'Flash Back' technique.

Figure 5.28   Internal behaviour of the animator.

M2PO). The events are mostly from the user. One of the macro-places is shown in detail to illustrate the possibilities of hierarchical decomposition.

5.3.3 Debugging techniques

In order to obtain a high model verification potential, it is fundamentally necessary to include verification techniques within the dynamic animation objects. To do this, each behaviour of a dynamic object is modelled, as recommended by M2PO, by means of an interpreted and communicating Petri net, capable of giving a precise error message in the event of inconsistency. In fact, each object, knowing the precise state it is in, is capable of determining whether the message from the simulator is correct. In the event of inconsistency, the user knows the object concerned, the type of error and the simulation time at which the error occurred. For example, it is absurd to ask a lift object to open its doors at the second floor, if it is currently between the tenth and ninth floors. Figure 5.29 shows a communicating Petri net simplified to describe the internal behaviour of a line object. The inclusion of debugging techniques within the objects, depending on their class, is one of the contributions of GIGA which assumes that the domain and design analysis of the behaviours of the objects have been completely validated by the experts in the domain. These techniques have become very important in the verification of simulation models. This does not mean that simulation objects must strictly include the same behaviours, for animation objects only reflect a consistent visual behaviour of the objects of a real system.

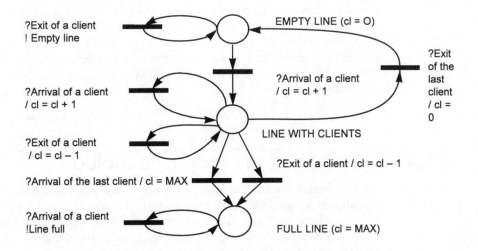

Figure 5.29 Internal behaviour of a queue object with limited capacity specified with an M2PO Petri net.

5.3.4 Hypergraphics

Another interesting function is based on hypertext techniques. It gives a user the possibility of distributing his or her graphic model over different planes. 'Hypertext style' navigation is authorized between these various planes by means of dynamic access objects, peculiar to the domain of the application, which incorporate other objects (dynamic and static). Each animation object specific to the domain may become an access object; the links are not strictly hierarchical, allowing reuse of graphic submodels made up of static objects. This technique may be used, for example, in a model based on queueing networks where a server may incorporate a sub-network of queues (Figure 5.30).

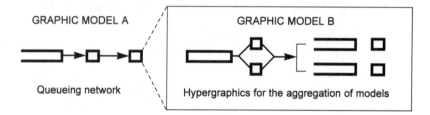

Figure 5.30　An example of hyperlinks used for aggregation.

5.3.5 Technical characteristics

The first version of GIGA was developed in 1989 on an IBM PS/2 running under MS-DOS with the C++ language and represented 20 000 lines of code. For this version no mathematical co-processor was necessary and the size of the object files (resulting from compilation) did not exceed 300 Kb. The graphics card should be VGA compatible. A Microsoft or compatible mouse is also necessary. The software also operated on Apollo Domain 30xx stations and on the series of HP/Apollo 400 stations. The present version of the GIGA toolbox is still used on UNIX workstations.

5.4　Limitations of the proposed toolbox

For the moment the majority of the operations necessary to create an editing and animation software for a domain are manual. The domain and design analysis of specific objects, including the discovery of the main visual behaviours of real objects, remain arduous tasks requiring both simulationists and experts in the domain concerned. The graphic representation of dynamic objects peculiar to a system and their animation methods must be at once clear, realistic and symbolic, in order to possess a high level of significance for a user. This type of consideration is based on ergonomic choices which are tricky to assess and which have to be discussed with domain experts. For example, a conveyor in a manufacturing system must be capable of being easily identified as a conveyor in a graphic model, and in addition, if it is an accumulating conveyor, it must be animated like an accumulating conveyor. This does not, however, mean that these objects must be drawn with CAD software (GIGA is not a CAD tool). We believe in addition that an excessive level of graphics may be harmful to the productivity of most simulation projects. The time spent drawing may be considerable if the system is complex; moreover, all the tools which provide this type of function have the defect of only presenting demonstrations of small models possessing very few dynamic objects. This level of detail is more oriented towards selling to a decision-maker than towards simulation model validation and verification. For our part, we limit ourselves to symbolic graphic representations which are realistic and which for the moment satisfy experts in the domains we have tackled.

The number of objects which may be manipulated with GIGA is not limited from the start, for it is always a matter of dynamic memory allocation, thus relying on the hardware configuration.

Only the size of the memory limits the size of the models. Industrial cases processed with the manufacturing systems editor/animator constructed on the basis of GIGA sometimes use over 300 objects specific to the domain, and only consume 10% of the dynamic memory remaining in a microcomputer which has 340 Kb of usable memory (after loading the animator (running under MS-DOS)).

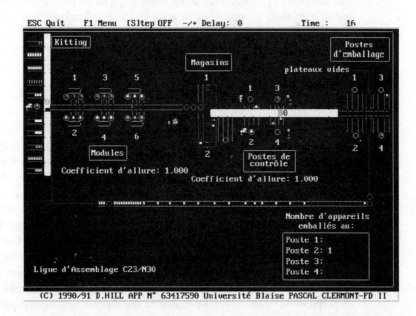

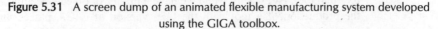

Figure 5.31 A screen dump of an animated flexible manufacturing system developed using the GIGA toolbox.

Amongst other limitations, we have already stated that we do not offer any real possibilities of visual interactive simulation (allowing a user to modify the process during simulation). This arises mainly from one of our objectives, which is to remain independent of the simulation tool.

We must point out that GIGA versions in C++ do not allow 100% reusability. In fact, the components that manage graphic capture of the objects and persistence must be edited when a tool is constructed for a particular domain.

It is necessary to add a portion of code specific to the classes of the domain dealt with so as to know what objects to construct when the user makes a choice, or when a model is loaded.

The problem does not arise under NeXTStep, thanks to the dynamic typing of Objective-C which allows more flexible management of persistence, making it possible, for example, to recover the name of the class of the object to be created in the tool palette proposed by a graphic objects editor component (Figure 5.31). The same type of technique is of course applicable to Smalltalk. The risks involved in not checking types are then the responsibility of the developers.

◁ 5.5 Conclusion

We have presented the GIGA toolbox with its reusable software components which are independent of any simulation software. The major objective was to be able to assist specialists in modelling to achieve valid animations. We have shown what a graphic animation may contribute in terms of validation and verification. The choice of an object-oriented approach makes it possible, amongst other things, to work at the level of abstraction of the entities of the real system, which are monitored visually, with animated graphic objects. To increase the chances of detecting inconsistencies in simulation models, we have organized the classes that manipulate GIGA components into graphic objects dependent on the domain and objects independent of the domain. The GIGA animator component, which receives the messages from the simulator, gives the objects of a graphic model the possibility of reacting to the messages they receive. We therefore bring the essence of validation techniques to the graphic objects dependent on the domain. The behaviour of these objects must be defined carefully by experts in the domain, who are best suited to finding valid forms of behaviour. The visual behaviour of these objects must correspond to states which are of significance to the experts.

To produce a hybrid animation tool, which has the features of general software while still having the power of dedicated tools, a modelling specialist may now concentrate on the domain of his or her choice and reuse the editing and animating components of objects supplied by GIGA. With our choices, the quality of preparation of the objects peculiar to the domain will determine the potential of the final tool. At present, when we have a library of objects peculiar to one domain, the production of a tool with the C++ version of GIGA passes through a set of manipulations which may take a whole day. With dynamic inheritance techniques it would be possible to supply an automatic tool, giving users the possibility of choosing and loading a library of objects peculiar to one domain, then using the tool they have just built dynamically.

In what follows, we will use the GIGA toolbox for two domains: flexible manufacturing systems and Petri nets.

We will then deal with the problems of automatic simulation code generation from graphic specifications of models based on the editing components of the graphic objects proposed in GIGA.

◁ KEY POINTS

- Techniques of animating simulation results become accessible to the widest number of people with the appearance of low-priced microcomputers and workstations which have good quality graphics cards.
- The principal contributions of graphics in a simulation project concern: the debugging and verification of simulation programs, the validation of knowledge and action models, the analysis of results and the design of experiments, communications and presentation of results.
- The principal errors which animation makes it possible to discover are: programming errors, errors made at the time of building the knowledge models, and errors involved in failing to take account of certain reactions of the system which might manifest themselves visually by unusual behaviours.
- Gains perceived by graphic animation users concern mainly gains in confidence, gains in understanding and increases in the involvement of system experts who wish to become more involved in the projects.
- The various simulation animation techniques are simulation animation using a post-processor, direct simulation animation and visual interactive simulation.
- Management of time in an animation is of capital importance in order to gain a real verification and validation potential. It is absolutely necessary to effect a transformation of the discrete time of the simulation events into a continuous time for animation.
- Multitasking systems pose problems for the animation of simulation results, because the periodic interruption of the processes may disturb the visual understanding of the system functioning. This problem is only really resolved on powerful types of architecture which have powerful graphic co-processors which assist the central processor.
- The animation of simulation results may be dangerous if the user 'forgets' or does not realize that what he or she is observing is only a small sample of a stochastic process.
- Visual interactive simulation is very well suited to the animation of deterministic simulations but presents dangers if, without precaution, we modify the sensitive parameters of a stochastic simulation.

◁ Exercises

5.1 Explain what the contributions and disadvantages of animation might be in analysing the transient results of a system.

5.2 What are the advantages and disadvantages of using animation as a communications and results presentation tool?

5.3 What solutions can artificial intelligence not provide for the intrinsic problems of visual interactive simulation?

5.4 What would be the advantages in the design of GIGA of dedicating this toolbox to specific simulation software, rather than making it independent of simulation tools?

5.5 What are the various types of interaction between a simulator and the animation kernel? How can we determine which simulation events are triggering events for the animation?

5.6 GIGA uses virtual C++ functions as parameters with 'iterative' methods. What are the advantages and disadvantages of this choice and what substitute technique may be proposed?

5.7 Amongst the M2PO message stream diagrams presented in this chapter, some use the concept of an 'abstract object'. Try to construct similar diagrams without these abstract objects, and compare them with the first ones.

5.8 The technique of a flashback during the simulation time of the 'animation film' is implemented in the GIGA animation kernel. What are the advantages of an object-oriented approach for this type of technique?

5.9 Propose constraints for the 'graphic_obj' class described by the instance card in Figure 5.15.

5.10 Justify the use of a macro-place in the M2PO RdP of Figure 5.28 (if necessary, redraw the network without this macro-place).

5.11 Give an example of the possible use of GIGA hypergraphics for animating flows of persons in a 20-storey building.

6

Generation of simulation animation code

◁ OBJECTIVES

This chapter presents various applications of the GIGA toolbox. These applications mainly concern the automatic generation of simulation code from a graphic model specification. The simulation code generated then allows us to animate the graphic model. We will first describe the design of this software with the M2PO notation, giving a summary presentation of testing techniques from software engineering which have been applied in an industrial environment. We will also present a case study of the modelling of a flexible workshop illustrating the code-generating possibilities. We will describe how we have adapted the possibilities of the QNAP2 simulation software language to take account of polymorphism, delegation and dynamic classification. Finally, different techniques of generating simulation code from a Petri net animator/editor are proposed, illustrating the multi-domain aspect of the GIGA toolbox.

◁ 6.1 Introduction

The first application concerns the generation of object-oriented QNAP2 code for flexible manufacturing systems. Initially, we describe how GIGA allows us to produce an animator for simulating models of manufacturing systems for the VALEO group (VALEO is a car parts manufacturer). We reuse the results of the GIGA study (from domain analysis to implementation) and the results of the domain analysis carried out for the SIGMA project. This last analysis made it possible to identify the object classes of the domain of discrete flow assembly systems, as well as the relationships which exist between these classes.

Following this stage of reuse, it is necessary to design a set of graphic objects adapted for animation and specify their behaviours so as to increase the validation and verification potential of the final animation software. We will give a general description of software, called GAME, which we designed for the VALEO group; a detailed description of it may be found in Hill and Junqua (1990). This software communicates with the simulator in accordance with protocols established for GIGA, and it must be capable of detecting and signalling the inconsistencies of a simulation program (programming or modelling errors). The analysis for the production of GAME, as well as the specification of animation object behaviours, uses the M2PO graphic notation. The GAME software is then tested on industrial cases.

We then adapt the GAME software, in order to be in a position to generate object-oriented QNAP2 simulation code automatically from a graphic model of a manufacturing system. We present the choices made and more particularly the codes specific to the physical, logical and decisional subsystems on a flexible manufacturing line. The technique proposed uses a combination of the transaction approach and the station approach. The generation of simulation code allows us to avoid most of the errors in the programming of a simulation model. Animation then facilitates the highlighting of modelling errors, thereby assisting in the validation of the knowledge model of a system.

The generation of object-oriented simulation code has allowed us to identify gaps at the level of the object-oriented functions of the QNAP2 language, in particular as regards dynamic classification and polymorphism. We offer a solution which will allow these gaps to be filled, using a compromise between the implementation of delegation techniques and dynamic inheritance of methods.

Another use of the GIGA toolbox has been produced for Petri nets. We shall not deal with the network editing and animating part which we have already detailed in Caux *et al.* (1991), but we describe the possibilities of generating QNAP2 code, SIMAN IV code and more particularly Occam 2 code. We describe the techniques used to model the operation of a set of interpreted and communicating Petri nets on a network of transputers.

◁ 6.2 Generation of object-oriented simulation code and animation of manufacturing systems

6.2.1 The editing and animation of discrete flow assembly system models

INTRODUCTION To satisfy the needs of the market, industrialists are using increasingly complex means of production: automated assembly systems, flexible workshops, and so on. In order to resolve problems which modern manufacturing systems throw up (dimensioning, understanding and improvement of their operation, evaluation of their performance, ...), the industrialists modify the topology and/or the rules of management of their systems. In most cases, they discover that their actions are not always convincing: the number of events to be understood, the correlation between most of these events, the difficulty in gaining an overall view of a system, and so on are such that empirical methods are no longer sufficient. For all these reasons, industrialists are increasingly seeking methods which will allow them to solve effectively these problems of the design, dimensioning, reconfiguration and analysis of the operation of a manufacturing system. We have chosen discrete event simulation to evaluate performance, to study flows in workshops (parts, materials, ...), to study resources (human resources, stocks of machines, transport systems, ...) and to predict behaviour. When studying flexible manufacturing systems by simulation, it is sometimes interesting, indeed necessary, to study the transient behaviour of these systems by means of realistic graphic animation so as to better understand certain critical situations (the influence of breakdowns on the operation of the system, ...). In this context, the VALEO industrial group wanted to have user-friendly and interactive animation software to assist the experts in interpreting the statistical results of simulation. We therefore developed the GAME animation software (Hill and Junqua, 1990; Breugnot *et al.,* 1991a) at the Computer Science Laboratory of the University of Clermont Ferrand II, in close collaboration with the experts on the various VALEO sites which exist in France, the UK and Italy. The industrial version of this software bore the name of VIEWMOD (Breugnot *et al.,* 1991d; Gourgand *et al.,* 1992).

TARGETS SET FOR SOFTWARE FEATURES

All of the GAME functions arise out of the possibilities of editing and animating models as described for the GIGA toolbox. These functions are in accordance with the requirements expressed by the experts of the VALEO group. These requirements were compiled, when visiting sites of the VALEO group, by analysing the results of a sounding grid and by establishing specifications validated by all the experts concerned. The validation of the requirements needed close collaboration between the designers and future users of the software. The stages which were used to define the requirements are given in Sommerville (1988).

The availability of the GIGA toolbox greatly simplifies the production of the GAME software, whether at analysis, design or implementation level. The achievement of GAME consists of including all of the GIGA tools and of adding all of the classes peculiar to the animation of flexible manufacturing systems (FMS). These classes must be organized hierarchically around an abstract superclass of graphic manufacturing objects, which will take the place of the superclass of domain-dependent objects mentioned in GIGA. The interface of the graphic manufacturing objects superclass includes the interface defined by GIGA. Furthermore, all the subclasses must provide a GIGA-compatible interface. Figure 6.1 shows the class of manufacturing objects. To obtain this type of class, a domain analysis should be carried out for the class of discrete flow manufacturing systems, followed by an object-oriented analysis and design adapted to the animation of simulation results.

ANALYSIS OF THE MANU-FACTURING SYSTEM DOMAIN

An analysis of the manufacturing system domain was carried out as part of the SIGMA project (Breugnot *et al.,* 1990). It is based on object-oriented analysis methods and the specification of manufacturing systems (Kellert, 1992), making it possible to describe the topology and operation of these systems as well as flows passing through them. It must be remembered that these methods are based on E/R diagrams designed following an analysis of 10 plants of the VALEO group (Kellert,

Name of the class: MANUFACTURING_OBJECT
Reference to superclass: DYNAMIC_OBJECT
Persistent objects: YES   Active objects: NO

Instance attributes:
state   entire (indicator of breakdown, blockage etc...)
dmem   index to find again the components dealt with by the object
nbpcrt   Instant number of components
state_phmc   Double the object state to safeguard an animation state
                      in main memory
nbpcrt phmc   Ditto for the instant number of components
                      Maximum capacity of number of components
                      Size in pixels

Instance methods:

virtual load (client *)   Load the component on a manufacturing object
virtual unload ( )   Unload components
virtual listobj (FILE *)   List the characteristics of the object on a file
virtual move ( )   Move the object on the screen
virtual breakdown (int, char*)   Management of breakdowns
virtual affanim ( )   Display of the object with the components
virtual animinit ( )   Initialization before animation
virtual saveshot (FILE *)   Save the animation state of the object on a file
virtual loadshot (char *)   Load it
virtual savephmc ( )   Save the animation state in main memory
virtual loadphmc ( )   Load it
virtual init ( )   Load the object before animation
getsize ( )   Access to the size in pixels
getnbpcrt ( )   Enter the capacity of the manufacturing object

Constraints: NONE

Figure 6.1 M2PO card for the abstract class of manufacturing objects.

1991). Transmitting the analysis results to an expert turned out to be easier with the assistance of an E/R diagram, rather than with graphic formalism from another object analysis method. Decomposition into three subsystems gave respectively an E/R diagram for the logical subsystem (ranges and schedules), an E/R diagram for the physical subsystem (topology) and an E/R diagram for the decisional subsystem (rules of management and control). Figure 6.2 gives the M2PO scheme of the physical subsystem deduced from the SIGMA E/R diagram.

In this illustration, the physical subsystem of the domain of discrete flow manufacturing systems is considered as a manufacturing (or storage) unit, which can be broken down hierarchically into other manufacturing units. Each manufacturing unit may contain machines, resources, paths, storage areas, conveyors, sensors and actuators. The machines have posts and/or stations (stations are completely automatic and posts are manual). The tools, workers and conveying supports (pallets, ...) are considered as resources. A path may, for example, be allocated to an accumulating conveyor (which would derive from the class of static conveyors) and

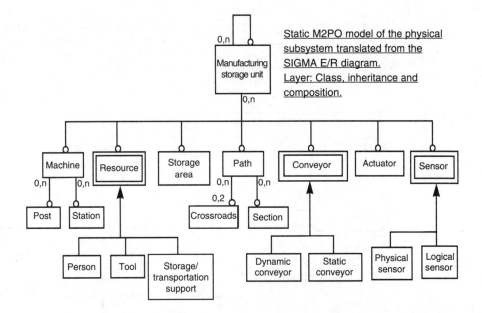

Figure 6.2 M2PO translation of the E/R diagram of the physical subsystem prepared for the SIGMA project.

possibly have several sections with the possibility of junctions. A section is a portion of a path on which only a pure conveying phase is encountered.

The sensors (photoelectric cells, counters, bar code readers, various contacts, ...) provide details to the decisional subsystem concerning the state of the physical subsystem and the actuators (stops, jacks, ...), allowing us to apply the decisions taken. The logical sensors have no physical existence but calculate the values necessary for an understanding of the system. These may be performance criteria evaluated by the experts. The details of these classes and the relationships which link them together may be found in Breugnot *et al.* (1990) and Kellert (1992).

Figure 6.3 represents the logical subsystem and shows flow elements from which components are derived (equipment flows), the information flows (manufacturing order, delivery order), and the labels (Kanban, whether throw-away or not). The composition relationships are used to give the schedules of components, as well as the concept of a range. The schedules show the practical order of utilization of components. The notion of hierarchy is used to represent schedules. Ranges are sets of cycles. Each cycle combines a set of operations of the same type and must be carried out entirely on a single machine. Operations are the elementary processing applied to one or several components (machining, inspection, assembly, ...).

We use the layers 'class', 'inheritance', 'composition' and 'common relationships' simultaneously in Figure 6.3 to represent the logical subsystem (see Section 4.4.5, subsection 'The graphic notation for the static object'). This makes it possible to obtain the same level of information as with the initial E/R diagram (SIGMA project) given in Figure 6.4. In practice, we prefer to work with the M2PO

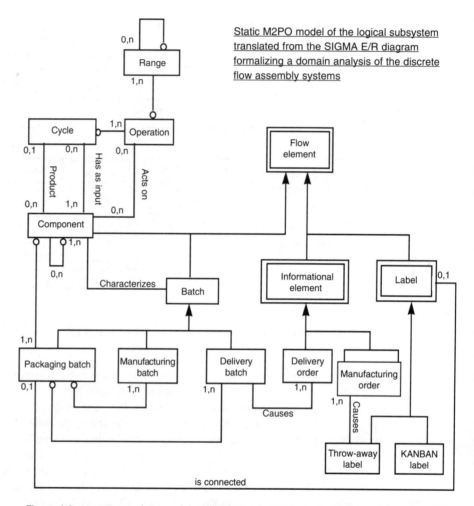

Static M2PO model of the logical subsystem translated from the SIGMA E/R diagram formalizing a domain analysis of the discrete flow assembly systems

Figure 6.3 M2PO translation of the E/R diagram of the logical subsystem prepared for the SIGMA project.

layers (superimposing only a few layers in order to avoid an overload of information). Figure 6.5 gives a separate view of the 'inheritance' layer of the logical subsystem which is much clearer than that which may be seen in Figure 6.3. For the subsystem presented, it is therefore preferable to have three views (class, inheritance; class, composition; class, association) rather than manipulate all layers. It does, however, remain possible to superimpose everything, but the superimposition of views must be generated by a CASE tool.

In Figure 6.6, which presents the decisional subsystem, the only object actually belonging to the decisional subsystem is the decision centre; other objects belong either to the logical subsystem or to the physical subsystem. The decisional subsystem consists of all of the system management and control rules. Each rule has a set of premises and consequences. Figure 6.6 shows the various relationships between the hierarchized decision centres and the other classes of objects from the

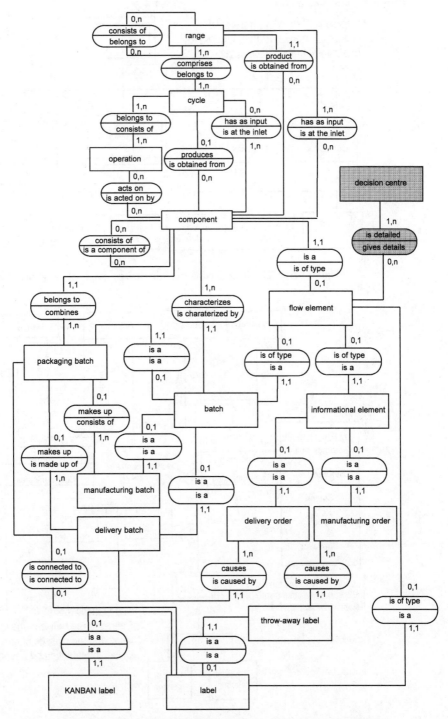

Figure 6.4   E/R model of the logical subsystem prepared for SIGMA .

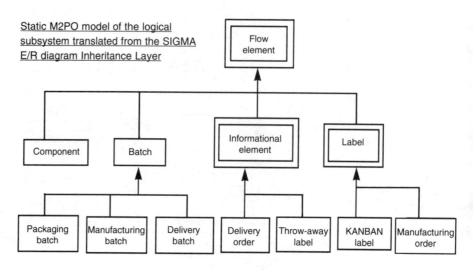

Static M2PO model of the logical subsystem translated from the SIGMA E/R diagram Inheritance Layer

Figure 6.5 M2PO layer giving the inheritance graph of the logical subsystem.

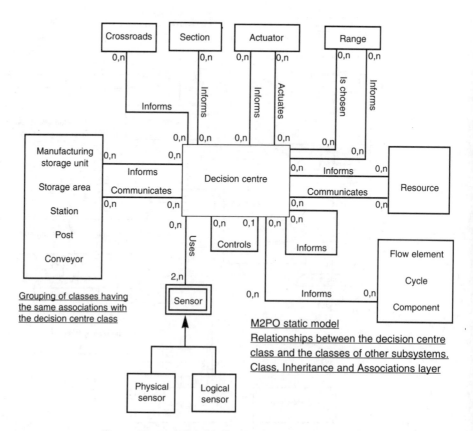

Grouping of classes having the same associations with the decision centre class

M2PO static model
Relationships between the decision centre class and the classes of other subsystems. Class, Inheritance and Associations layer

Figure 6.6 Decisional subsystem prepared for SIGMA.

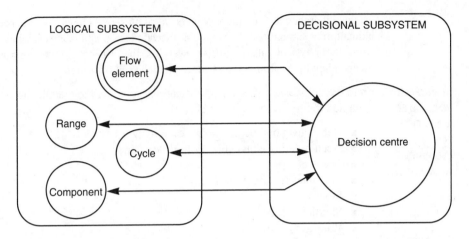

Figure 6.7 M2PO MFD between the logical subsystem and the decisional subsystem.

decisional subsystem. The decision centres manipulate the management and control rules of the system (with premisses and consequences). The communications between the decision centres and the other subsystems may be given in the form of a diagram with M2PO MFDs. Figure 6.7 shows the possible communications between the logical subsystem and the physical subsystem. Communications are effected on the one hand with sensors and by means of the attributes of the objects of the physical subsystem, and on the other with actuators and the aforementioned object methods.

Objects compiled in the translated E/R diagrams allow the deduction and design of the mechanism objects necessary to effect simulations as well as the graphic objects necessary for the production of animations. All the objects designed may therefore be combined in three separate sets, each having common intersections (Figure 6.8) as well

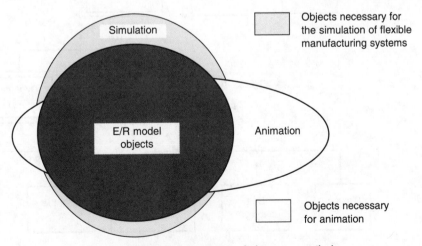

Fig 6.8 The three sets of objects compiled.

as the inherent parts (certain objects, attributes or behaviours are peculiar to the animation or simulation). The GAME software uses graphic objects which are deduced from the physical subsystem, as well as the set of graphic animation objects independent of the domain introduced with the GIGA toolbox.

MANUFACTU- RING OBJECTS IDENTIFIED FOR THE GRAPHIC ANIMATION

From the domain analysis and specifications submitted to manufacturing experts, we compiled the following specific classes:

- Belt conveyors (using chains, or conveyor belts, ...)
- Accumulating conveyors (with rollers, hooks, ...)
- Trolleys
- Machines (posts, stations, ...)
- Stocks
- Shuttles
- Wire-guided trucks and AGVs.

The design of a graphic tool for editing and animating simulation results involves the creation of abstract classes which make it possible to simplify the model which is the object of the solution. Figure 6.9 shows the inheritance hierarchy for the graphic manufacturing objects using M2PO notation. We will identify the following abstract classes for animating manufacturing systems:

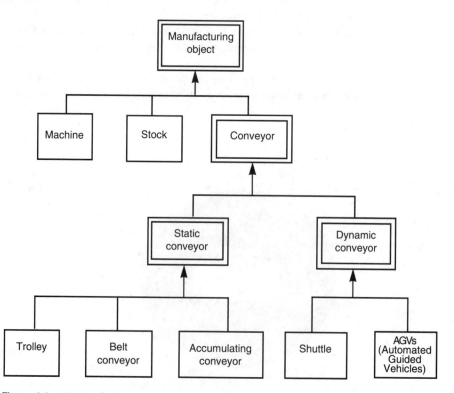

Figure 6.9 M2PO inheritance hierarchy for the classes of graphic manufacturing objects.

- Manufacturing object: this is the abstract superclass which will be equated with the abstract superclass specified in GIGA for domain-dependent objects.
- Conveyor: this is a class combining the characteristics common to two large families of transportation means, namely:
  - Static conveyors which guarantee conveying of components without moving;
  - Dynamic conveyors which move within manufacturing units to carry the components.

The internal behaviour of each class of object is described by an interpreted and communicating Petri net (in accordance with M2PO). The modelling of this behaviour must be fairly fine in order to be able to detect possible errors, mainly due to simulation model developers. These errors take the form of simulation messages for the animation which are inconsistent with the current state of the system or with the capabilities of the objects to which they are sent.

Figure 6.10 shows the Petri net associated with the shuttle class. It is, for example, inconsistent to ask a shuttle to unload a component when it is in movement. An M2PO file for the shuttle class is given in Figure 6.11.

SOFTWARE
TESTS
EFFECTED
FOR GAME

The test phases have made it possible to progress reliably in the writing of the source of the GAME software. Our software is organized both around classes of objects presented for GIGA and around the classes defined in the previous section. In the same way that the design of software follows a certain number of stages, the testing

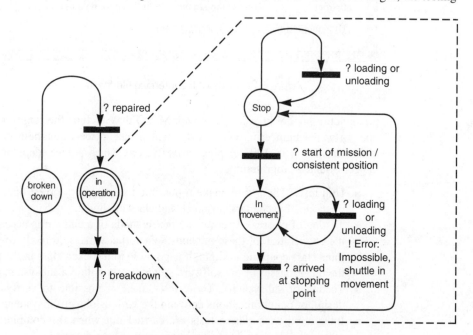

Figure 6.10 Simplified specification of the internal behaviour of shuttles.

```
Name of the class:   SHUTTLE
Reference to superclass:  MANUFACTURING_OBJECT
Persistent objects:  YES              Active object:  NO

Instance attributes:

taillep_chemin      Size of the path of the shuttle in pixels
tailler_chemin      Real size of the path
speed               Speed
chpoint             Character string of stop points
point []            Relative position of the stop points in pixels
poscrt              Current position in pixels
derp                Last stop point
crt                 Current stop point
dest                Destination stop point
ianim               Animation indicator
pas                 Movement step in pixels
crt_phmc            Current positions
dest_phmc           to be saved in main memory

Instance methods:

shuttle             Constructor and destructor of shuttle
affnavpix           Display the path of the shuttle in pixels
deplnav             Move the shuttle on the path during an animation
affstruct           Display the shuttle with the components transported

(The inherited methods are not described).
```

Figure 6.11 Code of the interface file for the shuttle class.

of an action model in accordance with M2PO may include the stages, specified by the software engineering community, which take place throughout development. Sommerville (1988, 1992) distinguishes five test stages and we adapt these stages to object-oriented programming:

- Unit tests. These tests make it possible to verify the correct operation of the methods of each class (instance and class methods).
- Testing of classes. After testing the methods of a class, it is necessary to test the cooperation of these methods. When the work is correctly organized and inter-class coupling is slight, it is possible to test each class in the presence of the other classes of the software system (tests within a subsystem of objects).
- Testing of subsystems. These tests make it possible to verify the correct design of communications between the various object subsystems.
- Integration tests. These tests are carried out when the complete system is assembled. Design or coding errors may still be detected.
- Acceptance tests. These tests are carried out by comparing the software with

real data. They may highlight errors in the definition of the requirements, which may not satisfy the level of functions or performance expected by the user. This type of test is effected by means of an operating prototype.

Tests on real industrial cases We give details here of the last phase of tests, called acceptance tests. To be deemed valid, software must be compared with data from real cases. We have undertaken this validation by supplying a prototype of the software to the potential users of the VALEO group. According to Sommerville, prototyping principally makes it possible:

- to highlight misunderstandings between users and developers during demonstrations of the functions of the prototype;
- to detect missing functions;
- to identify and improve the functions which appear difficult to use;
- to identify incomplete or inconsistent requirements during the development of the prototype;
- to have operating software very quickly, although limited, showing the feasibility and usefulness of the application to the persons concerned.

The use of the prototype in real cases improves the detection of possible weaknesses (or even errors), which are not always obvious to the designers. A prototype of the VIEWMOD software (called GAME) with its user manual was handed over to software engineering students studying at the CUST of Clermont Ferrand, who had to model, simulate and animate manufacturing systems of the VALEO group, in collaboration with the experts of the group. Subsequently, the final software was called VIEWMOD and was used at other sites of the VALEO group; it is still in service today. It was also used to animate various models from SAGEM, from the RATP, the EDF (French Electricity Company) and Manufacture Michelin.

The generic nature of GAME (built with the aid of GIGA) made it possible to tackle domains other than that of manufacturing systems. Figure 6.12 summarizes the models simulated and animated with GAME.

The industrial tests were of tremendous help. They made it possible, in particular, to modify and correct certain functions which did not always do what the user was entitled to expect. In this respect, the use of the prototype was beneficial for debugging the program. As far as the users were concerned, the animation gave a better view of the simulation models by making it possible to understand the transient operation of systems. It was possible to detect numerous coding errors in the simulation programs written by engineering students, thus assisting in verifying the action models.

6.2.2 Generation of object-oriented simulation code from a graphic specification

INTRODUCTION The generic nature of the GIGA toolbox made it possible not only to construct the GAME software relatively easily, but also to extend this software to take into

Year	Site and/or Company	Duration of the study	Number of animated models	Subject of Study
1990	VALEO Amiens	6 months	1	Modelling of a prop store for clutches
	VALEO Chatellerault	6 months	5	Study of different topologies for the manufacture of windscreen wiper motors
	VALEO L'Ilse d'Abeau	2 months	1	Herrkommer machine
	VALE Ste Florine	6 months	3	Three ignition coil systems
1991	VALEO	5 months	2	C23/N3O line for the thermal cómpartment
	VALEO La Suze	2 months	1	Assembly of high performance radiators
	VALEO Amiens	3 months	1	Clutch production line
	SAGEM Ste Florine	3 months	1	Assembly of coils
	EDF Equipment + Sub-Prefecture of Compiegne	1 months	1	Ground floor flows of the prefecture
1992	SAGEM Ste Florine	2 months	1	Assembly of coils
	EDF equipment + BASTIA Hospital	2 months	1	Emergency service
	EDF + AIA in Bordeaux	10 months	1	Aircraft component degreasing system
	EDF + Commercial Chamber of Dieppe	10 months	1	Modernization of the fishing port of Dieppe
	VALEO L'Isle d'Abeau	5 months	2	Two quality control lines

Figure 6.12 Summary table of industrial models animated with GAME.

account the generation of simulation code. The procedure used consisted of extending the classes of graphic objects (by adding attributes necessary for simulation) and of associating with them classes of simulation objects, taking into account the behaviour of the manufacturing objects. The target simulation language for the generation of code is QNAP2. This choice is justified for the following reasons:

- This software was retained for the SIGMA project.
- It has been validated by the industry for over ten years.

- It has powerful statistical tools and in particular proposes numerous confidence interval calculation techniques.
- The algorithmic language of QNAP2 has good legibility and can implement the principal concepts of the object model. It is possible with the same language to use powerful analytical resolution methods, discrete event simulation and Markovian analysis. With simple systems these techniques allow repetitiveness validation by comparing the simulation models with analytical or Markov models.
- The experience acquired in the laboratory on this software with several dozens of models, as well as our connections with the company SIMULOG (which maintains and distributes this software), allow excellent back-up.

We use an industrial system to present the various stages which make it possible to end up with an action model, using the object-oriented possibilities of the QNAP2 language. The industrial system in question is a toy assembly line.

The study is intended to analyse the performance of the line and if possible to increase the number of toys produced.

ANALYSIS OF THE SYSTEM

An analysis of the manufacturing systems domain having already been carried out, it is sufficient to extract, from the domain knowledge model, the classes of objects found in the system. We will now present the system in terms of objects. Decomposition into three subsystems is of course preserved.

The physical subsystem

The real system is very simple and comprises:

- 8 machines, 4 for assembly, 2 for machining and 2 for inspection;
- 4 accumulating conveyors; the first has 2 sections (1 and 2), the second has three sections (3, 4 and 5), the third is connected to section 6 and the fourth to section 7;
- 24 sensors; a sensor is positioned before and after each machine, in order to determine respectively whether the components are at the inlet of the machine and if there is space on the conveying section which follows the machine (Figure 6.13). In addition, sensors are necessary in order to know at any moment the number of components on the conveyors;
- 8 actuators; one stop is connected to each machine to block the components at the inlet while the machine is not free.

Amongst the objects compiled in this physical subsystem, only the machines and sections of the conveyors are shown on the graphic model built with GAME. The topology is given in Figure 6.13. To model the machines and conveyors with QNAP2 we have chosen to describe an abstract superclass called 'manufacturing object'.

This class possesses a semaphore signal which will be inherited and used for the take-up and return of the spaces present on machines and conveyors. We give the QNAP2 object code for this abstract class in Figure 6.14. It is important to note that for the effectiveness of the simulation model, the access methods to object attributes are not implemented (QNAP2 is interpreted).

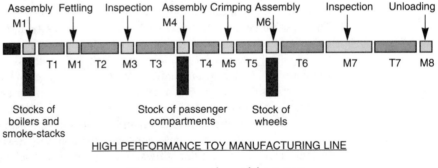

Figure 6.13 Topology of the system.

```
&--------------------------------------------------------------------------&
&               Abstract Class of Manufacturing Objects                    &
&--------------------------------------------------------------------------&
/DECLARE/                                      & Attributes ----------&
    OBJECT OBJ_PROD;
       QUEUE   SEM_NBPL;               & A semaphore giving access
                                       & to a manufacturing object
       INTEGER NBPL;                   & Capacity of the manufacturing
                                       & object
    END;

/STATION/
    NAME =*OBJ_PROD.SEM_NBPL;
    TYPE = SEMAPHORE,MULTIPLE(NBPL);
```

Figure 6.14 QNAP2 code for the abstract class of manufacturing objects.

The 'machine' class as modelled with QNAP2 possesses two stations (server(s) with the associated queue). It derives from the abstract superclass of manufacturing objects (inheritance of a semaphore with its number of places). The first station, called ENTRY, describes the processing sequence that a flow element (components, parts, finished products, ...) is to receive. It is mainly a matter of executing an upstream rule (belonging to the decisional subsystem), of carrying out all the operations of a processing phase (which correspond to a part of manufacturing routing in the logical subsystem), and then of executing a downstream rule (belonging to the decisional subsystem). The second station, called BREAKDOWN, is dedicated to generating random breakdowns in accordance with a statistical law (or in accordance with a distribution in the form of a histogram if it was not possible to find any law). Figure 6.15 gives adequate code for a machine class adapted to the problem posed. The code for managing breakdowns is not completely parametrized for greater legibility. In addition, where you might wish to model the destruction of the component during treatment in the machine, on the occurrence of a breakdown, it would be appropriate to use the preemption policy available with QNAP2 for the management of queues.

```
&-----------------------------------------------------------------------&
&                        CLASS OF MACHINE objects                       &
&-----------------------------------------------------------------------&
/DECLARE/                                 & Attributes -------------------&
     OBJ_PROD OBJECT MACHINE;
        QUEUE       ENTREE,PANNE;     & QNAP2 stations for machine class
        FLAG        LANCER;           & processing synchronization (def=FALSE)
        REAL        T_PAN,T_REP;      & inter-failure and repair time
     END;

/STATION/
NAME    =*MACHINE.ENTREE;                 & Stations --------------------&
TYPE    = MULTIPLE(NBPL);

SERVICE =
     BEGIN
        TC_REGAM(CUST_IND)(INCLUDIN(CQUEUE)::OBJ_PROD,TC_PATH(CUST_IND));
        TC_PHASE(CUST_IND)(TC_PAR1(CUST_IND),TC_PAR2(CUST_IND));
        TC_REGAV(CUST_IND)(INCLUDIN(CQUEUE);;OBJ_PROD,TC_PATH(CUST_IND));
     END;

/STATION/
NAME    =*MACHINE.PANNE;
INIT    = 1;
SERVICE =
     BEGIN
        EXP(T_PAN);                       & Inter-failure duration
        BLOCK(ENTREE);                    & Block the machine
        UNIFORM(0.85*T_REP,1.15*T_REP);   & Repair time
        UNBLOCK(ENTREE);
        TRANSIT(PANNE);
     END;

&--------------------- Machines Construction Macro --------------------&
$MACRO GEN_MAC (NAME,M_P,M_R,M_PL)

     /DECLARE/ MACHINE NAME;
     /EXEC/    BEGIN
                       NAME.T_PAN   := M_P;
                       NAME.T_REP   := M_R;
                       NAME.NBPL    := M_P
               END;
$END
&-----------------------------------------------------------------------&
```

Figure 6.15 Example of QNAP2 code simplified for a machine class.

The 'conveyor' class is also modelled by QNAP2 stations (Kellert, 1987). In order to guarantee an output flow of correct parts it is important to use several servers, and in particular to separate the first and last place of the accumulating conveyor sections. An example of a possible queuing network separating only the last place is given in Figure 6.16; Figure 6.17 gives the corresponding QNAP2 code.

The logical
subsystem

The range/schedule is simple; the manufacture of a toy (steam locomotive) on this line requires four wheels, a smoke-stack, a passenger compartment and a boiler. The operations associated with this manufacture total eight and are sequential. The inspection operations generate reject flows which are not recycled.

(1) Assembly of the smoke-stack boiler
(2) Fettling
(3) Inspection
(4) Assembly with the passenger compartment
(5) Crimping
(6) Assembly with the wheels
(7) Inspection
(8) Unloading of toys

The circulation of flow elements through objects of the physical subsystem is shown in Figure 6.18. When components arrive they are taken over by stocks which are considered to be infinite for the duration of the simulation (one day). This type of hypothesis is considered as realistic by experts. At the level of the QNAP2 software, we are able to represent classes of flow elements by various classes of clients (of queuing networks). For the model we are dealing with, two classes of clients are sufficient (one class for the toys and one for the rejects). However, these statistics are necessary for each type of component of the toy; it is sufficient to associate a client class with each elementary flow (wheel, boiler, smoke-stack and passenger compartment).

With a simple system of this type, we only identify one path comprising eight elementary phases. In order to adopt a transactional approach we associate with each class of clients:

- a table of paths, consisting of manufacturing objects, to be travelled by the clients;
- a table of pointers to the procedures to be executed in the manufacturing objects for each treatment phase;
- tables of pointers to param eters of these procedures;
- tables of pointers to upstream and downstream rules of the manufacturing objects.

Each client possesses an index which allows it to find the manufacturing object in which it is located, what processing phase it is to undergo, and the rules applicable to it. Figure 6.19 gives the QNAP2 code for the declaration of tables associated with the flow class as well as the index associated with the client.

The code consists of adding to the classes of clients (CLASS) and the instances of these classes (CUSTOMER), predefined by QNAP2, attributes making it possible

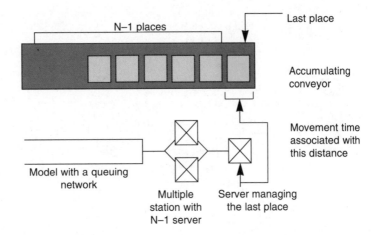

Figure 6.16 Possible queuing network model for an accumulating conveyor.

```
& ---------------------------------------------------------------------- &
&            Class for sections of accumulating conveyors               &
&                                                                        &
& NBPL, which is passed as a parameter at the time of construction of a &
& conveyor, is in fact only the number of real places - 1. This is due  &
& to the internal choice of modelling a conveyor by a station with a    &
& multiple server plus a single server for the last place.              &
& ---------------------------------------------------------------------- &
/DECLARE/                               & Attributes ------------------- &
    OBJ_PROD OBJECT CONV;
    QUEUE   INLET, LAST,                & QNAP2 stations for conv_acc class
            D_SEM;
    FLAG    STOP;                       & Stop (FALSE by def)
    REAL    T_DEP;                      & Movement time to 1 place
    END;

/STATION/
    NAME =*CONVI.D_SEM;                 & Stations -------------------- &
    TYPE = SEMAPHORE,MULTIPLE(1);

/STATION/
    NAME   =*CONVI.ENTRY;
    TYPE   = MULTIPLE (NBPL);
    SERVICE =
      BEGIN
        TC_REGAM(CUST_IND)(INCLUDIN(CQUEUE)::OBJ_PROD,TC_PATH
        (CUST_IND));
        CST(NBPL * T_DEP);
        P(D_SEM);                       & Request for the last place
        V (SEM_NBPL);
        TRANSIT (LAST);
      END;
/STATION/
    NAME =*CONVI.LAST;
```

```
SERVICE =
  BEGIN
    CST(T_DEP);
    TC_REGAV(CUST_IND) INCLUDIN(CQUEUE) :':OBJ_PROD,TC_PATH(CUST_IND));
  END;
```

& ------------------------Section constructor------------------------- &

```
$MACRO GEN_CONV(NAME,CO_NP,CO_TDEP)

/DECLARE/       CONV NAME;
/EXEC/  BEGIN
            NAME.NBPL   := CO_NP;
            NAME.T_DEP := CO_TDEP;
        END;
$SEND
```

& -- &

Figure 6.17 QNAP2 code for a conveyor section.

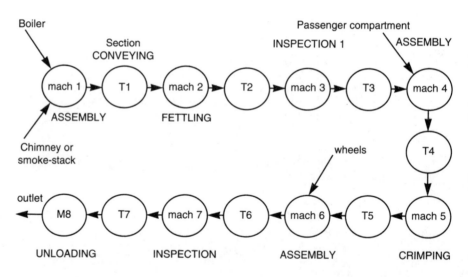

Figure 6.18 Circulation of flows and processing within objects (M2PO MFD).

to describe the behaviour of different classes of clients while retaining the separation between the physical, logical and decisional subsystems. This technique, based on the use of the transaction approach, is possible in the QNAP2 language and in combination with the station approach natural in QNAP2.

The decisional subsystem

The operation of the manufacturing system must respect the following constraint: machine 7 can only commence its service when four parts are available on conveyor 3 (section 6). We include the classification of the rules prepared for the SIGMA project. We therefore separate the local rules, controlling the inlet and the outlet of

```
& --- Declaration of the attributes associated with the flow class --- &
    CLASS REF OBJ_PROD    PATH_TC (LGGAMME);    & Routing tables
    CLASS REF PHASE       PHASE_TC (LGGAMME);   & Phase table
    CLASS REAL            PAR1_TC  (LGGAMME);   & Table of phase parameters
    CLASS REAL            PAR2_TC  (LGGAMME);   & 2 possible parameters
    CLASS REF RULE        REGAM_TC (LGGAMME);   & Table of upstream rules
    CLASS REF RULE        REGAV_TC (LGGAMME);   & Table of downstream rules
    CUSTOMER INTEGER IND_CUST;   & Each flow element possesses an IND_CUST
                                 & to know the object describing the phase
                                 & which it has to undergo and its position
                                 & on its path
    CLASS TOY,REJECTS;           & Class of toys and rejects
```

Figure 6.19 QNAP2 declaration of attributes necessary for a transactional approach.

the components on the manufacturing objects in terms of the number of places (resources) available, and the global operating rules scrutinizing and modifying the state of several objects. The global rules are associated with a decision centre. Local default rules are present upstream and downstream of each manufacturing object. In the majority of cases, they are used for taking up and returning resources as well as issuing messages for animation. One of the important functions of these rules is connected with their location within the services rendered by the manufacturing objects, which allows assertions (preconditions and post-conditions) to be taken into account. Assertions are a powerful software verification technique and therefore a technique for verifying action models (programming as contracting (Meyer, 1988)). As we have stated, not only do assertions make it possible to verify that the model is behaving correctly, but in addition they document the model. Figure 6.20 gives an example of a simple local rule between a conveyor and a machine.

```
& --------------- Global declarations for animation ----------------- &

INTEGER STEP   = 10;                & Ratio between T anim and T simul
FILE    ANIM_F;                     & File for anim messages
BOOLEAN ANIM_B = TRUE;              & Switch for animation

.... Other declarations

PROCEDURE CTM_R (SOURCE_O,DEST_O);  & Rule downstream of conveyor
    REF PROD_OBJ SOURCE_O,DEST_O;
BEGIN
    P (DEST_O.NBPL_SEM);            & Request machine access
    IND_CUST := IND_CUST + 1;       & Client => following phase
    V(SOURCE_O::SEM_D.CONVI);       & Return last CONV place
                                    & Message for the animation

    IF ANIM_B, THEN WRITELN(ANIM_F,'2',TIME*STEP,SOURCE_O, DEST_CCLASS);

    TRANSIT(DEST_::MACHINE STOP.ENTRY); & Go into the following station
END;
```

Figure 6.20 Local default rule for transfer from a machine to a conveyor.

```
&   --------------------------------------------------------------- &
&                   Classes for decision centres                    &
&   --------------------------------------------------------------- &


DECISION OBJECT;
    QUEUE          ENTRY;                  & Station for scrutiny
    REF PROD_OBJ   OBJ_AM, OBJ_AV;         & Scrutinized objects
    REF RULE       RULE_P;                 & Scrutiny rule
    REAL           POOL_T;                 & Scrutiny interval
END;


/STATION/NAME    =*SUPERVIS.ENTRY;        & Station --------------------- &
         INIT    = 1;
         SERVICE = BEGIN
                     P_REGL(OBJ_AM,OBJ_AV);
                     CST(T_POOL);
                     TRANSIT(ENTRY);
                   END;


& --------------- Constructor of decision centre objects -------------- &


$MACRO GEN_CDES(NAME,S_OAM,S_OAV,S_PR,S_TPOOL)

    /DECLARE/ DECISION NAME;
    /EXEC/ BEGIN
             NAME. OBJ_AM := S_OAM;
             NAME.OBJ_AV  := S_OAV;
             NAME.P_REGL  := S_PR;
             NAME.T_POOL  := S_TPOOL;
          END;
$END
```

Figure 6.21 Code for the class of decision centres.

A class is specified to model the decision centres of the logical subsystem (taking over the global rules). Each decision centre has a list of objects it is managing, as well as a rule comprising a premiss and a consequence. The premiss and the consequence of the rule may use sensors and actuators (stops), which are modelled with flags in QNAP2. The decision centres activate every 'dt' simulation time intervals ('dt' being a parameter of the model). Figure 6.21 gives the QNAP2 code for a decision centre. The decision centres are generally associated with complex upstream or downstream rules, managing sensors and actuators, which are activated by the flow of clients.

To take into account the constraint on machine 7, two decision centres are used. The first is given the task of lifting the stop of conveyor 3 (section 6) and the second is given the task of lowering it. The inter-scrutiny time set for the decision centres is 4 seconds. The QNAP2 code for the global rules associated with this constraint is given in Figure 6.22.

```
&  ------------------------------------------------------------------  &
&                       Declaration of global rules                    &
&  ------------------------------------------------------------------  &
PROCEDURE R_LB(O_SOURCE,O_DEST);          & Lift the conveyor stop
    REF OBJ_PROD O_SOURCE,O_DEST;
BEGIN
    IF (O_SOURCE::CONVI.ENTREE.NB > 3)AND (O_DEST::MACHINE.ENTRY.NB = 0)
    THEN SET(O_SOURCE::CONVI.STOP);
END;
PROCEDURE R_BB(O_SOURCE,O_DEST);          & Lower stop
    REF OBJ_PROD O_SOURCE,O_DEST;
BEGIN
    IF (O_DEST::MACHINE.ENTRY.NB = O_DEST.NBPL)
    THEN BEGIN
      RESET(O_SOURCE::CONVI.STOP);
      SET(O_DEST::MACHINE.START);
    END;
END;
```

Figure 6.22 Global management rules for machine 7 and section 6.

Code
generation

The domain analysis of manufacturing systems made it possible to obtain all of the classes necessary for the automatic creation of QNAP2 action models. The detailed design of these objects makes it possible to obtain a simulation code which best models the behaviour of real objects, from the point of view of the experts. Implementation using a transaction approach makes it possible to describe the manufacturing objects of the physical subsystem generally, independently of the client behaviours which carry their own information. The objects designed, if they are sufficiently general, may therefore be reused for several models.

The GAME software presented above makes it possible to capture the topology of a model (physical subsystem). Likewise, the logical subsystem is partially present since the list of flow elements is known (icons are associated with them). We have extended this software so that a graphic specification makes it possible to generate most of the QNAP2 code of the models. The extended version of this software is called EMMAUS. Extensions mainly concern the logical subsystem. For each class of client the user specifies the sequence of objects of the physical subsystem (constituting the paths). This capture comprises both a graphic selection by mouse of the manufacturing objects concerned, and the specification of the processing phase associated with the flexible manufacturing objects, the service of which varies according to the class concerned.

The creation of a model by generating code is then resolved by producing the macro-instructions necessary for the instantiation of the objects of the physical subsystem and by initializing the tables of the client classes (with the paths, phases, rules, ...). The decisional subsystem is not, however, taken into account totally by the EMMAUS software. In fact, the global rules of operation should be specified with a rule editor (achieved with SIGMA). However, local default rules are generated automatically and allocated to the respective locations of the manufacturing routing specified (stock to machine, machine to conveyor, shuttle to machine, ...). The percentage code generated remains greater than 90% of the total code for the cases

```
&  ---------------------- Instantiations of machines -------------------- &

   $GEN_MAC   (MAC_8,3600,11.88,1)
   $GEN_MAC   (MAC_7,9000,59.4,4)
   ...

&  --------------------- Instantiations of conveyors ------------------ &

   $GEN_CONV  (T_7,5,0.11)
   $GEN_CONV  (T_6,5,0.11)
   ...
```

Figure 6.23 QNAP2 code making it possible to generate the physical subsystem of a model.

```
RADIA.TC_PATH   (1) := T_1;        & Object following Section 1
RADIA.TC_PHASE  (1) := LCST;       & Service time according to a
RADIA.TC_PAR1   (1) := 6.9;        & constant law of 6.9 secs.
RADIA.TC_PAR2   (1) := 0;
RADIA.TC_REGAM  (1) := R_VIDE;     & Upstream rule step
RADIA.TC_REGAV  (1) := R_M2C;      & rule for transfer of a machine
                                   & to a conveyor
```

Figure 6.24 Initialization of a part of toys manufacturing routing.

studied. The remaining part is the responsibility of the specialists and experts who implement complex management policies within the decision centre object.

Figure 6.23 gives an example of macro-instructions which have been generated; the code of the initialization of tables associated with client classes is given by Figure 6.24: an extension of the manufacturing objects available in the EMMAUS software shows up the notion of a source of flow elements. Sources make it possible to specify distribution laws of arrivals, rules of arrivals and flow element arrival messages for the animation. Likewise, an output of the model may be specified in the list of objects of a path for a class of clients.

The automatic production of this type of code assumes an extension of the C++ code of the object peculiar to the domain of manufacturing systems. It is necessary to add a virtual instance method which will make it possible to generate macro-instructions for each manufacturing object, and a method is needed for each class of manufacturing objects making it possible to supply the code of the QNAP2 classes (already designed). If a class of manufacturing objects possesses one or more instances in a model, it is then necessary to 'bind' the QNAP2 code of this class in the QNAP2 source generated. Examples of C++ code which must be added to the interfaces of the classes are given in Figure 6.25. The principal stages of QNAP2 object-oriented code generation are:

- the declaration of general variables and constants as well as the experimentation framework;
- the declaration of code for QNAP2 classes which appear in the system studied;
- the declaration of code for local rules necessary in terms of the classes present and the manufacturing routing;
- the creation of instances in terms of objects compiled in the system;
- the initialization of the manufacturing routing.

```
// ------------------------------------------------------------------- //
//                 Extract from Object of Production Class             //
// ------------------------------------------------------------------- //

class obj_production : public obj_dynamique {
    protected:
        ...
    public:
        ...
    virtual void gen_instance_QNAP2(FILE *);      //each subclass
                                                  //generates its
                                                  //QNAP2 macro calls
    };
// ------------------------------------------------------------------- //
//                     Extract from Machine Class                      //
// ------------------------------------------------------------------- //

class machine: public obj_production {        //example for 1 subclasses of
        protected:                            // obj_production
            ...
        static unsigned int nb_instances:     //number of
public:                                       //instances of the
                                              //machine class

            ...
        static void gen_classe_QNAP2(FILE *); //QNAP2
        void gen_instance_QNAP2(FILE *);      //machine class code
                                              //supplies the QNAP2 code
        };                                    //for creation of a machine
        ...
// ------------------------------------------------------------------- //
//             Generation of QNAP2 code as part of table              //
// ------------------------------------------------------------------- //
...
void hash::gen_source_QNAP2(FILE * fsource_QNAP2);
{

    declaration_QNAP2(fsource_QNAP2);

    if (machine::nb_instance) machine::gen_classe_QNAP2
        (fsource_QNAP2);
    if (shuttle)::nb_instance) navette::gen_classe_QNAP2
        (fsource_QNAP2);
...
    local_rules_QNAP2(fsource_QNAP2);

    iteration(&obj_production::gen_instance_QNAP2);

    range_QNAP2(fsource_QNAP2);

}
```

Figure 6.25 Extract of C++ code for the automatic generation of QNAP2 source code.

The simulation control parameters, like the duration of the simulation, the choice of confidence interval calculation methods, and the possibility of generating animation messages, are also taken into account by a dialogue window. The content of this window makes it possible to effect the automatic generation of the corresponding QNAP2 declarations.

The separation brought about between the logical subsystem, the decisional subsystem and the physical subsystem is taken into account, in order to be able to carry out several experiment plans for one and the same topology.

USE OF THE SIMULATION RESULTS

A first study of the model presented was effected from a set of parameters proposed as the initial configuration. This configuration is given by the table in Figure 6.26. It is the grouping of attributes of the M2PO instance cards for the machine class and accumulating conveyor section. With this configuration, 20 714 toys leave the system each day and the highest rate of occupation is that of machine 5 which controls the crimping (94.1%). The aim of the study is to improve production by taking into account topological constraints.

Description	Distance	Entry step	Frequency speed	Capacity	Interval between breakdowns	Repair duration
M1 assembly	0.3 m	0.6 m	6.9 s	1	23.66	3600 s
Section 1	1.48 m		0.25 m/s	0 to 3		
M2 fettling	0.3 m	0.6 m	5 s	1	59.4	18000 s
Section 2	1.48 m		0.25 m/s	0 to 3		
M3 inspection	0.3 m	0.6 m	3.5 s	1	11.88	1200 s
Section 3	2.08 m		0.25 m/s	0 to 5		
M4 assembly	0.3 m	0.6 m	7 s	1	11.88	1800 s
Section 4	1.48 m		0.25 m/s	0 to 3		
M5 crimping	0.5 m	0.6 m	7.45 s	1	7.2	720 s
Section 5	1.48 m		0.25 m/s	0 to 3		
M6 assembly	0.8 m	0.6 m	7.53 s	1	59.4	18000 s
Stop section 6	2.68 m		0.25 m/s	0 to 6		
M7 inspection	2.12 m	0.6 m	22.4 s	4 by 4	59.4	9000 s
Section 7	2.68 m		0.25 m/s	0 to 6		
M8 unloading	0.5 m		6.64 s	1	11.88	3600 s

Figure 6.26 Initial configuration of the system.

The tests carried out concern first the frequency of entry into the system. Successive tests showed that the frequency of entry could be brought down to an arrival of joints and a bundle every 6.8 seconds (instead of 8 seconds). The following test takes into account a reduction in the entry step of the machines. This notification involves a substantial increase in the number of components (10%, that is, 22 595 toys per day). The speed of the conveyors was then increased up to 0.33 metres per second. This new speed allows an increase in the entry frequency up to an arrival every 6.4 seconds, making it possible to obtain 23 485 toys per day. It is also desirable to observe the effect of breakdowns. The model was therefore simulated without breakdowns, and then with breakdowns, these having a minimal effect on the system. The table in Figure 6.28 gives the results of various configurations of the system.

The use of the EMMAUS tool makes it possible to reproduce the results obtained with a QNAP2 model produced manually. The search for the parameters that make it possible to improve the system is easier with EMMAUS than with a simple source and the QNAP2 software, because knowledge of the simulation language is not necessary and the user only manipulates one 'user-friendly' interface. Furthermore, coupling with the animation is immediate, because the messages, which are peculiar to the animation, are inserted automatically. An EMMAUS prototype which generated simulation code for the SIMAN IV, SLAM II software was also produced. Generation of Simula-67 code was also carried out, out of respect for this pioneering language which, even today, is still far from being obsolete. The Simula code generated for a manufacturing system with two machines (with breakdowns) and two stocks is given in Figure 6.27; it uses a library of queuing network objects developed at Clermont-Ferrand. The results of various configurations are shown in Figure 6.28.

```
!WIDGET.SIM;

    external class QNOPTOOL;
    QNOPTOOL begin

    ref (cr_s2m)     r_s2m;
    ref (cr_m2s)     r_m2s;
    ref (cr_m2c)     r_m2c;
    ref (cr_c2m)     r_c2m;
    ref (cr_2out)    r_2out;
    ref (cr_vide)    r_vide;
    ref (cr_s2obj)   r_s2obj;

    ref (client)     GADGET;
    ref (stock)      STK_2;
    ref (stock)      STK_1;
    ref (machine)    MAC_2;
    ref (machine)    MAC_1;
    ref (src)        S_FLUX;

    GADGET :- new client (100);
```

```
%  ----------------- Creation of local rules objects ------------------- %
      r_vide        :- new cr_vide;
      r_c2m         :- new cr_c2m;
      r_m2c         :- new cr_m2c;
      r_s2m         :- new cr_s2m;
      r_m2s         :- new cr_m2s;
      r_2out        :- new cr_2out;
      r_s2obj       :- new cr_s2obj;

%  -------------- Creation of 'production systems' object ------------- %
      STK_2 :- new stock;
      gen_stk (STK_2,"STK_2",10);
      STK_1 :- new stock;
      gen_stk (STK_1,"STK_1",19);
      MAC_2 :- new machine;
      gen_mac (MAC_2,"MAC_2",1,lexp,lunif,100.00,0.00,5.00,15.00,1);
      MAC_1 :- new machine;
      gen_mac (MAC_1,"MAC_1",1,lexp,lunif,150.00,0.00,200.00,250.00,1);

      S_FLUX :- new src;
      gen_src (S_FLUX,"S_FLUX",lexp,10.00,0.00,STK_1GADGET,r_s2obj);

      GADGET.tc_path       ( 1)       :- MAC_1;
      GADGET.tc_regam      ( 1)       :- r_vide;
      GADGET.tc_regav      ( 1)       :- r_s2m;

      GADGET.tc_path       ( 2)       :- STK_2;
      GADGET.tc_phase      ( 2)       :- LEXP;
      GADGET.tc_par1       ( 2)       := 6.00;
      GADGET.tc_par2       ( 2)       := 0.00;
      GADGET.tc_regam      ( 2)       :- r_vide;
      GADGET.tc_regav      ( 2)       :- r_m2s;

      GADGET.tc_path       ( 3)       :- MAC_2;
      GADGET.tc_regam      ( 3)       :- r_vide;
      GADGET.tc_regav      ( 3)       :- r_s2m;

      GADGET.tc_path       ( 4)       :- NONE;
      GADGET.tc_phase      ( 4)       :- LEXP;
      GADGET.tc_par1       ( 4)       := 8.00;
      GADGET.tc_par2       ( 4)       := 0.00;
      GADGET.tc_regam      ( 4)       :- r_vide;
      GADGET.tc_regav      ( 4)       :- r_2out;

      simperiod:=1000;
      hold(simperiod);
end of model;
```

Figure 6.27 Simula code for a manufacturing system with two machines (with breakdowns) and two stocks.

Configuration	Number of toys produced per day	
Initial model entry frequency = 8 speed = 0.25 entry step = 0.6	20714	
Improved model entry frequency = 6.4 speed = 0.33 entry step = 0.4	23062 with break- down on all machines	23485 no breakdown

Figure 6.28 Results of various configurations.

◁ 6.3 Implementation of polymorphism and dynamic classification in QNAP2

6.3.1 The choices made: a compromise between inheritance and delegation

The algorithmic language of QNAP2 has a simple static inheritance mechanism but does not allow dynamic classification. Furthermore, as dynamic binding is not implemented, it is not possible to send polymorphic messages directly. We wish to be able to send polymorphic messages to a QNAP2 object and also to have dynamic classification techniques.

For this purpose, we have implemented dynamic binding with the 'dispatch tables' technique. A first solution consists of associating a table of methods *with each class* (dynamic inheritance of methods, Figure 6.29). A second solution, approximating actor models, consists of associating *with each object* tables of methods (selector and reference to the method) and a reference to another object which will be used as a delegated (or proxy) object.

The QNAP2 language is a queuing network declaration language. However, it is possible to create QNAP2 objects which may be considered as actors (active objects). These actors define their scripts by means of the 'SERVICE' clauses of the queue servers. An object possessing a single server therefore becomes active from the moment a client, emulating a control flow, passes through it. It is possible to have a dummy client locked within these objects, with time only being advanced when a call on an explicit modification function of the simulation time is made (Figure 6.30). The language of the QNAP2 simulator uses a process approach and the

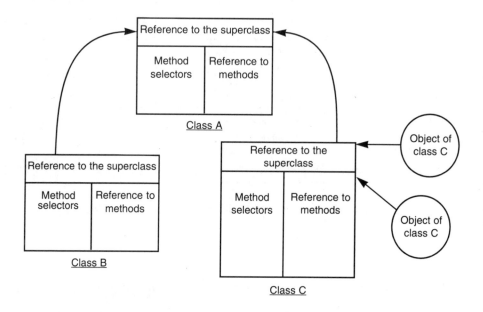

Figure 6.29 Diagram of the references between 'dispatch tables'.

synchronizing kernel takes over management of the quasi-parallelism. It therefore becomes possible to simulate networks of actors.

We propose to separate two types of models:

(1) The references associated with each object reconstruct a dynamic inheritance of method hierarchy and are based on the static inheritance of the attributes proposed by QNAP2.

Thus we are able to inherit polymorphic methods and redefine them.

(2) References associated with each object are used to implement delegation as presented by Johnson and Zweig (1991).

The second model concentrates on objects present during execution and no longer on classes. The assumptions retained are the following: each object has a reference to a delegated object. When it receives a message, either it knows how to deal with it directly, or it passes it on to its delegate which in turn can pass it on to its own delegate. An object at the end of the chain responds by signalling an execution error. An object therefore 'inherits' the methods of the objects to which it delegates its messages. A state may be inherited in the same way, since the encapsulation and abstraction of data involves the use of messages to gain access to the attributes of the object. The creation of actor objects by making differential copies may be implemented by means of QNAP2 macro-instructions.

```
&  ------------------------------------------------------------------  &
&       Example definition of a prototype of an actor object           &
&  ------------------------------------------------------------------  &

ACTOR OBJECT;
    QUEUE               SCRIPT;       & Station QNAP2 defining
    REF ACTOR           PROXY;        & the script
                                      & proxy of the actor
    & Attributes and references for the methods
END;

/STATION/NAME     =*ACTOR.SCRIPT;
    INIT          =1;
    SERVICE       = BEGIN
                      & Code QNAP2 corresponding to the script.
                      TRANSIT(SCRIPT);
                  END;
```

Figure 6.30 QNAP2 prototype for the definition of actor objects.

Delegation supplies the power of inheritance by allowing code sharing. It also becomes possible to change the behaviour of an object dynamically. This change in behaviour is effected by changing the delegated object and is the same as a change of class. Delegation not only eliminates the complexity of metaclasses without losing their power, but also makes it simpler to model objects which change behaviour according to their state.

There is a shade of difference between pure delegation and the simple onward transmission of messages. With delegation, an object that delegates a message must continue to play the role of message receiver, even after it has delegated a message.

If a method corresponding to a delegated message involves sending a message to the current object, this must be addressed to the object which initiated the delegation, and not to the delegated object which is dealing with the message. It is important to note that this message may be further delegated.

6.3.2 Implementation of method lookup

For the two models presented, the sending of a message to an object must pass through a procedure acting as a messenger, as in Objective-C (Cox and Novobilski, 1986). The implementation of the messenger is performed with the QNAP2 language. We will limit ourselves to method selectors in the form of a character string (in the usual implementations, these selectors are compacted). Figure 6.31 gives the QNAP2 code for a messenger supporting the inheritance associated with polymorphism, not delegation.

The technique that allows the implementation of pure delegation consists in adding to the messenger procedure parameters a reference to the object initiating delegation. The first time a message is sent, this reference is initialized with the reference of the receiving object, but it is not modified if the message is delegated. The messenger procedure must therefore take into account any reference to 'SELF'

```
&  ------------------------------------------------------------------------  &
&        Procedure for sending a message and seeking a method in            &
&                      a dynamic inheritance tree.                          &
&  ------------------------------------------------------------------------  &

PROCEDURE SENDMSG( POBJ, SELMV);         & Ptr  on  the  message  receiving
object
          REF BASE        POBJ;
          STRING          SELMV;         & Selector of mode (textual)

& -------------- Declaration of local variables ----------------------- &

INTEGER        I;                         & loop index
BOOLEAN        FOUND;                     & Method found and executed

BEGIN
          I                 := 1;
          FOUND   := FALSE;
          WHILE  (I<= POBJ.NBMETH) DO     & The Boolean is not used
          BEGIN                           & in the exit text
               IF POBJ.TSEL(I) = SELMV    & for reasons of efficiency
               THEN BEGIN
                    POBJ.TMV(I);          & Execute the method
                  I := POBJ.NBMETH+1;     & to get out of the loop
                  FOUND := TRUE;
               END
               ELSE I:= I+1;
          END;
          IF NOT FOUND
          THEN BEGIN
                    IF POBJ.ISA = NIL THEN WRITELN (SELMV,"Run time error...")
                    ELSE SENDMSG(POBJ.ISA,SELMV);
               END;
END;
&  ------------------------------------------------------------------------  &
```

Figure 6.31 QNAP2 polymorphic messenger.

(or equivalent), which identifies the current object, in order to be able to return this type of message to the initiator of the delegation (Figure 6.32).

The model we have chosen uses dynamic typing (we cannot modify the QNAP2 interpreter), although the delegation techniques do not exclude the use of static typing (Johnson and Zweig, 1991).

6.3.3 Performance

Using the solutions proposed, execution times are much longer than those which can be obtained with a language such as C++. Not only is the QNAP2 language interpreted, but it is also necessary to search for a method dynamically. This search

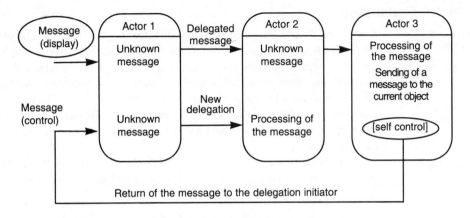

Figure 6.32 Example of delegation with return of a new message to the delegation initiator.

may be a long one, since a larger number of selector and linking comparisons may be needed, and an indirect procedure call is also required. To substantially improve performance, a global cache for the methods may be added, following the technique used by Brad Cox for Objective-C (Cox and Novobilski, 1986). A hashing table is used in the cache to find methods via their selector (Figure 6.33).

Each entry in the table comprises the class of the initial message receiver object, the method selector (here in a textual form) and the reference to the method. When a method is called up, the search is first carried out in the cache. If the entry in the cache corresponds to the method sought, it is executed; if not, the search uses the 'dispatch tables', and the cache is updated before the method found is executed.

It is not necessary to deal with collisions because it is sufficient to replace the entry in the table whenever an unsuccessful call is made.

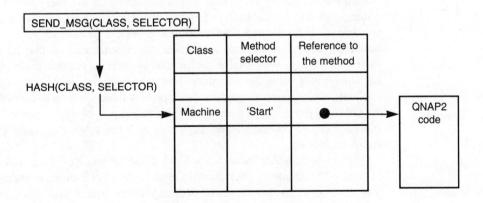

Figure 6.33 Cache for access to methods.

6.3.4 Constraints

Since the QNAP2 language does not directly support dynamic classification and polymorphism, the programmer must do part of the work. He or she has a global procedure which plays the role of messenger and defines the tables of polymorphic methods. However, these tables must be initialized in accordance with the classes, or in accordance with the actors designed by the programmer. To make a change of class, the programmer must modify the reference to the proxy or to the superclass. With dynamic typing, responsibility for consistency in message sending rests with the programmer.

As regards the techniques presented, we consider delegation as a way of implementing inheritance, when the objects being handled might change class.

◁ 6.4 Generation of simulation code from a graphic Petri net specification

6.4.1 Introduction

Amongst the modelling tools for parallel systems, Petri nets (hereafter PN, see Chapter 4) allow the modelling of sequential and concurrent operations, taking into account the phenomena of contention and the problems of synchronizing (Brams, 1983). These models are often analysed in order to determine their properties (to know whether they are alive, restricted, whether or not they have conservative components, ...). However, it is only possible to carry out these analyses on standard PNs.

When studying Petri nets, it may be useful to understand their behaviour by using discrete event simulation. It would be interesting to have a graphic Petri net editor coupled to a simulation code generator. The target code chosen must be that of a known and validated simulation tool, so as not to have to write a dedicated simulator, and also so that it can be integrated easily within a modelling environment. It is also useful to be able to have a graphic trace giving 'the animation' of a Petri net execution (movement of the tokens), if only from a teaching point of view. To produce this type of software, it is quite possible to reuse the GIGA object editor and animator. The techniques of hypergraphics moreover allow the capture of hierarchical Petri nets with the notions of macro-places and macro-transitions.

Petri nets which have been tackled are generalized PNs, coloured and stochastic PNs (Molloy, 1982; Ajmone *et al.*, 1984). For p-timed or stochastic Petri nets, timing is effected in places. When a token arrives in a place, it remains unavailable until timing is completed. During this timing, there can be no downstream transition. We present various techniques to simulate Petri nets with examples of code generated for the QNAP2 and SIMAN IV discrete event simulation software, as well as for the Occam 2 language.

6.4.2 Identification of object classes

Classes to be identified here are limited. It is sufficient to create an abstract 'Petri net object' superclass which must be 'grafted' to replace the superclass of domain objects according to the GIGA design. The diagram of Figure 6.34 gives an inheritance view of the classes identified, using M2PO notation. For each of the classes ('place', 'arc' and 'transition') it is possible to derive subclasses peculiar to each target simulation language.

The dynamic graphic behaviour of the objects identified is very simple; the Petri net in Figure 6.35 models the behaviour of a 'place' class object during the animation of a simulation trace. The size of the source code of the PSA Petri Network editing, animation and simulation tool (Petri net Simulation Animation) does not exceed 11 000 lines of C++, and we only needed a week of development with the GIGA toolbox (Caux *et al.*, 1991) (not all the GIGA classes are necessary).

6.4.3 Simulation of Petri nets

DEDICATED SIMULATION TOOLS

Existing tools for simulating Petri nets, such as SEDRIC (Vallett *et al.*, 1985), LORIC (Leopopoulos, 1985), PETRI-S (Tankoano *et al.*, 1991) and OR (Song and Poeley, 1992), are based on a synchronizing code written with a universal procedural language (Pascal, Fortran, C, ...). This type of code is very powerful and allows the use of numerous extensions of Petri nets. The interfaces proposed do, however, lack user-friendliness. The graphic editors are sometimes used upstream of

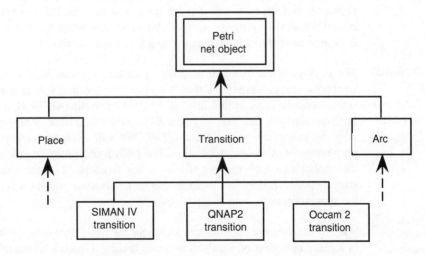

Figure 6.34 Inheritance graph of the graphic Petri net.

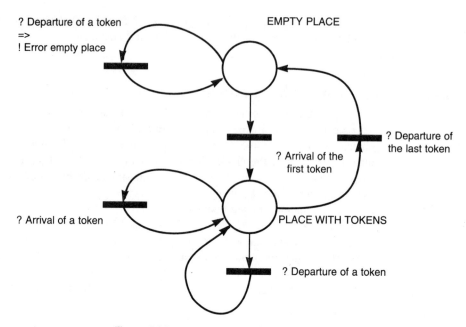

Figure 6.35 M2PO Petri net for the place class.

the simulation and Markovian analysis tool (Song and Pooley, 1992). (Stochastic Petri nets are isomorphic with first-order discrete Markov chains (Molloy, 1982).) In general, there is no animation in existing tools because it is of limited interest. The PSA software which we present does not seek to compete with existing software, but should be seen as a feasibility study concerning the reusability of the GIGA toolbox. PSA is not in any way a tool for verifying the properties of a basic Petri net, nor for reduction of Petri nets, but may be integrated in a modelling environment, or be reused for student projects (specification and simulation of protocols, ...) for it is dedicated neither to a language, nor to a particular simulator.

TECHNIQUES OF SIMULATING PETRI NETS   The PSA software makes it possible to capture a generalized Petri net, which is stochastic and coloured. We then translate this specification into a discrete event simulation language, in this case either QNAP2 or SIMAN IV (Caux *et al.*, 1991). Simulation results may possibly be used to constitute a trace, which can be animated with the animation kernel from GIGA. We will examine various techniques of translating the graphic specification. The main problem lies in guaranteeing that all the transitions which may be 'fired' at any moment 't' of the simulation will be started up in parallel. This problem can be resolved in various ways, depending on the simulation tools used.

Classic appointment technique   We will describe the appointment technique for basic Petri nets; each token arriving in a place upstream of a transition (modelled by a queue) scrutinizes all the other places upstream (queue) of the same transition modelling the appointment. In the case of a pure appointment, the selection structure of Petri nets (a place shared by two transitions) is impossible. If the token sees that the other places upstream contain at least one token, then the token activates the transition; otherwise the token is blocked on a flag. This method is perfectly suited to simulation languages; however, the resulting code is long because part of the code of the appointments must be implemented in each place.

Technique using a sequential supervisor

A dummy entity manages the activities of a supervisor, whose objective is to scrutinize the network sequentially, looking for transitions that can be fired. Here too, queues represent the places of a network, and the transitions are considered to be a set of upstream places and downstream places. With this technique the resulting code is shorter than that generated with the classic appointment method. However, it does introduce implicit priorities between the transitions due to the sequential operation of the supervisor. This resolves Petri net selections in a deterministic manner, which is not always desired.

Parallel supervisors

To avoid these implicit priorities, a supervisor can be introduced for each transition. All the problems of priorities, parallelism and synchronization are then referred to the simulation software. This is one of the approaches we use for simulating Petri nets with the SIMAN IV or QNAP2 languages.

The technique of guarded tasks

There is also a solution offering a good compromise for a great number of Petri net extensions. This is the technique of guarded tasks which are presented in Gourgand and Hill (1990b), which was implemented on a parallel transputer-based architecture. Each transition is a process guarded by all of its preconditions. Parallel execution is guaranteed by an adapted material architecture. The partitioning problems on physical processors are not negligible and we will not tackle them directly. Stochastic methods adapted to these types of problems are proposed in Norre (1993).

6.4.4 Production of code to simulate a Petri net

This section deals with the production of QNAP2, SIMAN IV and Occam 2 code to simulate the operation of a Petri net. In all cases, an object containing the graphic specification (place objects, transitions and arcs) is created by PSA. This container is a list indexed by transition, making it possible to obtain for each transition a list of the upstream and downstream places. This simplifies the creation of parallel supervisor code with the QNAP2 and SIMAN IV software, as well as the codes for guarded tasks in Occam 2.

TRANSLATION TO QNAP2

In our case, we have only created two QNAP2 classes: place and transition. A token which arrives in a place object sets a flag called *marked* to indicate its presence, and then waits until the associated transition is fired on a flag called *fire*. When the transition is fired, the token is released from the *fire* flag and leaves the system (the supervisor is given the task of creating the tokens for the downstream places).

A supervising dynamic entity, belonging to instances of the transition class, scrutinizes the preconditions of a transition. When all preconditions are verified, the supervising entity deletes all the tokens waiting on the *fire* flag in the places upstream. Then it creates the number of tokens required for the downstream places and returns to scrutinizing.

When the code for the place and transition classes has been written, the creation of a QNAP2 program consists simply of creating instances of these classes. The object-oriented approach simplifies this translation by using polymorphic methods for each class. Figure 6.36 gives the QNAP2 code for the place and transition classes.

```
&  ----------------------------------------------------------------------- &
&                         Class defining the places                        &
&  ----------------------------------------------------------------------- &
/declare/

    object place;
         queue    place;                    & Server associated with the place
         flag     marked;                   & Flag for the
         flag     fire;                     & firing
         real     tempo;                    & Timing for stochastic Petri net
         integer  initialmarking;           & Number of initial tokens
    end;

/station/

    name =*place.place;
    type = single;
    init = initialmarking;
    service =
      begin                                 & Message for the animation
        writeln("1 ",TIME," ",includin(cqueue), "token");
        exp(tempo);                         & Timing
        set(marked);                        & Presence signal
        wait(fire);                         & Awaiting firing
        reset(marked);
        transit(out);
      end;

&  ----------------------------------------------------------------------- &
&                    Class defining the transition objects                 &
&  ----------------------------------------------------------------------- &
/declare/
    object trans;
         queue                trans;        & File supervisor
         queue integer        nbup;         & Number of upstream places
         integer              nbdown;       & Number of downstream places
         ref place            pin(10);      & References to the upstream places
         ref place            pout(10)      & References to the downstream places
         integer              i;            & Local counter
    end;
```

```
/station/ name   = *trans.trans;
    type         = single;
    init         = 1;
    service      =
        begin                             & Preconditions
        for i := 1 step 1 until nbup do
        begin
          wait(pin(i).marked);
        end;                              & Moving tokens

        for i := 1 step 1 until nbup do   & Movement of tokens

        begin                                       & Animation message
          free(pin(i).place.first,pin(i).fire);
          writeln("3 ",TIME," ",includin(cqueue)," TOKEN");
        end;

        for i:=1 step 1 until nbdown do   & Creation of tokens
        begin                                       & downstream
          transit(new(customer),pout(i).place);
        end;
        transit(trans);
      end;
```

Figure 6.36 QNAP2 code for the place and transition classes.

TRANSLATION TO SIMAN IV

With SIMAN IV, the translation code follows the same principle as with QNAP2, with one exception: SIMAN IV does not have an object language, so as much code must be written as there are places and transitions. The places are represented by queues from which tokens are removed (REMOVE block) and to which they are sent (BRANCH block). Figure 6.37 shows the SIMAN IV code for a Petri net junction structure. For this example, there is only one transition (Q_TRANS1). Q_PLACE1 and Q_PLACE2 are upstream places of this transition and Q_PLACE3 is the downstream place. With the Petri net objects container structure supplied by PSA, it is relatively simple to generate the SIMAN files. The PSA queue file corresponds to a trace file which may be used by the animator. Codes of triggering events for the animation are: '1' for a token which enters a place and '3' to leave a place.

TRANSLATION TO OCCAM 2

Adaptation to the transputer architecture

For a translation to Occam 2 making the best possible use of the transputer architecture, it is important to explain the technique which allows us to test whether data is ready on a channel without being blocked (Occam 2 communications usually being synchronous). We will explain this technique in relation to the classic problem of readers/writers reading the marking of a place in parallel.

All parallel readers must be able to test whether data is ready on a channel without being blocked: when processes work in parallel through an Occam 2 'PAR'constructor, if just one of the processes is blocked, all the other processes of the 'PAR' will also be blocked at the end of their work. The usual solution to the

```
        begin;
          create,10;                                    ! Initial marking

        Q_PLACE1
          write, PSAfile, '(' 1',£12.4,'Q_PLACE1 TOKEN')':tnow);
          delay:50;                                     ! Timing
          queue,Q_PLACE1:detach;

          create,10;
        Q_PLACE2
          write,PSAfile,'(' 1',£12.4,'Q_PLACE2 TOKEN')':tnow);
          delay:20;
          queue,Q_PLACE2:detach;


        Q_PLACE3
          write, PSAfile, '(' 1',£12.4,'Q_PLACE3 TOKEN')':tnow);
          delay:10;
          queue,Q_PLACE3:detach;


          create,1;

        Q_TRANS1
          delay:0.0;
          queue:Q_TRANS1;
          scan :
                nq(Q_PLACE1)>0 .and. nq(Q_PLACE2)>0;
          remove:1,Q_PLACE1,out;
          write,PSAfile,'(' 3',£12.4,'Q_PLACE1 TOKEN')':tnow);
          remove:1,Q_PLACE2,out;
          write,PSAfile,'(' 1',£12.4,'Q_PLACE2 TOKEN')':tnow);
          count:C_TRANS1;
          branch:
                always,Q_PLACE3:
                always,Q_TRANS1;

        OUT
          count:OUT:dispose;
        end;
```

Figure 6.37 SIMAN IV code for a junction.

problem of readers/writers in Occam is to use the 'ALT' constructor to guarantee mutual exclusion between the readers and the writers (this is the same as the Hoare (1978) solution with CSP (Communicating Sequential Processes), but a single reader may read at a moment 't'. We wish to have a really parallel solution making use of the possibilities offered by the hardware. To this end, we will use only a few data duplications and a channel testing technique. Figure 6.38 shows our Occam 2 solution for the 'reader/writer' problem (variables are assumed to be declared).

```
&-----------------------------------------------------------------&
&                  Server for the marking of a place              &
&-----------------------------------------------------------------&

PROC CTRL ()
  WHILE TRUE                              — marking [ ] value of the marking
    PRI ALT                               — duplicated in a table
      ALT i = 0 FOR nb.writers            — More important priority
        write [i] ? newvalue              — for the writers
          SEQ j = 0 FOR nb.readers        — Duplication for the
            marking[j]:= newvalue          — parallel readings
      TRUE & SKIP
        PAR j = 0 FOR nb.readers
          PRI ALT                         — Parallel reading
            read[j] ? any                 — if it occurs
            data.read[j] ! Object[j]      — several readers
          TRUE & SKIP
            SKIP
```

Figure 6.38 Occam 2 code for the server of a Petri network place.

```
PRI ALT
  channel ? any
    . . .
TRUE & SKIP
  SKIP
```

Figure 6.39 Occam 2 code making it possible to test a channel.

Each iteration of the main body of the loop uses the construction in Figure 6.39. The priority alternative means having to test first whether an issue is present on the 'channel'; if there is nothing, the other alternative is executed (it is then a matter of continuing in sequence).

The guarded tasks technique   We can now present our guarded tasks technique. With this technique, Occam channels are used for marking servers and communications between communicating Petri nets, if we wish to model them. The solution proposed remains very close to Occam 2 possibilities, which offers guards for processes using both a Boolean expression and a single receipt on a channel. We consider all transitions as being processes which may work in parallel, the exception to this rule being the presence of the Petri net selection structure (one upstream place shared by several transitions). Transitions that share an upstream place may not be executed in parallel; they are grouped together in an 'ALT' constructor. Most of the Occam 2 compilers implement the ALT constructor as a 'PRI ALT', and the conflict is then settled by using the specified priority.

For each transition, a Boolean expression involving all the preconditions of the transition (availability of tokens, evaluation of predicates, if necessary, ...) is

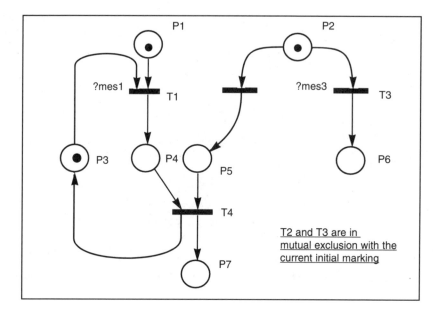

Figure 6.40 Example of Petri net with selection structure.

evaluated; it does not include the receipt of messages. A marking server process is associated with each place. We find parallelism at two levels: transitions and marking servers. Sequential accesses are compulsory when two transitions wish to modify the marking of the same place at the same moment. An abstract Occam 2 code is given in Figure 6.41 for the Petri net of Figure 6.40.

For an implementation on a network of transputers, a configuration file to place the parallel processes of the Petri net must be constructed manually, using the 'PLACED PAR' instruction.

An Occam 2 algorithm to execute all the transitions in parallel within a loop is possible only if all the transition processes are completed (whether the transitions have been fired or not). The technique used is the same as that proposed for the reader/writer problem allowing testing of preconditions, including the arrival of messages on channels, without being blocked. Managing several Petri net extensions involves managing the data structures associated with these extensions, and taking them into account when evaluating preconditions. Such structures are proposed in Leopopoulos (1985).

Modelling several interpreted and communicating Petri nets

The Occam 2 code for managing several interpreted and communicating Petri nets is identical to that proposed for a single Petri net Figure 6.42 shows the interpreted and communicating Petri nets. One of the nets manages the machining (physical subsystem) and the other models the control of the machine (logical subsystem).

```
&-------------------------------------------------------------------------&
&                    Example of parallel transitions                      &
&-------------------------------------------------------------------------&
   PAR                                   -- Parallel transitions
    PRI ALT                              -- Code of transition 1
     fire.condition[1] & mes1 ? any
      PAR                                -- Updating of a marker
        server.place[1] ! -1
        server.place[3] ! -1
        server.place[4] ! 1
    TRUE & SKIP
      SKIP
    PRI ALT                      -- Transitions 2 and 3 in exclusion
      fire.condition[2]          -- Guard without message
        do.work.2()
      fire.condition[3] & mes3 ? any
        do.work.3()
      TRUE & SKIP
        SKIP
```

Figure 6.41 Occam code of transitions in parallel.

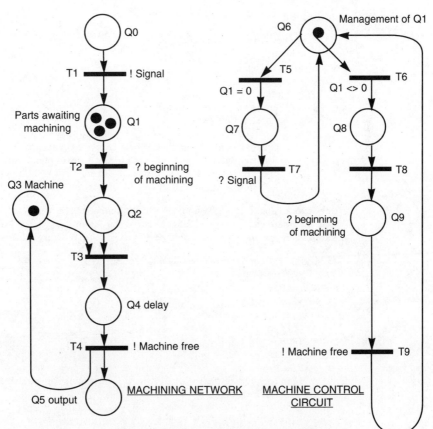

Figure 6.42 Two communicating Petri nets.

These communicating nets allow the modelling of a flexible MICHELIN line (Barnichon, 1990). The general Occam code adapted for these two Petri nets is given in Figure 6.43.

The study of the generation of Occam 2 code for Petri nets was carried out on a microcomputer fitted with five T800 transputers. It showed that the Occam 2 language may be used to model the operation of the Petri nets effectively, if we have suitable equipment. Even though the Occam 2 language does not offer all the facilities of a high-level language (structures, dynamic allocation, recursion and function pointers are absent), it may be used as a formal tool for the specification of parallel systems communicating by messages, because it is based on a well-defined mathematical concurrency model (CSP (Hoare, 1978)). Implementing coloured Petri nets with Occam 2 requires the use of structures on the transition communication channels, which we also tested (Gourgand and Hill, 1990a).

```
&----------------------------------------------------------------------&
&         Template for the model of communicating Petri nets           &
&----------------------------------------------------------------------&

PAR
  ... Servers for the marking of the places
  SEQ
    ... Fix the initial marking
    not.finished := TRUE
    WHILE not.finished
      SEQ
        PAR
          ... Process for evaluating the preconditions
          ... of the two Petri nets
        PAR
          ... Process modelling the transitions of the matching Petri net,
          ... and of the controlled Petri net, only those of which the
          ... preconditions are valid are fired
        ... Give the marking and instant statistics

-- The two transitions T5 and T6 which share place Q6
-- are automatically in exclusion for they have
-- exclusive Boolean conditions concerning the number of tokens of Q1.

-- Example of transitions for the 2 Petri nets
    PAR
        PRI ALT                              & Transition T1
          fire.condition[T1] & SKIP
            ... Maj marking
            Signal ! Ok
          TRUE & SKIP
            SKIP
        PRI ALT                              & Transition T2
          fire.condition[T2]                 & beginning of machining ? any
            ... Maj marking
          TRUE & SKIP
            SKIP
```

```
... Other transitions T3 and T4 of the machining Petri net

PRI ALT                          & Transition of the control Petri net
  fire.condition [T5] & SKIP     & The firing condition takes into
    ... Maj marking              & account testing of the marking
  TRUE & SKIP                    & of the place Q1 (Q1 = 0)
    SKIP
... Other transitions T6, T7 and T8 of the control Petri net

PRI ALT                          & Transition T9
  fire.condition[T9] & machine free ? any
    ... Maj marking
  TRUE & SKIP
    SKIP
```

Figure 6.43 Occam 2 code for modelling several communicating Petri nets.

◁ 6.5 Conclusions

GIGA has proved its usefulness and its reusability potential in two application domains. The GIGA toolbox not only enabled us to produce the Petri net simulation tool in less than one week (PSA, 11 000 lines of C++), but it is also the basis for GAME, which turned out to be a powerful tool for animating the simulation results of flexible assembly system models (20 000 lines of C++). This tool was validated on numerous industrial sites of the VALEO group. The biggest animated system is that of Nogent Le Rotrou, which has over 300 graphic manufacturing objects (almost all classes available in GAME were used). Studies carried out with GAME in domains other than that of manufacturing systems (administrative systems, data processing systems) show not only the interest of this tool, but also the generic nature of software built with GIGA. These software items allow the desired model verification and validation tests to be integrated in the behaviour of domain-specific objects. In this way the power of dedicated tools is obtained while maintaining the ergonomics and user-friendliness of a family of tools.

One of the interesting aspects of the tools built concerns the automatic generation of object-oriented simulation code for industrial cases from a graphic model. The approach used recommends decomposition into three subsystems (physical, logical and decisional) and combines a station and transaction approach. We took advantage of the contributions of simulation languages (like QNAP2, Simula, SIMAN) while proposing techniques making it possible to use dynamic classification and polymorphism with the QNAP2 language. In addition, simulation codes that can be generated for various software show the openness and compatibility of tools built with GIGA.

We have illustrated various analysis and design results with the graphic notation proposed by M2PO. The static part was used to reuse a domain analysis carried out using E/R diagrams. The dynamic part was used to represent interactions between different subsystems, transactions and the internal behaviour of objects.

◁ KEY POINTS

- Domain analysis allows a very high degree of reusability because it may be exploited by many applications. The domain analysis carried out for the SIGMA project allows rapid design of simulation models, graphic object models for editing, animation and code generation.
- The superimposition of several M2PO graphic layers (inheritance, association, composition, ...) is possible, but in practice, to keep the diagrams legible it is often preferable to concentrate on a few types of relationships.
- The library of domain objects necessary for the construction of an editing/animating tool with the GIGA toolbox is deduced from the domain analysis.
- Classes of graphic objects of a domain must present a visual behaviour consistent with reality and integrate error checking features in order to have techniques for model verification and validation, therefore presenting finer techniques than those usually proposed. The behaviour and consistency checks are specified by means of M2PO Petri nets.
- The generation of object-oriented simulation code from a graphic specification facilitates the design of models by non-specialists and increases the reliability of simple simulation programs by avoiding programming errors.
- Decomposition into three subsystems and domain analysis with M2PO facilitate the writing of simulation code generators.
- The object-based languages are often flexible enough to be able to implement polymorphism, delegation and dynamic classification which are sometimes not directly available.

◁ EXERCISES

6.1 Criticize the M2PO diagram of Figure 6.2. Would it be interesting to specialize the static and dynamic conveyor classes? If so, give examples of subclasses.

6.2 In the domain analysis carried out in the SIGMA project for flexible discrete flow assembly systems, quote the various flow elements. To what subsystem do these elements belong?

6.3 What types of inconsistency between a simulation model and reality may be detected by specifying the behaviour of the graphic objects of a domain with M2PO Petri nets?

6.4 Do the M2PO Petri net in Figure 6.10 again, taking into account the management of errors arising from loading a component on a full shuttle and unloading an empty shuttle (use a new macro-place). Take into account references to stopping points in the mission orders of a shuttle and verify the consistency of the requests.

6.5. Modify the QNAP2 code in Figure 6.15 to take into account the fact that the machine can only break down if it is working.

6.6 Propose a model of an accumulating conveyor using a queuing network which, unlike Figure 6.16, takes into account the conveyor's first place. What are the special cases of this modelling (take into account the place number of the conveyor)?

6.7 Give the disadvantages of automatic generation of simulation code.

6.8 Propose a general technique for taking account of global rules (touching several objects). Adapt this technique to take account of metarules.

6.9 Modify the QNAP2 code of the messenger in Figure 6.31 in order to take account of delegation (it is necessary to add a parameter specifying the initiator of the delegation). What effect does the deletion of the recursive call by a 'while' or a 'goto' have on the messenger's effectiveness?

6.10 Compare the elegance of the code generated for QNAP2 with that generated for SIMAN for a Petri net specification comprising many places and transitions. To what are the differences due?

6.11 The number of Occam 2 channels making it possible to read the marking of a Petri net place in parallel corresponds to the number of duplications of the shared information. This number corresponds to the number of transitions this place possesses upstream. It is preferable for reasons of effectiveness that this number be low. Is this realistic? Knowing the number of transitions which might be fired in parallel, what are the problems encountered if you wish to partition these processes on a network of transputers?

7

Conclusions and prospects

◁7.1 Conclusions concerning the possibilities of the tools designed

In this book, we have tried to bring together the advanced techniques of software engineering and those of discrete event simulation by making use of the object model used by the specialists in both domains. We first of all propose an object-oriented modelling method based on a modelling process which integrates domain analysis upstream of the object-oriented analysis and design phases. The modelling process presented adapts to the modelling of complex systems and the production of the corresponding simulation programs (by including the notions of knowledge and action models). The analogy between software systems and models of real systems has allowed us to identify invariants of the object-oriented analysis and design methods. The main contributions concern the modelling of dynamic aspects of the systems, as well as the decomposition of a system into three subsystems (physical, logical and decisional). The principal characteristics of the M2PO method are:

- the recommendation of domain analysis (and of the reusability which arises from it);
- an improvement in the traceability of the objects;
- the decomposition of a system into three additional subsystems (for simulation) introduced in the SIGMA project;
- the taking into account of the principal concepts of the object model and the separation of static aspects (using different layers) from the dynamic aspects of a real system to be modelled (handled with adapted tools: message flow diagrams, interpreted and communicating Petri nets, ...);
- the covering of the whole object modelling cycle proposed, while remaining independent of the various object-oriented languages;
- the intensive use of abstract classes, both for the static and dynamic aspects, imposing a high level of abstraction;

- simple graphic and textual notations which are not mandatory;
- the establishment of paths and phases for the flow elements, thereby detailing the logical subsystem and facilitating the use of object-oriented simulations using a transaction approach.

The various types of results obtained with M2PO have turned out to be useful to handle either a simulation project or general software. We may therefore consider that the M2PO method is open to other domains.

Like inheritance, domain analysis must be considered as a form of factorization necessary in the medium and long term for the collection and formalization of the knowledge of a system. It is now a good idea to validate, refine and supplement this method on projects of an industrial scale. Our method does not claim to be universal, but it tries to facilitate the use of software engineering techniques which may satisfy the requirements which exist in the simulation community.

We are also interested in the validation and verification of simulation models using automatic code-generation techniques and graphic model animation. The GIGA toolbox which we have produced provides assistance for modelling specialists who wish to have valid animations, while remaining independent of the simulation software. The transient behaviour of the entities of the real system is understood, visually, by means of animated graphic objects. The level of abstraction obtained for the development of a simulation model is then greater than that of a simulation language. In order to increase the chances of detecting inconsistencies in simulation models, we have separated the graphic objects which depend on the domain from those which are independent of it. Specification of the internal behaviour of graphic objects of a domain makes it possible to integrate the ability to react to any programming or modelling errors. The user then has information to assist the validation of the knowledge model as well as the verification of the action model. The GIGA toolbox was used to produce a tool for simulating and animating Petri nets (PSA, over 10 000 lines of C++), but it is also the basis of the VIEWMOD software. This software turned out to be a powerful tool for animating the simulation results of flexible assembly systems (20 000 lines of C++). This tool was validated on numerous models of industrial systems in the VALEO group.

The ease with which it was possible to produce the VIEWMOD and PSA applications shows the usefulness of domain analysis as carried out for GIGA. Applications arising from this kind of design may have the power usually found with dedicated tools, while enjoying the ergonomics and user-friendliness of a family of tools.

We also tackled the automatic generation of object-oriented simulation code for the QNAP2 software. The code generated is that of industrial models of manufacturing systems, specified by means of a graphic interface. The case presented showed the usefulness of decomposition into three subsystems (physical, logical and decisional). To resolve the problem of the automatic generation of the simulation code of a system, we propose a solution which combines a

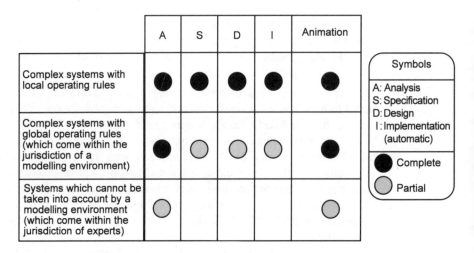

	A	S	D	I	Animation
Complex systems with local operating rules	●	●	●	●	●
Complex systems with global operating rules (which come within the jurisdiction of a modelling environment)	●	○	○	○	●
Systems which cannot be taken into account by a modelling environment (which come within the jurisdiction of experts)	○				○

Symbols

A: Analysis
S: Specification
D: Design
I: Implementation
  (automatic)

● Complete
○ Partial

Figure 7.1   Objectives achieved in terms of the category of system.

transactional specification of a system with a station approach necessary for obtaining a QNAP2 model. Simulation codes of non-object-oriented languages such as SIMAN IV or Occam 2 were also obtained automatically from a specification produced by means of Petri nets. As regards code generation, the solutions we propose, although they increase the reliability of action models, none the less remain inaccessible to non-specialists in modelling (unlike the SIGMA environment which must be within reach of industrial experts).

Figure 7.1 gives a reminder of and supplements the objectives which we set in Chapter 1. We have design tools allowing an analysis of complex systems and the specification of their behaviour in order to build knowledge models and deduce from them the corresponding action models, to implement them automatically and animate them. For systems including global operating results, we have been able to exceed our targets. We are in fact capable of analysing and animating complex systems and we can also automatically generate the major part of the code.

◁ 7.2 Prospects

One of the most complex theoretic problems after a domain analysis is to propose a structure which makes it possible to formalize to the best advantage the generic knowledge model of a domain. Since this is intended to be instantiated, it is necessary to guarantee the consistency of the translation of a domain into a knowledge model. That is why we envisage specifying and resolving theoretical problems concerning software engineering and modelling. In fact, if we wish to achieve the modelling of systems comprising very complex decisional parts, it will be necessary to be capable of proposing structures and interfaces (graphic languages? automatic code generation? formal languages such as Object-Z?) which 'easily' and reliably bring about the implementation of solutions based, for example, on communications between a simulator and an expert system or on a distribution of simulation objects with an architecture supporting Time Warp.

The tools we have proposed are mostly prototypes demonstrating the feasibility of the ideas put forward and it will be possible to use them to solve these theoretic problems. The M2PO method proposed in 1992 needs to be applied to a great many examples in order to determine and correct its weaknesses. In order for it to be fully usable, a CASE (Computer Aided Software Engineering) tool is necessary. This tool must be sufficiently general to be able to accept other object-oriented analysis and design methods. Like GIGA, which may be associated with libraries specific to domains, the CASE tool must be capable of supporting different methods and different simulation languages. It is therefore appropriate to produce a domain analysis for this type of tool first of all.

As regards the GIGA toolbox, we believe that it is a good idea to design software which allows the user to create interactive editors/animators. This software should be capable of managing the library of standard GIGA components as well as a set of object libraries peculiar to the domains already studied. The user would then be in a position to construct interactively a tool such as GAME. To do that, it seems to us an interesting idea to be able to specify graphically and interactively the objects peculiar to a domain, in order to construct a new library. The following stage consists of associating an object-oriented simulation code with each of the classes constructed. We also wish to invest in visual interactive simulation and programming techniques (taking care with regard to the statistical results supplied). Visual programming, which makes use of the composability of objects, illustrates what our future modelling tools will be.

The procedure we have adopted, which is similar to factorizing, tends to lead us into concentrating on one type of problem to analyse its domain. When various domain analyses have been carried out, we think that it will be interesting to tackle domain analysis of entire classes of problems.

APPENDIX A

Introduction to C++

◁ A.1 Introduction

This short introduction to the C++ language is intended for developers familiar with the C language. It is impossible to cover all the aspects of the language in so few pages, but we will try to deal with the main characteristics as well as certain special features.

The C++ language is the result of the work of Bjarne Stroustrup in the Bell laboratories (Stroustrup, 1986, 1992). The educated reader will know that this language is inspired mainly by SIMULA-67 (Dahl *et al.*, 1968) for the notions of classes of objects, inheritance and polymorphism. In return, numerous simulators are now based on the C++ language (C++ Sim, SIMEX 3.0, Sim++, DEVS/C++, ...). The C++ language incorporates the C language with very few exceptions; in fact the C language was preserved because of its multipurpose nature, its brevity, and its capacity to carry out low-level system tasks efficiently (which is why it was designed). Another important asset is the fact that the C language, which is used as the basis for most C++ compilers, runs on any hardware, which guarantees very considerable portability (without being perfect). Finally the current mass of C developers are susceptible of changing easily from structured programming to object-oriented programming, by reusing millions of lines of C code which exist in the form of utilitarian applications or system libraries. It therefore seemed interesting to try to compensate for the C language defects while preserving the definite advantages.

The first rough draft of C++ was called 'C with classes' and it was only after numerous developments of the language that the subtle name of C++ was suggested. The various interpretations of this name are given in Stroustrup (1986). The basic objective of this language is to make it possible to express the concepts of a solution in a language close to the problem to be solved, without losing its efficiency.

The presentation of the C++ language which we are going to give could not replace a reading of works such as Ellis and Stroustrup (1990), Stroustrup (1992), Lippman (1992) or Coplien (1992). The object languages involve a modification of the way in which a designer must reason; it is not simply a matter of learning a new language. It is necessary to agree to change a certain number of habits acquired in structured programming during a great many years of experience. Stroustrup states in particular that the better you know C, the longer and more difficult it seems to change your programming style in order to draw any advantage from the potential of C++. However, by means of a reasonable effort, many C developers rapidly agree that C++ is a tool which has a great power for tackling the design of complex problems.

Below, we shall present the C++ language around examples drawn from the design of a simplified manufacturing objects graphic editor such as the GAME/VIEWMOD software.

◁ A.2 The modelling of a problem by means of classes

A.2.1 Abstraction and encapsulation

One of the aims of the C++ language is to express its ideas directly in the language of the problem with which you are faced, and in a practical and safe way without conceding anything as regards the level of efficiency. The programmer must therefore be able to define abstractions of the reality, which are called classes in C++, and then manipulate the instance objects of these classes.

Let us suppose that we are trying to construct an editor of graphic entities. We will define an abstraction of the entities we wish to manipulate. One of the solutions consists in finding the minimum characteristics of an object class which will serve as a base class from which to derive all the other classes. The first object class we will manipulate will be called `graphic_obj`.

We know that one of the central concepts of object-oriented programming is based on a unifying theory which consists of grouping together the code and the data in an entity called an object. In C++ attributes are called data members and methods are called member functions.

C++ gives the possibility of merging the code and data by extending the structures and unions concepts of the C language with the concept of SIMULA classes.

```
class graphic_obj {      // declaration of the graphic_obj class
    // attributes
    // methods
} ;
graphic_obj circle;      // declare an instance of the
                         // graphic_obj class
```

Note: the comments '//' are single line. If you generalize their use in your programs, you can comment entire zones of code with the classic comment symbols of C, /* and */, which can help with debugging.

It is possible to use this class of object as a new type and so declare tables of graphic objects and pointers to graphic objects as we would have done on simple integers. The C++ language being considered as a hybrid, it is not possible to consider all types as classes of objects; the predefined types are not classes. With a very high degree of flexibility it is possible to control access to the data and to the member functions of a class. The visibility of class members may be modified by means of the private, protected, and public keywords.

The private keyword only applies to the declarations of classes and structures and means that all members (data and functions) declared behind private (and right up to the next protection keyword) would only be accessible to the member functions of the object undergoing declaration.

The protected keyword only applies to class declarations. It is equivalent to private for the members of the class declared but it also allows member functions of derived classes to gain access to members of the base class. This mechanism will be taken up again when we deal with the notion of inheritance.

The public keyword specifies that all members declared between public and another protection keyword or an end of declaration are visible to all, with no restriction other than the scope of the object.

The default forms of protection are as follows: for classes the protection is private; for structures it is public; the members of a union will always be public and that cannot be modified.

A.2.2 Declaration of classes

We have already begun to pose for ourselves the problem of a graphic objects editor. Let us reason initially as we would have done with C. The majority of graphics editors on the market reference-mark graphic objects by means of two coordinates which specify a window in which an object is contained. This classic approach for graphic objects is included and justified by Gorlen (1987). Let us bring these coordinates together in a structure so that we can declare a certain number of entities for this new type.

```
struct graphic_obj {
      char name[30] ;     // name of the object
      int  xig , yig ;    // bottom left-hand coordinates
      int  xsd , ysd ;    // and top right-hand.
      } ;
graphic_obj     circle, * ptr_obj , tab_obj[ 10 ] ;
```

C programmers will have noted the absence of the keyword struct at instance declaration level. We have defined a new type without having explicitly used the keyword typedef. In fact the structures and unions may be considered as special object classes with which it is impossible to construct a hierarchy of classes.

Therefore `circle` is an instance of the class `graphic_obj`, `ptr_obj` points to a graphic object and `tab_obj` is a table of 10 graphic objects.

A.2.3 Methods

Let us now look at what we wish to do with these graphic objects. Initially we will only look at simple actions. It would be interesting to know the name of an object or to know whether it has just been selected with a mouse. By means of member functions it is possible to specify these actions in the declaration block of a class, of a structure or of a union.

```
struct graphic_obj {
      char name[30] ;               // name of the object
      int   xig , yig ;             // top left-hand coordinates
      int   xsd , ysd ;             // and bottom right-hand.

      int   contains ( int x , int y ) ;  // methods or member functions
      char*itsname ()   { return name; }
      } ;
graphic_obj::contains (int x = 0, int y = 0)
{
      if ( x >= xig && x <= xsd && y >= yig && y <= ysd )
         return 1;
      else return 0;

}
```

This example means that we discover new aspects of the C++ language.

First of all it is possible to define the body of a function in a declaration of methods. Here the member function `itsname` is described as an implicit `inline` type declaration when the instructions of the function body are explained in the class declaration; it is then of no use to specify the keyword `inline`. The `inline` functions correspond in fact to intelligent macros with typing facilities; they are used for reasons of efficiency and generally for very short functions, the code being copied. The example given above shows an ideal use of an `inline` function for an access method to a particular member. This allows at once an elegant style of programming, respecting the principles of encapsulation, without however sacrificing efficiency. Any function may however be declared `inline` outside a class definition; it is sufficient to have the declaration of the function preceded by the keyword `inline`.

Another novel notion is that of the scope resolution operator `::`, which makes it possible to name the class, the structure or the union owning the member functions which are then called deported functions. The term 'deported' is used because the content of these functions is not detailed in the class declaration but outside this declaration.

Here `graphic_obj::contains ()` makes it possible to clearly identify the `contains()` function because other functions could have the same name in other classes or simply in the body of the program. The scope resolution operated may also be applied to all class members.

You will doubtless have noticed that the default values (implicit) may be given to the arguments of the `contains` function. In fact, as in the C language, it is possible to call up a function without giving all of its parameters, indeed without giving any! Implicit values will be allocated to parameters which would not be specified when calling up a function.

Let us now study access to class members. As in the case of the members of a C structure, the resolution operator . allows a class instance (an object) to gain access to attributes and methods. The pointed notation `->` of the C language is still valid; a pointer to an object class will gain access to members by means of this pointed notation.

```
circle.contains(76,235);        // test if the circle contains
                                // this coordinate
graphic_obj * ptr_obj;          // pointer to a graphic object
ptr_obj = new graphic_obj;      // memory allocation
ptr_obj->contains(100,200);     // call up of the member
                                // function contains by pointed
                                // notation
```

A.2.4 The construction and destruction of objects

When declaring a class instance, the space necessary for data members and for pointers to member functions is allocated. As in any structured approach, it is a good idea to decide on the initialization of members. As in C, we may write the code necessary for the initialization after each instance creation. This procedure is very heavy, so a function which would do this work would be very welcome. Provision was made for this in the C++ language which proposes using a special member function called a 'constructor' of a class. The name of this constructor is that of the class to be constructed; if the programmer forgets to specify a constructor, it is generated automatically by default without arguments.

The C++ source extract which follows gives the code of a constructor for the `graphic_obj` class. This constructor may be called up in two ways: either on the occasion of a static object declaration, or with a dynamic object declaration. (The operator `new` advantageously replaces the function `malloc()` of the C language for several reasons which will be explained to you later on).

```
class graphic_obj {
  protected :
      char    name[30] ;                  // name of the object
      int     xig , yig ;                 // bottom left-hand and top
                                          // right-hand coordinates.
  public :
      int     contains( int x , int y ) ;
      char*   its name() { return name ; }
```

```
     graphic_obj ( int x1, int y1, int x2, int y2, char *name);
     ~graphic_obj() { }
} ;

graphic_obj::graphic_obj (   int x1,  int y1,
                             int x2,  int y2, char *name)

{
  xig   =      x1 ;
  yig   =      y1 ;
  xsd   =      x2 ;
  ysd   =      y2 ;
  strcpy(nom, name)  ;
}
```

The destructor is also a special member function: its role is to erase the data members and restore the memory allocated to the object. The name of the destructor is that of the object class but it is preceded by a tilde (~) to distinguish it from the constructor.

If we omit to declare a destructor, C++ creates one (as in the case of constructors). Destructors are automatically called up when an object goes outside its scope or earlier if we use the operator delete (the counterpart of new).

In this example, we have used a class definition instead of a structure definition. For a structure the members are public. Data members are placed behind a protected specification so that member functions of a derived class may gain access. In fact, if nothing is specified, the data members of the class are private and the derived classes would not have access. On the other hand, member functions were specified public, so as to be accessible from any location of a future program.

It is possible to specify as much access control as you wish, although it seems more consistent to group together in the same place all the members benefiting from the same type of protection.

```
class example_class {
private :
      // members (data and functions) visible only from
      // instances of the example_object class
   protected :
      // members (data and functions) visible from instances of
      // the example_class and instances of objects
      // derived in public from the example_class
   public :
      // Members (data and functions) visible to all
   }
```

A.2.5 Class declarations and modules

In a C++ program, convention requires that class declarations be grouped together in 'header' files which must be included in the program body files. The first type of file (headers) uses the extensions '.h', '.hpp' or '.hxx' and only allows us to glimpse the design side of a class; the second type (bodies) uses the extensions '.cpp', '.c' or '.cxx' and develops the implementation of the class. Obviously separate compilation is recommended with, if possible, a header file and a body file per class.

Modularity still remains one of the key elements of object-oriented programming. If it is difficult for an average developer to understand a program of a million lines of code written all at one go, it is easier for him or her to understand many modules of a thousand lines.

◁ A.3 The notion of inheritance and hierarchy

A.3.1 General aspects

Complex system modelling is facilitated by the possibilities of abstraction and encapsulation which make it possible to mask the internal representation of programs.

In addition, program modularity allows us to break down a complex problem logically until we obtain elementary problems. Despite that, it remains difficult to understand a set of abstractions without a hierarchical approach. It is therefore a good idea to try to classify these abstractions, and this process of classification makes use of taxonomy. Biologists propose the classification of insects according to their families; Andrew Koenig proposes to classify vehicles (Koenig, 1988), while seeking to show that the construction of genealogical trees of graphs, applied to object-oriented programming, contributes a powerful method of representing knowledge. The principle of inheritance may be expressed in simple terms as follows: an object 'o' has a set of basic characteristics and we seek to extend these characteristics by adding to it a number of attributes and a number of methods. Instead of modifying the initial object class, it is sufficient to create a new type of object which possesses all the characteristics of the initial object plus the new ones which we are seeking to add to it. In C++ we use the term base class for a superclass and derived class for all the subclasses which inherit the base class.

The trees are not all strictly hierarchical: a simple hierarchy allows children to inherit from their mother (hence the notion of simple inheritance) but there are more complex problems involving multiple inheritance (inheritance from both the father and the mother) which give rise (for computer science) to a certain number of problems which we will subsequently mention.

A.3.2 Extension of a class and simple inheritance

The class we previously defined is not in itself very useful. In fact, it is a base class from which it becomes possible to construct a myriad of derived classes. We will try to construct a general class for manufacturing objects. This class will be capable of accepting machines, stocks, trolleys and other types of objects which would be found in a manufacturing system. It is a matter of enriching the base class graphic_obj with new attributes and new methods. Here is how we are able to write this new class from our current knowledge of graphic_obj.

```
class graphic_obj {
  protected :
      char          name[30] ;        // name of the object
      int           xig , yig ;       // top left-hand side and bottom
      int           xsd , ysd ;       // right-hand side coordinates.
  public :
      int           contains( int x , int y ) ;
      char          its_name() { name return; }
      graphic_obj ( int x1, int y1, int x2, int y2, char *name) ;
      ~graphic_obj() { }
      } ;

class manuf_obj : public graphic_obj {
  protected :
      int           colour ;
      int           size ;
      int           capacity ;
      int           state ;
  public :
      manuf_obj (int      x1,int y1,int x2,int y2,
                 char *n,int c,int t,int s,int e) ;
      ~manuf_obj() { }
      int           its_colour()     {colour return; }
      int           its_size()       {size return; }
      ...
      void          broken down()    {state = 0 ; }
      } ;

manuf_obj::manuf_obj (int x1,int y1,int x2,int y2,
                            char*n,int c,int t,int s,int e)
      :graphic_obj (x1,y1, n2,y2,n)
{
      colour    = c ;
      size      = t ;
      capacity  = s ;
      state     = 1 ;                 //the manufacturing object functions
}
```

Derivations are declared by specifying the derived class, then the base class preceded by : and the base class access modifier.

For this portion of code, it is graphic_obj which is the base class and manuf_obj which is the derived class.

Here the derivation is effected with the public access modifier, which means that the members of the base class will be viewed as follows in the derived class:

public if they were declared public in the base class, invisible if they were declared private in the base class, protected if they were declared protected in the base class.

If the access modifier was private, members of the base class would be viewed as follows in the derived class:

private if they were declared public in the base class, invisible if they were declared private in the base class, private if they were declared protected in the base class.

This is summarized in Table A.1.

Table A.1　Access rights of the classes.

Base class	Access modifier	Derived class
public	public	public
private	public	not accessible
protected	public	protected
public	private	private
private	private	not accessible
protected	private	private

To summarize, member functions of the manuf_obj class may here have access to all data members and all member functions of the graphic_obj class. Of course, they also have access to all the new members declared (one member function may call up another, indeed call up itself ...).

Note: the constructor of the new class calls on the constructor of the graphic_obj base class. This avoids rewriting the initialization lines of the coordinates of the graphic object as well as the initialization lines of the object name. This type of code economy may appear fortuitous in this precise case but, for examples of a large size, it is a good idea not to neglect it. What is more, the initialization of each data member is only effected in one place, the effect of which is to increase the reliability of the program and reduce the code size.

Now let us look at how we may construct machine and stock objects from this new class.

```
class machine : public manuf_obj {
  protected :
     float     machining time ;

  public :
     machine(
         int x1,int y1,int x2,int y2,    // coordinates
         char *n,                        // name of the machine
         int c, int t, int s, int e,     // colour, size,
                                         // capacity, state
         float ts) ;                     // machining time
         ~machine() { }
         float its machining time() {machining time return; }
} ;
```

```
machine::machine
   (int x1,int y1,int x2,int y2,char*n,int c,int t,int s,int e,float u)
   :manuf_obj ( x1, y1, x2, y2, n, c, t, s, e)
{
   machining time = u ;
}
class stock : public manuf_obj {
   protected :
      char      policy ;           // stock management policy
   public :
      stock(
         int x1, int y1, int x2, int y2,
         char *n,
         int c, int t, int s, int e,
         char p ) ;
      ~stock() { }
      char its_policy() { policy return; }
} ;
stock::stock(int x1, int y1, int x2, int y2, char*n,
            int c, int t, int s, int e, float u)
            :manuf_obj (x1, y1, x2, y2, n, c, t, s, e)
{
   policy = p ;                          // LIFO,FIFO or BULK policy
}
```

It is important to remember that the machine and stock constructors call up the `manuf_obj` class constructor which itself calls up the `graphic_obj` class constructor. In order to get our ideas straight, let us give some code examples which may be written concerning stock and machine objects.

```
machine m (0,0,100,10,'MACHINE1', BLUE, 5, 1, START, 45.876);
stock * ptr_stock ;

ptr_stock  = new stock (5,10,200,40,'STOCK A', YELLOW,7,10,START,FIFO);
machine.contains(2,2) ;

ptr_stock->broken down() ;
float time = machine.its machining_time() ;
```

A machine or a stock may easily call up the member function `contains()`. In fact, this code is common to all the objects deriving in `public` from the `graphic_obj` class. Likewise, the member function `broken_down()` is shared by all the objects deriving in `public` from the `manuf_obj` class, but only one machine gives access to the machining time data member. In fact, the inheritance mechanisms provided by the C++ language allow the programmer to follow an object-oriented design method which avoids the usual redundancies of classic structured programming while very substantially increasing the reliability of the code produced.

A.3.3 Multiple inheritance

In a flexible manufacturing system it is a frequent occurrence to come across robots. Now, these robots often behave both like machines and stocks (indeed even frequently like conveying systems, ...). We are faced with a case of multiple inheritance; with the C++ language it is possible to express this fairly simply.

```
class robot : public machine, public stock {
  protected :
        float tps_extract_stock ;        // stock extraction time
  public :
        float itstps_ex_stk() { tps_extract_stock return ; }
        void modif_param_robot(float t, char p) ;
        robot(
                int x1, int y1, int x2, int y2, char *n,
                int c, int t, int s, int e,
                char p, float t,
                float t2
                ) ;
        ~robot() { }
  } ;

robot::modif_param_robot(float t1, float t2, char p)
{
  stock::policy = p ;                    // Change the policy of the
  machine::machining_time = t1;          // line, the machining time
  tps_extract_stock = t2 ;               // and the extraction of
                                         // the stock to manage a
}                                        // new type of parts
robot::robot(   int x1, int y1, int x2, int y2, char *n,
                int c, int t, int s, int e, char p, float t,
                float t2 )
    : stock( x1, y1, x2, y2, n, c, t, s, e , p) ,
    : machine ( x1, y1, x2, y2, n, c, t, s, e ,t )
{
  tps_extract_stock = t2 ;
} ;
```

Access to the actual class members defined is effected as in the case of simple inheritance; on the other hand, on the occasion of access to inherited members, it is the responsibility of the programmer to specify from what class of parents they come, which is done in the function modif_param_robot(). The scope resolution operator : : indicates from what parent class we wish to recover members. It is in an explicit way that the conflicts of multiple inheritance are sorted out in C++, indeed, it is possible to add the keyword virtual to the derivation instruction:

```
class machine : virtual public manuf_obj
{
...
}
```

Thanks to the virtual keyword, the constructor of this robot class calls up the two constructors of direct superclasses. The C++ compilers will only call up the constructor of the base class manuf_obj once, thereby avoiding repetitive inheritance.

We advise readers who are interested to refer to the reference manual of the ANSI version of the language (Ellis and Stroustrup, 1990) for further details.

◁ A.4 Polymorphism and virtual functions

A.4.1 General aspects

The polymorphism mechanism must be present in all object-oriented languages (Masini, 1988; Meyer, 1988; Booch, 1991). This mechanism comes directly from the SIMULA language (Dahl *et al.*, 1968; Birtwistle *et al.*, 1973; Kirkerud, 1989). It makes it possible to give the same name to several member functions of the same hierarchy. Each member function executes a different code.

We must distinguish virtual functions from overloaded functions. In fact virtual functions express in different code forms (polymorphism) an action corresponding to the same semantic but authorizing access to dynamic binding. In addition, a virtual function must without fail have the same arguments in all its implementations (same number and same types of parameters). On the other hand, overloaded functions are distinguished by their argument signature.

To get our ideas straight, we will consider the display and erasure of graphic objects on which we are working.

A machine object will not have the same graphic formalism as a stock or a conveyor. However, we would prefer to display any object by means of a single code line specifying that we wish to display the object without bothering about its type. To do that it is necessary to have as many member functions as there are different types of objects (one function for the machine class, one for the conveyor class, and so on). Since all these functions satisfy the same semantic, it is a good idea to give them the same name: `display()`. Finally, in order to be able to start the display without bothering about the type of object, it is sufficient to declare the `display()` function as being virtual for the base class `graphic_obj`.

The code which follows gives an example of what that may give at the level of the classes we have already defined. It is important to note that no addition is made at the level of the `manuf_obj` class which already knows that it recovers by `public` inheritance a virtual member function `display()`.

```
class graphic_obj {
  protected :
        ...                             // data member previously
                                        // declared.
    public :
        ...                             // member functions
                                        // previously declared.
        virtual void display(int) ;
} ;
class machine : public manuf_obj {
  protected :
        float    machining time ;
    public :
        ...                             // member functions
                                        // previously declared.
```

```
              void display(int mode) ;
              } ;
      void machine::display(int mode)
      {
        gp_circle(x1, y1, x2, y2, mode);      // graphic display
      }                                       // function for a circle

      class stock : public manuf_obj {
        protected :
              char    policy ;
        public :
              ...                             // member functions
                                              // previously declared.
              void display(int mode) ;
      } ;

      void stock::display(int mode)
      {
        gp_rectangle(x1,y1,x2,y2,mode);       // graphic display
      }                                       // for a rectangle
```

This corresponds to the classic use of virtual functions; by means of this type of code within classes, we can use a principal code independent of the type of current object. In fact, let us assume that all graphic objects of any model are stored in a table; it is then sufficient, to display all the objects (of any type whatsoever), to call up the virtual function display() for each table entry. The resulting code could be as follows:

```
graphic_obj *tab [100];
machine       ma(.......);        // call up the machine and stop
stock         stk(.......);       // constructors with the
                                  // necessary parameters
...
tab[i] = &(graphic_obj) ma;       // storage of the table entries
tab[j] = &(graphic_obj) stk;      // with conversion of type

void display_all(int mode)
{
   for(int register i = 0 ; i<=MAXTAB ; i++) tab[i]->display(mode)) ;
}
```

In this example you will notice another special feature of C++, namely being able to declare variables (or objects) at any location in the source program.

A.4.2 Implementation at machine level

The code of the function display_all() is capable of correctly displaying any type of graphic object. However, when generating code the compiler does not yet know which display() function it should call up. Should it call up the display() function of a stock, of a machine, ...? It is only at execution time that the program will decide what member function of what class of object it has to call up. We talk of calculated call-up (at execution time) and late binding (or dynamic binding). Let us compare a simplified code which could be generated when calling up a simple function and that generated by calling up a single virtual function (we will use a pseudo assembler code).

```
C++ code                              Pseudo assembler code

simple function_object() ;            static link

              CALL     @fn

virtual function object() ;           dynamic binding

                           (1)    MOV     RBASE, @virtual_table_base
                           (2)    MOV     RINDX, method selector
                           (3)    MUL     RINDX, size
                           (4)    CALL    [RBASE + RINDX]
```

This code may be explained as follows: in the case of the classic call-up, the compiler knows the address of the function to be called up (&fn) and codes a simple subroutine call-up. In the case of dynamic binding, (1) the compiler can recover in a register the base address of a virtual function table for the class (more complete tables are generated automatically for all object classes (Ellis and Stroustrup, 1990)). It is the type of object we are manipulating (known at the time of execution of the program) which makes it possible to select the right function in the table. The method selector is placed in an index register (2).

This selector makes it possible to calculate the offset in the table of virtual functions (3). It is sufficient to know the overall memory size in bytes of a function address and then to multiply the code of the type by this overall amount. The multiplication would of course be effected by shifting to the left, not with a possible MUL operator, which is expensive in machine cycles, but it seemed clearer to describe the mechanism with a mnemonic MUL to specify the multiplication.

The fans of function pointer tables in the C language will have recognized in this mechanism concepts which they regularly handle. It should be noted that a simple call-up is more powerful than the calculated call-up with double indexing (one for the table, and one for the call-up). This efficiency is completely relative if we consider the software in its entirety (here we do not take into account the skill of developers in coding and choosing data structures).

It may be useful to give an example of standard C code and to compare it with its equivalent in C++. The code we propose as an example calls up the display () function for a certain number of object classes. In C the type of objects will be assumed to be known and stored in a type identifier.

```
switch(type.object) {                      // each type of object possesses
                                           // its display function
     case CIRCLE :             display_circle (object);
                               break;
     case LINE :               display_line (object);
                               break;
     case RECTANGLE :          display_rectangle (object);
                               break;

     ...

     case TEXT :               display_text (object);
                               break;
     default :                 break;
     }
```

This code, written in C++ with the hierarchy of classes and virtual functions, is summarized on the following line.

```
object.display();
```

The addition of a new type of object assumes the addition of a new 'case' in the 'switch' instruction for the classic C solution. On the other hand there is no need to modify the C++ line. It is of course possible to obtain almost equivalent coding in C, by explicitly writing the call-up to use a table of function pointers. Declarations, dimensions and initializations of the function pointer table must also be explained, by the C programmer.

```
// Declaration of a function pointer table

int      (*tab_ptr_fn[NB_MAX_OBJECT] )() ;

// example of initialization

*(tab_ptr_fn + CIRCLE) = &CircleDisplay;
...

// Call-up of the function corresponding to the type given
(* *(tab_ptr_fn + type) )() ;
```

You will have noticed that this code is not very clear (we intentionally selected less readable notations) and that the call-up of virtual functions advantageously replaces this type of source code at the level of legibility, reliability and maintenance.

The virtual function mechanism takes on its full scope when we realize that the display_all() function code will remain the same whatever the number of classes deriving from the graphic_obj class which we wish to add. It becomes possible to bring together all the definitions of classes previously described in a library (the source text no longer being essential). It is no longer necessary to forecast what derived object classes may be added, since the virtual functions take over responsibility for calling up the right method at the right moment. Combined with inheritance, polymorphism is the most powerful mechanism implemented by object-oriented languages; the developer may finally design classes and widely reusable code.

It is important to point out that the type of implementation which has just been described only concerns static typing languages (such as C++). For dynamic typing languages (Smalltalk, Objective-C), the mechanism is more complex and if it offers less efficiency and less security, it also proposes more flexibility and abstraction power.

It now seems necessary to give a reminder of what precautions should be taken when using virtual functions. Only the member functions of a class may be virtual, and all the virtual functions must have the same arguments signature, that is, the same parameters (with the same types) and the same type for the return value. In the case of different signatures, functions would no longer be virtual but simply overloaded.

A.4.3 The technique of redefinition (or substitution)

In an application it frequently occurs that a set of derived object classes uses a member function inherited from the base class. For example, the function `contains(int,int)` of the class `graphic_obj` tests whether a coordinate captured by means of a mouse is contained in the graphic object so as to select the object in question.

The application is then extended by the addition of a circle object class and a frame object class derived from the base class (`graphic_obj`). For these new object classes the member function `contains()` no longer fulfils its role for the circles, and frames may contain other graphic objects and mask them in the event of a selection by means of a mouse. To overcome this we will make the member function `contains()` a virtual function which will be redefined in accordance with the technique called substitution. Only circle and frame classes will have to redefine the virtual function `contains()` so that it tests only the contours of the circle and frame objects; all the other classes will use the code of the base class.

By means of this technique a set of objects share the same code, and the special cases specify their own codes without the principal modules having to take account of it. In fact, a principal module will simply call up the virtual function `contains()` without bothering about special cases.

```
class graphic_obj {
  protected :
     ...                                // data member previously
                                        // declared.

  public :
     ...                                // member functions previously
                                        // declared.
    virtual int contains( int x = 0, int y = 0 )
    {
       if ( x>= xig && x <= xsd &&y >= yig && y <= ysd ) return 1;
       else return 0;
    }
};
```

The circle and frame classes which follow will be derived in `public` from the `graphic_obj` base class.

```
class circle : public graphic_obj {
  protected :
        float    radius;
  public :
        ...
        contains(int,int);
}
circle::contains ( int x = 0,  int y = 0)
{
    ...                                 // algorithm testing that we are
    ...                                 // on the contour of the circle
}

class frame : public graphic_obj {
  public :                             // no other attributes
        ...
        contains(int,int);
}
frame::contains( int x = 0,  int y = 0)
{
        ...                            // algorithm testing that we are
        ...                            // on the contour of the frame
}
```

It is important to be aware that a virtual member function is more powerful than an ordinary function. For all situations capable of developing during the life of the software, it is preferable to use virtual functions so that future extensions do not raise questions concerning codes general to all objects. There are not yet any general rules to follow.

A.4.4 Pure virtual functions and abstract classes

An abstract class is only used as a base template for derived classes and has no instance. Such a class does, however, propose an interface common to all the derived classes by means of its virtual functions. These virtual functions may be declared as being pure virtual functions by allocating the function to 0 at the time of its definition. The presence of a single pure virtual function implies that the class is an abstract class.

```
class abstract {
    ...
    public:
        abstract() ;
        virtual void pure_virtual_function() = 0 ;
        };
```

◁A.5 Complements and special C++ features

A.5.1 References

A reference is a way of temporarily linking an identifier with an object name (Koenig, 1989). For example, if we write:

```
int   tab [DIMENSION] ;
int   i   = 10 ;
int & r   = tab [i] ;
```

we specify that r is another name for the object tab [i] which is of the class int. The reference type links are reference-marked by the symbol & following a type (or a class of object). Once a link has been made, the name r refers to the object i throughout its scope. The following code will make this clear.

```
int           i = 4 ;
int &         r = tab[i] ;

i++ ;
```

The value of i is now 5, but r continues to refer to tab [4]. People familiar with the C language are going to wonder what difference exists between a reference and a pointer to an object. In fact, at implementation level, there is no difference. Here is the coding in virtual assembler of a few sequences of C++ code:

```
int           i = 4 ;    MOV [@ i] , 4      // Initialization of i
int&          r = i ;    MOV RINDEX , @ i   // Initialization of
                         MOV [@ r] , @ i    // the reference to
r++ ;                    INC [RINDEX]       // the address of i
int           i = 4 ;    MOV [@ i] , 4      // Initialization of i
int *         p = &i ;   MOV RINDEX , @ i   // Initialization of
                         MOV [@ p] , @ i    // the pointer p to
(*p)++ ;                 INC [RINDEX]       // the address of i
```

As you can see, the implementation is identical, an index register RINDEX being used to store the pointer or the reference. The writing and the use of references is far more flexible than the explicit use of pointers. It is an additional level of abstraction borrowed from SIMULA.

One of the frequent uses of references may be that of argument passing by address. Argument passing by reference corresponds to passing by address, which avoids dragging along the pointed notations of the C language which become heavy when you exceed two levels of indirection. Here is a simple example.

```
pass by address in C ANSI        then by reference in C++
swap(int *x, int * y)            swap( int& x, int& y)
{                                {
        int     tmp = *x ;               int     tmp = x ;
        *x =*y ;                         x = y ;
```

```
*y = tmp ;                              y = tmp ;
}                                       }
swap( &a , &b );                        swap( c , d );
```

In C you will have noticed the indirection to gain access to the value specified by the pointers to x and y. With C++ a simple 'reference' is sufficient to access the value in question; there is no need to bother with the different levels of indirection. Moreover, the body of the function does not use the star notation which, if it is amusing, is none the less difficult to handle when using several levels. Performance remains identical in both cases.

Another frequent use of references consists in choosing this mode of parameter passing even for functions which do not modify their input parameters. In fact, the default argument passing mode in the C language is passing by value, which consists in working on copies of the arguments so as to restore the original values of the arguments on returning to the calling function. This argument passing mode (for parameters) is the least efficient; it is why, when certain arguments are not modified, it is interesting to pass by address (preferably by reference). When you choose passing by address for reasons of efficiency or quite simply because the type of parameter passed cannot be copied, it is recommended that you declare the arguments in the form of constant references. The following example illustrates this.

```
class machine : public manuf_obj {
  protected :
        float machining_time ;
  public :
        ...                             // member functions previously declared.
        set_time(const float & tps)     { machining time = tps }
        } ;
```

In the previous example a set_time (....) of the machine class for reasons of efficiency (in addition to its implicit on-line declaration) recovers its new value per address. Note the **const float &** which on the one hand ensures that the run argument is not modified and on the other reminds us that this run mode with the symbol & is chosen for reasons of performance.

Finally, *contrary to pointers, in C++ reference addresses give the addresses of the objects referred to*. The following example will illustrate this principle:

```
float          f ;
float&         ref= f ;
float*         ptr= &f ;

&ref           is the same as            &f
               and different to          &ptr (!...)
```

A.5.2 A simple form of polymorphism: function overloading

As in the case of the SIMULA language (Dahl *et al.*, 1968; Birtwistle *et al.*, 1973; Kirkerud, 1989), it is possible to declare homonymous functions. Virtual functions must have the same signature (same types of arguments and same number). But it may be useful to define a function which would effect an action of the same semantic for different types of parameters.

For example, we could try to calculate the average of a complete table, whether short or long, or single or double real numbers. The way in which the size of the table is delimited may vary.

```
short      average      (short  * table, const int & size);
long       average      (long   * table, int beginning, int end);
float      average      (float  * table, unsigned char  size);
double     average      (double * table, const int & t_size);
```

Such definitions 'overload' the meaning of the average function, which becomes sensitive to the context specified by call-up parameters. The compiler is in a position to know which of the four functions it must call up depending on the type and number of call-up parameters (or effective parameters). This feature contributes additional flexibility and better legibility provided it is not overused.

The overloading of functions with a number of different arguments is particularly interesting in defining several class constructors.

The classic example is that of the constructors of a `string` class to manage strings of characters (Koenig, 1990). Here are the three overloaded constructors proposed by Andrew Koenig:

- An initial `string::String()` constructor without parameter determines what value to give to a character string object which is not explicitly initialized.
- A second `string::String(char *)` constructor to be able to initialize a string from a parametrized text constant.
- A third `string::String(const String &)` constructor to initialize a string from the text of another string (copy constructor).

A.5.3 The recovery of the address of overloaded functions

To recover the address of overloaded functions, the name ambiguity must be resolved explicitly by specifying the argument types of the function pointer which will recover the address of the overloaded function. Here is an example which shows you the way to code this recovery:

```
void        function(char) ;
int         function(double) ;
void        (*ptrfn) (char)      =      &function ;
char        (*ptrfn2) (double)   =      &function ;
```

A.5.4 Overloading operators

As well as overloading user functions in C++, it is possible to overload many operators of the language. The number of operators of the C++ language being vast, there is no shortage of interesting examples (Eckel, 1989; Koenig, 1989;

Stroustrup, 1986). However, only the ANSI reference manual (Ellis and Stroustrup, 1990) gives special features of the operator overloading such as indexing [], the assignment operator =, or the function call-up (). We will redefine the indexing and addition operator for tables. Contrary to the C language tables, this new class indicates how the validity of indexes given at the time of addressing may be tested at runtime.

```
class table {
  protected :
        void* tab ;       // the starting address of the table
        int   size ;      // size of the table
  public :
        table(int) ;
        ~table() { delete tab }          // space restoration
        int     get_size() { return size; }
        void&   operator[] (int) ;       // overloading of the
                                         // indexing []
        void    operator=(table &) ;     // of the assignment =
        void*   operator&() { return tab } ; // and of the address
} ;                                      // operator
table::table( int t )
{                                        // it is assumed that
  if (t <= 0) exit (ERRTABLE) ;          // ERRTABLE is already
  size = t ;                             // defined
  tab = new void [t] ;
}
table::operator[] (int i)                // OUTOFBOUNDS assumed to
{                                        // be defined
  if (i >= size && i < 0) exit(OUTOFBOUNDS) ;
  return *(tab + i) ;
}
```

The indexing operator [] is redefined for this class; the index used is tested to ensure that it is within the limits defined when constructing the table object.

The redefinition of the assignment operator is written as follows:

```
table::operator= (table & tabtmp)        // SIZEDONTMATCH assumed to
{                                        // be defined
  if (this->size != tabtmp.get_size() ) exit(SIZEDONTMATCH) ;
  for(int register i=0; i<size; i++) *(this->tab + i) = *(tabtmp + i);
  return *this ;
}
```

You have just noticed with the declaration of operator = the use of the undeclared variable this which is a pointer. It is the pointer to the current object (precisely this one, whose operator member function is being declared =). This pointer does not have to be declared and it is a reserved word of the C++ language.

The assignment operator operator = () has a set of characteristics which make it a special case:

- It can never be inherited.
- It behaves like a destruction of the variable we wish to allocate (with return

of the dynamic memory if necessary) and then construction of a new object per copy.

■ It has a return value. Constructors return **this** implicitly without the programmer having to check it, but for the assignment operator it is advised that ***this** be returned. This allows sequential allocation of complete structures, which is not possible in C (struc_a = struc_b = struc_c;).

A number of limitations concerning the overloading of operators exist. When overloading ++ or -- operators, the C++ language no longer distinguishes between the prefixed and postfixed versions of the new operators (Ellis and Stroustrup, 1990). Generally, priority rules are not modified by operator overloading.

Since version 2.0 of ANSI C++, it is possible to overload the ',' operator used for sequential evaluation from left to right, and the operator '->' so as to implement what are called 'smart' pointers. It is also possible to overload the operator '->*' for the use of pointers to members.

A.5.5 Overloading the new and delete operators

The new and delete operators may be overloaded locally at each class and become member functions. This is effected without losing the global new and delete operators.

The new operator must accept a long type and return a pointer to void. Likewise the delete operator must accept a pointer to void and return nothing. In the following example, note the use of the scope resolution operator to gain access to the global new and delete operators.

```
class demo {
        static          int nbinstance ;
  public :
        void * operator new (long size)
                {
                        nbinstance++ ;
                        return ::new (size) ;
                }
        void    operator delete (void *ptr)
                {
                        nbinstance-- ;
                        ::delete( ptr ) ;
                }
        } ;
```

It is also possible to define the delete operator with a second argument indicating the size of the object to be destroyed. This size may be automatically calculated by the compiler if the program adheres to the rules given about this in Ellis and Stroustrup, (1990).

A.5.6 Friend functions

If we want to write an addition operator for the class table, we need access to the data members of two instances of the table class. In fact data members of the table are protected and it is recommended not to violate the table class's access protection by using the interface of member functions. This is why C++ proposes friend functions of one or several classes. These friend functions, although not members of this or that class, can gain access to attributes and to private or protected methods of the class or classes concerned.

```
class table{
  protected :
        void     * tab ;          // the starting address of the table
        int      size ;           // size of the table
    public :
        friend operator+ ;
        table(int) ;
        ...
        } ;
table operator+ (const table & t1, const table &t2)
{
    if( (int size = t1.get_size()) != t2.get_size())
    exit (SIZEDONTMATCH) ;

    table& tmptab = * new table(size) ;
    while (size--) tmptab[size-1] = t1[size-1]+t2[size-1];
    return tmptab ;
}
```

This friend function coding example is a good performance compromise in terms of execution speed and the amount of memory taken up.

Now let us look how it is possible to declare a member function f1 of a class c1 as a friend of the table class:

```
class table {
  protected :
        ...
    public :
        friend void c1::f1() ;// f1 member of c1 table friend
        ...
};
```

We may finally declare an entire class as a friend of another class by means of the following declaration:

```
class table {
  protected :
        ...
    public :
        friend class    c1;
        ...
};
```

After this declaration all the c1 instance methods may gain access to all the attributes of the table class.

A.5.7 Genericity

There exist at least three ways of programming genericity, including the use of templates, which are very flexible despite the fact that they are sometimes laden with syntax.

The first solution consists of using inheritance to emulate genericity (see Meyer, 1988), the second is based on the notion of macro-instructions and has already been used in C. It was necessary to include a very simple header file <generic.h> which contains the two macro instructions given below.

```
#ifndef GENERIC_H
#define GENERIC_H

#define name2(n1, n2) n1 ## n2 // ## Concatenation operator
#define declare(a,type) a ## declare (type)

#endif  GENERIC_H
```

To give an example, when we write name2 (float, gentab) the macro instruction develops floatgentab. Likewise declare(gentab, float) is developed as gentabdeclare (float).

The purpose of this solution is to be able to declare an object class by manipulating a generic type as follows:

```
generic_class(type)      object ;
```

Operations to emulate genericity are complex, which is why Bjarne Stroustrup proposed parametrized types in the form of templates. This is the third solution available and it is now standardized. These templates are object classes on functions for which the types are parametrized; the use of these templates is simple. Parametrized classes are also used in Algol 68, Ada, Eiffel (Meyer, 1988).

```
template <class T> class vector {
        T        *      v;
        int      size;
  public:
        vector(int);
        T&       operator[] (int) ;
        T&       element(int i) { return v[i]; }
        }

vector < complex >      v(10) ; //define a vector of 10 complexes
vector < char >         v(80) ; //and one of 80 characters

template <class T> T & <T> vector::operator [] (int i)
{
  if (i < 0 || size <= i) error(OUTOFBOUNDS);
  return v[i];
}
typedef <char *> vector tptchar;
tptchar table(50);
table[3] = table.element(4);
```

To these notions of templates the notions of type equivalences between templates are added as well as the notion of template functions for a family of functions. Any reader interested in genericity with C++ should refer to Ellis and Stroustrup (1990).

A.5.8 Streams

It is a good idea to discuss the stream library supplied with C++. The C language is linked to a standard input–output library `<stdio.h>`. This library is preserved by C++, but a stream library `<iostream.h>` is supplied. This library proposes a simpler syntax based on the overloading of the >> and << shifting operators (respectively to right and left). These operators may be used for all standard data types, which is far more flexible than the use of `printf` and `scanf` formats. The >> and << operators remain overloadable for the user-defined types.

C++ ANSI proposes three channels:

- the standard input, `cin`
- the standard output, `cout`
- the standard errors output, `cerr`

We give a brief example of their use; any reader interested will refer to Stroustrup (1986, 1992), Ellis, (1990), Eckelt (1989) or Hansel (1990).

```
main()
{
        int             x;

        cout << 'Enter x :' ;
        cin  >> x ;
        if (x > 255) cerr << 'x is too big' ;
        cout << 'x * x =' << x * x ;
}
```

A.5.9 Explicit inline declarations

`Inline` functions were reviewed at the time of their implicit utilization in certain member functions. This new type of function arises from the fact that there is anxiety concerning the costs of calling-up numerous small functions in a program. If performance is required, it may be interesting to develop small size functions in the body of the program (1 to 4 lines). This was usually the role of the #*define* macros of the C language. It is recommended to avoid declaring `inline` functions which have loops, since there is no gain in efficiency. Here is an example.

```
Inline  mulpar8(int val) { return (val << 3) ;}
...
```

```
source code              real code

mulpar8 (j) ;            j << 3 ;         // no further function
i += j;                  i += j ;         // call-up
```

A.5.10 Static members

Static members belong to classes and not to instances. Whether it is a matter of data members or member functions, here again we meet up with the Smalltalk model where classes are also objects. In C++, classes are not objects, but for obvious reasons of analysis and design (the global functions and data pollute the object approach) the notions of class variables and class methods have been introduced. Static members are identified by using the keyword static at the time of their declaration in a class. This static member function may only act on the static member data (or on global variables).

```
class example {
      static  int nbobj ;
      ...
public:
      static  void inc_nbobj() { nbobj++ }
  } ;
```

A.5.11 Automatic generation of the assignment operator and the copy constructor

Copy constructors (&) are used to make copies for argument passing on initialisation. Both copy constructors and the assignment operators can be created by the compiler if the programmer has not defined them.

Copying and initialization are effected automatically and 'intelligently' on all class members, but it is advised to write a copy constructor and an assignment operator for each class manipulation dynamic memory with its data members (see Ellis and Stroustrup (1990)).

A.5.12 The tasks

As in the case of the C language, it is necessary to use a task management library (for example, the AT & T Bell task library which has the header <task.h>, described in Hansen (1990) and based on the concurrence of UNIX). Different concurrence mechanisms have also been proposed in the Bell laboratories at Murray Hill by Gehani and Roome (1988). Significant examples of the construction of classes with different degrees of protection are proposed in Gorlen (1987) which provides a library of C++ classes called OOPS for 'Object Oriented Program Support'. In it there is a set of simple classes, most of which are inspired by Smalltalk-80. There are also classes dealing with character strings, date, time, linked lists, hashing tables, and so on. In addition, it includes classes like 'processes', 'scheduler', 'semaphore' and 'queueing line' which support multiprogramming facilities with co-routines on queue.

A.5.13 Exceptions

The management of exceptions was presented in the conference minutes of the USENIX C++ conference, held in San Francisco in 1990, as well as in Ellis and Stroustrup (1990). In C++ the termination model of exception handling is provided. This error management mechanism seems to us to be powerful and the majority of compilers should soon support it. Management of exceptions is typed. Exceptions are typed by the type or class of object triggering the exception with the instruction `throw`. They are recovered by a parametrized `catch` expression in the same way as a function by stating the type of exception to be intercepted and the object or reference concerned. The catch instructions supply the code of the exception handler. The C++ code dealing with the exceptions must be inserted in a 'try' block.

An exception handler which has a type `C`, `const C`, `C &` or `const C &` (C frequently being a class) will be called up by the `throw` instruction of an object of type `O` only in the following cases:

- The types `O` and `C` are identical.
- `C` is a base class derived in public which `O` inherits.
- `C` and `O` are pointer types and `O` may be converted into `C`.

This means that the management of exceptions follows the inheritance hierarchy. If an object of a subclass raises an exception and there is no exception handler for its class, then the exception handler of its base class is called up. In order that the inheritance hierarchy be complied with, it is necessary to place the subtype handlers upstream of the base class handler, because the catch instructions are tested in the order in which they appear in the code. In the event that no handler is found, the special 'terminate' function is called up. It may happen that an exception is raised for an unexpected type. This case may be handled by specifying with 'setunexpected' the 'unexpected' function which will be called up. In any case, management of any type of exception may be effected by `catch(...)`. The management of exceptions being powerful but complex, we prefer to refer the reader to Ellis and Stroustrup (1990) for precise examples.

A.5.14 Pointers to members

A pointer to a class member must always be associated with an object. At the time of its definition, it is also necessary to specify the exact type to which it points, without forgetting its class.

```
class object {
        ...
   public:
        int i;
        ...
        double function(float f) { return f -(double)i; }
        void            display();
        void            erase();
   };

int     object::*ptri ;                 // pointer to integer member

double (object::*ptrfn) (float) ;       // pointer to member
                                        // function

ptri = &object::i ;                     // Init of the address of the
ptrfn = &object::function ;             // pointers to members

// example of utilization with an instance then with a pointer
// to an instance

object  o ;
o.*ptri = 1 ;                           // pointer reference
double  d1 = (o.*ptrfn)(2.71828) ;

object *po      = new(object) ;
po->*ptri       = 2;
double d2       = (po->*ptrfn)(3.14159) ;
```

Let us now assume that we have an object collection class (list, table, tree) derived from an abstract `collection` class possessing the following pure virtual functions to effect an iteration of the collection.

end	:	indicates the end of the iteration
current	:	recovers the current element
next	:	goes on to the next.

```
class collection {
        ...
   public:
        virtual int     end() = 0 ;
        virtual object  *current() = 0 ;
        virtual void    next() = 0 ;
   } ;
```

We are now going to show how it is possible to give a pointer to a member function as argument to a collection iterator function (whatever the class of the collection) in order to parametrize the function to be applied to each iteration. It is preferable in practice to define iterator classes, especially for overlapping iterations in the same structure.

```
void run(collection & c, void (object::*ptrfn)())
{
  while (!c.end()) {
    (c.current()->*ptrfn)() ;   // Applies the function to
    c.next() ;                  // the object
    }
}
```

We may then use the iterator `run` on different structures with different functions to be executed:

```
run (tree, &object::display);
run (table, &object::erase);
run (list, &object::display);
```

This example of code is highly reusable; moreover, it is possible to parametrize virtual functions. We must, however, admit that the legibility obtained is not excellent. Furthermore, the implementation of this code requires a good compiler as well as good control of the language which possesses a considerable number of subtleties which it has not been possible to describe here.

◁ A.6 References forming part of the C++ appendix

Antebi M. (1990). Issues in teaching C++. *JOOP*, November/December, 11–21

Bezivin J. (1984). Simulation and object-oriented languages. *Bigre* No. 41, 194–211

Birtwistle G., Dahl O., Myhraug B. and Nygaard K. (1973). *SIMULA Begin*. New York: Petro-Chelli/Charter

Coplien J.O. (1992). *Advanced Programming in C++*. Wokingham: Addison-Wesley

Dahl O.J., Myhraug B. and Nygaard K. (1968). *The Simula Common Base Language*. Publication S-2, Norwegian Computing Centre. Oslo

Dewhurst (1987). Flexible symbol table structure for compiling C++. *Software Practice and Experience*, 17(8), 503–12

Eckel B. (1989). *Using C++*. Osborne: MacGraw-Hill

Eckel B. (1994). *Black Belt C++. The Masters Collection*. M & T Books

Ellis M. and Stroustrup B. (1990). *The annotated C++ reference manual*. ANSI Base Document. Harlow: Addison-Wesley

Gehani N. and Roome D. (1988). Concurrent C++: Concurrent programming with class(es). *Software Practice and Experience*, **18** (12), 1157–77

Gorlen K. (1987). An object-oriented class library for C++ programs. *Software Practice and Experience*, 17(12), 889–922

Hansen T. (1990). *The C++ Answer Book*. Harlow: Addison-Wesley

Jordan D. (1990). Implementation benefits of C++ language mechanisms. *Communications of the ACM*, **33**(9), 61–4

Kirkerud B. (1989). *Object-Oriented Programming with Simula*. Harlow: Addison-Wesley

Koenig A. (1988). Why I use C++. *JOOP*, June/July, 38–42

Koenig A. (1989). References in C++. *JOOP*, March/April, 43–5

Koenig A. (1990). Frequent questions. *JOOP*, November/December, 44–9

Lippman S.B. (1992). *Essential C++*, 2nd edn. Wokingham: Addison-Wesley

Meyer B. (1988). *Object Design and Programming*. Interedition.

Scott M. (1992). *Effective C++*. Harlow: Addison-Wesley

Stroustrup B. (1986). *The C++ Programming Language*. Harlow: Addison-Wesley

Stroustrup B. (1992). *The C++ Programming Language*, 2nd edn. Harlow: Addison-Wesley

APPENDIX B

A number of simulation languages

◁ B.1 Introduction

In this appendix we study a number of the best known and most used simulation languages. First of all we present a number of general non-object-oriented performance evaluation software such as GPSS, SLAM and SIMAN. Widespread tools such as SIMSCRIPT or WITNESS are not dealt with here; anyone interested may refer to various references including Gilman and Billingham (1989) and Brian (1989). A study of 26 tools and simulation environments may also be found in Hill *et al.* (1992). Finally we deal with a number of object simulation languages, especially Modsim III and Simula 67. The ROSS language and recent tools such as Sim ++, C++ Sim or SIMEX 3.0 are not dealt with in this book; they are available on the Internet and offer considerable conceptual, financial and educational interest, though they are not very widespread. The QNAP2 object-oriented language is described in somewhat more detail because it has been widely used in this book. General languages such as Smalltalk can also deal with simulation problems (Bezivin, 1984). A description and an interesting mini-tutorial concerning discrete event simulation software is given by Banks (1994) and a history of simulation languages is provided by Law (1991).

◁ B.2 GPSS

B.2.1 History of GPSS

The GPSS language was introduced in 1961 at IBM (Gordon, 1962). It has developed into different versions (GPSS II, GPSS III, GPSS/360 and in 1970 GPSS V). The last version proposed by IBM is therefore version V (Gordon, 1978). Along with IBM quite a number of software companies developed more evolved versions. We may mention GPSS/H by Wolverine which came out in 1977 and was updated in 1988. Since it is distributed by quite a number of companies, GPSS is available on a considerable number of platforms (Schriber, 1989). Recent versions of GPSS generate either a code which is compiled or a pseudo-code which is fast to interpret. These solutions are more powerful than the simple code interpretation which was used in the first versions. What is more, it is also possible to find GPSS versions integrated in programming languages such as GPSS APL, GPSS PL/1 or GPSS FORTRAN (Schmidt, 1980).

B.2.2 Modelling with GPSS

GENERAL
ASPECTS

GPSS (General Purpose System Simulator) is a very rich language which may be used to model a wide range of classes of systems. It is the language which has been used and tested for the longest period of time.

GPSS uses a process approach for discrete event simulation (McHaney, 1991). It is a structured language in the form of parametrized blocks which, when assembled, constitute a network. There are dozens of different types of blocks in order to represent the various notions or actions which a simulation expert may need. Dynamic entities called transactions describe the way in which you move in a network of previously organized blocks, so as to represent the system to be simulated. GPSS is said to be 'transaction flow based'. The time management, the movement of transactions in the system, the collection of information necessary to obtain statistical results, and the editing of these results is automatic (Gourgand, 1990). The calculation of confidence intervals is also available using the replication method.

In addition to blocks, GPSS uses a control language which makes use of a series of instructions to initialize the model, fix the parameters of experiments, produce reports, and so on. These control instructions are executed first and are used to start the 'network of blocks' part of the model.

THE
CATEGORIES
OF ENTITIES

We have seen that dynamic entities are called transactions; five other categories of entities are also available: the equipment, calculation, statistics, storage and group entities.

The meaning of transactions is set by the simulation expert when he or she constructs a model. They are often created to represent active objects such as a client in a prefecture, an aircraft in an airport or a truck in a workshop. Of course, with GPSS it is possible to generate as many transactions as you like. It is this approach which allows GPSS to simulate parallel systems sharing resources. Each transaction has a list of parameters which may be allocated according to the logic of the model. These parameters may be used especially to shunt movements in the networks of blocks. One of the attributes of a transaction is its level of priority, which is fixed with a PRIORITY block or, at the time of creation of a transaction,

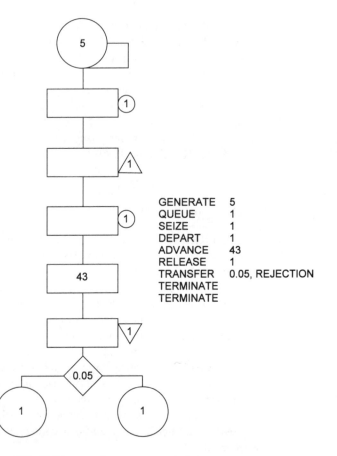

Figure B.1 GPSS example program and diagram.

with a GENERATE block. The greater the value, the closer the transaction comes to the top of the list of current events, the top of the list corresponding, of course, to the event processed by the synchronizing kernel of the simulator. The transactions are created with GENERATE or SPLIT blocks and are destroyed with TERMINATE or ASSEMBLE blocks.

The advancement of transactions in the network of blocks is automatic; they are stopped either by the ADVANCE blocks which set a time and progress the simulation time or when they enter into competition for a resource and this is not available.

Equipment type entities are used to model resources. This category of entity comprises the 'facilities' used to model simple servers, the 'storages' used to model multiple servers, the 'logic switches' used to represent switches and the 'user chains' used to model resources which have infrequent queue management disciplines. These 'user chains' are controlled with the LINK and UNLINK blocks.

Another category of entity is that of the calculation and processing entities. This category comprises variables, Boolean expressions and functions. The details of these entities are clearly given in Schriber (1991). The category of data storage entities is used to store the state of variables and other information generated and used by the model. This category contains the 'savevalues', 'matrix savevalues', the 'ampervariable' and the 'synonyms' (sort of equivalence declaration). Another category used is that of groups which are used to construct sets of transactions (McHaney, 1991).

The category of statistical entities is used only for the deduction of information from the model. Amongst other things we find in this category the lines (associated with the QUEUE block) and the tables (TABULATE block). A QUEUE block is used by a transaction which must enter a line and the DEPART block is used to specify the start of a line. Lines are used to collect information concerning the delays encountered by transactions during their run through the network. It is therefore possible to obtain information concerning a line, such as the maximum and average numbers of transactions in the line over the simulation time, the total number of transactions passed through the line, the average time spent by these transactions in the line, the content of the line at the end of simulation, and so on. The tables are used to collect more specific information concerning the model functioning.

THE
CONTROL
LANGUAGE

The GPSS language may be considered as having two sets of separate instructions, one associated with instructions describing the model of a system with its transactions, and the other used to fix the parameters of experiments, fix initial conditions, allocate memory or control the editing of results. The compilation directives form part of this category and in particular make it possible to define macro-instructions. In the GPSS/H version from Wolverine, debugging instructions have been added, as well as interactive variable capture/modification instructions.

B.2.3 Animation and interactivity

It is possible to animate models with some of the GPSS versions, for which GPSS/PC supplies integrated animation primitives. These primitives, however, remain limited to the displaying of variables, curves, histograms and graphic objects on two-dimensional drawings. It is also possible to animate the passage of transactions on the blocks, but there is not much interest in this because this type of visual debugging remains limited. The GPSS/H version has an interface for TESS (see SLAM). By means of input/output primitives it is also possible to control certain generalized animators. The AUTOGRAM animator may therefore produce three-dimensional colour animations for models written with GPSS/H.

As regards interactivity, to our knowledge it is a little limited; only the GPSS/H version allows it, by means of primitives (GETLIST and PUTPIC ...) for controlling interactions with the screen, the keyboard or files. This technique slightly resembles that available with SLAMSYSTEM.

◁ B.3 SIMAN, CINEMA and ARENA

B.3.1 History

SIMAN (SIMulation ANalysis) is a general simulation language despite its orientation towards manufacturing systems. Introduced by Pegden (1982), the functions of SIMAN make it possible to model discrete systems, continuous systems or combined. It is also possible to describe discrete changes of state in a system with either an event or a process approach; continuous models are described by means of differential equations. SIMAN is available on large computers, on workstations and mainly on microcomputers. Since its introduction in 1982, SIMAN has been constantly maintained and updated. The present version is SIMAN V. The ARENA simulation system distributed by System Modelling Corp. integrates an interface allowing the construction of models and SIMAN experiments with a user-friendly interface. It integrates animation tools (based on CINEMA software, presented later on) finalizing data for results presentation.

B.3.2 Modelling with SIMAN

GENERAL
FUNCTIONS

Modelling with SIMAN is based on the theoretic concepts of Zeigler (1976) according to which a distinction is made between a model and the experimentation frame of this model. The model of the system defines the static and dynamic characteristics of the system. The experimentation frame defines the conditions under which the model is executed to generate specific data. It is therefore possible to carry out a great many experiments without having to modify the model.

As in the case of GPSS or SLAM, SIMAN uses a network of blocks to model a system. Diagrams which are produced are linear and describe the flow of SIMAN entities through the system. These are transactions in the GPSS sense. Each entity may possess its own attributes which characterize it. There are ten types of blocks having a different base: OPERATION, HOLD, TRANSFER, QUEUE, STATION, BRANCH, PICKQ, QPICK, SELECT and MATCH. The OPERATION, TRANSFER and HOLD blocks are split up into a certain number of functional blocks where the type of associated operation is specified as being the first operand of the block. For example, the DELAY block of the OPERATION type specifies that it is a block where the entities will have to wait a certain time. Each base block has parameters or a label if necessary. The block diagram obtained possesses its equivalent in SIMAN instructions which are used to constitute a portable source file of the model. Experimentation conditions give experiment files (Pegden and Sturrock, 1989).

FUNCTIONS DEDICATED TO MANU- FACTURING SYSTEMS

The SIMAN language proposes a set of functions which are also used for modelling manufacturing systems. It is therefore possible to have submodels using the STATION block to take account of various workshops or manufacturing islands. Entities enter into submodels by means of the TRANSFER block, and the ROUTE block then makes it possible to shunt to other workstations, islands or workshops in a plant. This allows a hierarchical approach to modelling manufacturing systems. To a certain extent it is possible to develop 'submodel' macros in order to have a semblance of genericity. After assembling a group of blocks, the whole group can be parametrized in order to create 'instances' of these blocks. This technique does, however, have a limit which is linked to the syntax of the SIMAN language – the resource capture instructions are not the same for all the SIMAN manufacturing 'objects': SEIZE/RELEASE for the resources, ACCESS/EXIT for static conveyors, and REQUEST/FREE for dynamic conveyors.

As regards the model/experiments separation, SIMAN proposes sequences of visits to the workstations associated with the processing time. Since SIMAN uses the SEQUENCE element which forms part of the experimental frame of a project, each workstation visited may be constituted of several SIMAN blocks. These sequences make it possible to describe mini-ranges which the parts of a manufacturing system must follow. A transactional approach is used here. Each SIMAN dynamic entity (parts, raw materials, clients, and so on) has two attributes as a standard feature. The first, NS, points to a visit sequence and the second, IS, points to the current workstation and is updated automatically when an entity arrives on a TRANSFER block. It is also possible to modify these attributes during simulation so as to repeat sequences or link up sequences to constitute complete ranges.

With SIMAN the experimental model authorizes the specification of a schedule of resource capacities in real time by means of SCHEDULES element. It is therefore possible to specify, for each resource or category of resources, an available capacity and to do this for either a fixed or a calculated duration with a statistical distribution law. It is therefore possible, for example, to simulate that we have 8 workers for 4 hours, then 0 workers for a duration uniformly distributed between 1 and 2 hours, then 6 workers for 2 hours.

The modelling of the manufacturing handling and conveying systems of a manufacturing system remains extremely important, for this is a critical function for many manufacturing systems (50–70% of activities).

SIMAN separates two basic functions in the matter of conveying: a function for conveying on various paths guaranteeing intermittent movements of a truck (the conveyor moves with its load), and a function for continuous conveying over a fixed path (the conveyors are fixed).

SIMAN experimental blocks and elements are provided to generate two basic conveying functions. The SIMAN dynamic conveyors propose the notion of guided conveyors which automatically take into account bottlenecks in a circulation network and intersections. SIMAN also distinguishes between accumulating and belt conveyors. Conveyors also may be decomposed into segments. These distinctions were not possible with the old versions of SIMAN (Pegden and Sturrock, 1989).

The set of SIMAN primitives does not, however, permit the modelling of systems with a very complex decisional part (including global rules associated with sophisticated management policies) without recourse to external subroutines written in C or in Fortran. As with SLAM this approach is fairly tedious. However, the set of concepts and solutions proposed by SIMAN remain very interesting; a powerful algorithmic language would be welcome.

ANIMATION WITH CINEMA (POORTE AND DAVIS, 1989)

CINEMA is an animation system associated with the SIMAN simulator. An editing module called CINEMA is used to construct graphic models consisting of static components (forming the images and background of a model) and dynamic components (queues stations, variable, routes, ...). The routes are used to specify paths used by icons representing the dynamic entities of the SIMAN model. It is possible with the new version of CINEMA to correctly animate the AGVs (automated guided vehicles), accumulating conveyors, and curves and histograms are now available in addition to the various gauges of previous versions. CINEMA also allows the loading of the background drawn with software such as AutoCad. Animation and simulation are effected concurrently with the CSIMAN module.

In addition to the fact that there are limited possibilities of visual interaction, the minor disadvantages of CINEMA are debatable management of the time scales (animation is not continuous) and the non-use of the object-oriented approach which limits its power. The accent is placed more on communication and presentation of animated results rather than on debugging.

◁ B.4 SLAM II and SLAMSYSTEM

B.4.1 History of SLAM (O'Reilly and Lilegdon, 1987)

The SLAM simulation language was introduced in 1979. It was the first language which made it possible to use three different modelling approaches. It is therefore possible to describe a system by using a process approach, an event approach, a continuous approach or produce any combination of these three points of view within a single model.

In 1981 significant improvements in the primitives offered by SLAM led to SLAM II. Since that date SLAM II has been regularly maintained and updated. The use of SLAM II on thousands of applications has shown the modelling power and flexibility of the language, but these applications have also shown the possible directions of extensions of SLAM II in order to supplement and improve its user-friendliness. This is why, in addition to the recent and impressive FACTOR/AIM the following software was developed:

- (The Extended Simulation System) TESS: Introduced from 1984, this extension offers interesting tools for the production of a complete simulation project. It is therefore possible to analyse data in order to fit laws of distribution probability, to generate and use a database for simulation results, to graphically construct models and analyse them, to obtain curves and graphs or to animate the results of models on workstations and on multi-user systems.
- (Material Handling Extension) MHEX: Designed in 1986, this is the extension for the detailed modelling of the regular or special resources of raw materials or components management (cranes, storage zones, automatically steered vehicles, ...).
- (Interactive Execution Environment) IEE: This extension was added in 1987 to allow interactive debugging. It is therefore possible to interrupt a simulation in order to examine the state of the system, allocate new values to variables, simulate in step by step mode or call up external routines.

B.4.2 Modelling with SLAM II (Hammesfahr *et al.*, 1989)

SLAM II
NETWORKS

With SLAM II, a simulation model usually begins with a flow diagram called a network in SLAM II terminology. This network must reflect the flow of entities (people, components or other information) which pass through the system studied. A SLAM II network consists of nodes (junction points) in which processes are carried out. Nodes are connected by arcs called activities and define the routing of entities in the system. Routes may be deterministic, probabilistic or based on the state of the variables in the system. The times associated with these activities may represent process, conveying or queuing times. Entities which pass over a network may have their own characteristics therefore constituting the attributes of an entity class.

The construction of a SLAM II network uses a set of predefined graphic symbols. The network of graphic symbols seems heavy and complex even for a very simple model. However, for simple systems, it is possible to rapidly and automatically obtain global statistical results of models designed solely with these graphic symbols using TESS.

The graphically constructed networks are translated into SLAM instructions to which a set of control instructions are added, making it possible to define the experimental conditions of a simulation (simulation duration, choice of statistical results, ...). A SLAM II model, once in textual form (a sequence of SLAM instructions), may be run on all computers which support the SLAM II simulation language.

TAKING
COMPLEX
MODELS INTO
ACCOUNT

Because the basic concepts of SLAM II and the symbols associated with it are limited, the modelling of complex systems which integrate sophisticated forms of decision logic sometimes mean that it is necessary to call up user routines written in Fortran (or any other language capable of being bound with Fortran). If it is interesting to have interfaces between SLAM II and user routines in order not to 'close' the simulation software, and so be capable of modelling complex systems, it is regrettable to have to write significant parts of models in a classic programming language thus opening the door to numerous development errors or modelling inconsistencies which it is difficult to control. However, this feature remains powerful, as with SIMAN. In fact, it is possible from a Fortran program to call up functions giving not only the state of the system during simulation, but also to modify this state in different ways. This last possibility, necessary to guarantee reasonable modelling power and flexibility, remains risky and fairly tedious even for simulation experts.

B.4.3 Modelling with SLAMSYSTEM (O'Reilly and Nordlund, 1989; Pritsker, 1989)

SLAMSYSTEM is software for PC/PS compatible microcomputers running under MS-Windows. This software is designed to manage the majority of complex activities of simulation projects consisting of one or several scenarios. Each scenario may consist of a SLAM network, control information, user data, Fortran user routines, a graphic model for animation comprising a background, a 'script' defining the routings, documentation concerning the model, and results of simulation experiments in the form of statistical summaries, graphics (histograms, pie charts, curves ...) or animation. An integrated project manager takes care of the consistencies of the various components of a scenario.

SLAMSYSTEM comprises a graphic SLAM II networks editor running under MS-Windows. This editor has three levels of detail making it possible to display hundreds of symbols simultaneously at the highest level. It also has a sensitive assistant as well as the syntax control necessary for the input of a consistent network. It is possible to input the SLAM II instructions directly by means of a text editor; this having been done, the graphic editor is capable of reconstructing the corresponding graphic network.

B.4.4 The animation possibilities (Pritsker, 1989)

An animator was marketed for SLAM II on a microcomputer in 1986. It was the SLAM II/PC Animation System. Since 1989, this animator has been improved and integrated in SLAMSYSTEM. The animator proposed may be run at the same time as the simulation, or after a simulation using the results produced.

The animator in its present state uses a background for each animation called 'Facility' coupled to a graphic editor called 'Facility Builder'. This is a graphic editor capable of loading backgrounds created with CAD software such as AutoCad (equivalent to CINEMA).

The script part specifies the animation actions to be taken when a particular simulation event occurs. A script is a collection of animation instructions associated with SLAM II animation triggering events. It is possible to specify complex rules by means of Fortran user routines to trigger animation instructions. However, the technique used does not facilitate verification of the consistency between the simulation model and the animated model. Flexible and powerful tools have also been available for some years for models integrating short-term schedules and interactive simulations (FACTOR/AIM (Grant, 1989)).

◁ B.5 Simula-67

B.5.1 History

The Simula language is derived from Algol 60 and certain GPSS concepts. It introduces all the principal concepts of object-oriented programming: encapsulation, the class–instance relationship, inheritance and polymorphism. This language was developed in the 1960s by Norwegian researchers (Dahl and Nygaard, 1966; Dahl *et al.*, 1968) and it is a development of the Algol language. The principal objective of the language was to deal with discrete event simulation problems but it is in fact a very powerful general language (Birtwistle *et al.*, 1973; Pooley, 1986). The book by Bjorn Kirkerud (Kirkerud, 1989) gives a complete description of the general functions of Simula which are far from being obsolete, so great was the advance made at the time of the definition of Simula-67. In fact, all class languages derive from Simula; even the languages which recommend dynamic typing such as Smalltalk, CLOS and Objective-C are greatly influenced by Simula (which has static typing).

One of the great characteristics of Simula remains the concept of active objects. They are considered as autonomous processes, which communicate and synchronize with each other. The terminology for sending messages is not used; in fact it is the Smalltalk language which has supplemented Simula with the idea that objects interact by means of messages, although the calling up of a virtual procedure of an object is strictly the same.

It may be interesting to note that with Simula, procedures declared as virtual may have different argument signatures. This delays verification until execution, which is not intended to displease enthusiasts of dynamic typing.

The Simula language, although it has not known the success it merited in its time, is far from having faded into oblivion; compilers are available on numerous platforms. It is standardized, taught in universities and even today continues to inspire numerous creators of object-oriented languages (Bertrand Meyer with Eiffel (Meyer, 1988) or Bjarne Stroustrup (1986) for example). The designers of Simula also presented the Beta language in 1987. Any reader interested in references to this subject may consult Masini *et al.* (1990).

B.5.2 Modelling with Simula–67

THE CO-
ROUTINES
(DAHL AND
NYGAARD,
1966; POOLEY,
1986)

The manipulation of active objects to model parallel processes is implemented in Simula by means of the co-routine mechanism. Co-routines emulate the parallel execution of processes on a sequential computer (we are talking of quasi-parallelism). Each co-routine is described as a sequential instance process of a class. Co-routines therefore make it possible to express several activities, each having their own logic; a co-routine transfers control to another by the 'resume' instruction. This instruction symbolizes both the control flow transfer point to another co-routine and the point of return of the control flow to the co-routine effecting the 'resume'.

A co-routine-based system written in Simula generally has a main program which creates the co-routines by effecting a 'new' for each one. The 'new' for an active object class has the effect of creating a co-routine instance and of starting its execution. If each co-routine actually executed the body of its program on the occasion of its creation, the main program could never create more than a single co-routine at the same time. Now, it is frequently necessary to have to 'initialize' a certain number before the actual starting of the program. In order to solve this problem the 'detach' instruction is inserted at the beginning of the body of the program of a co-routine in order to return the control flow to the entity which performed the 'new'. This means that the effective starting of the program in its totality is performed by a single 'master co-routine resume' in the main program. A simplified client/server example with just two concurrent instances is given below; in this case the master co-routine is the server.

```
begin
        class server
                effect_service procedure ;
                render_service procedure ;
        begin
                ... Body of the procedures
                detach ;
                while true do
                begin
                        effect_service
                        resume a_client
                end
        end server;

        class client
                request_service procedure ;
        begin
                ... Body of the request service procedure
```

```
        ... (call up a_server.render_service)
        detach ;
        while true do
        begin
                request_service ;
                resume a_server ;
        end
    end client ;

    ref (server) a_server ;
    ref (cliet) a_client ;
    a_server :- new server ;
    a_client :- new client ;

    resume a_server ;
end
```

THE CLASSES
AVAILABLE
FOR
SIMULATION

Simula supplies a SIMULATION class which may be used as the base class for other classes, as well as a real global 'time' variable taking into account the simulation time. The simulation class also describes a PROCESS class which authorizes the creation of processes. In addition, each instance of the simulation class has its own time schedule in the form of a linked list of events. Each event is represented by a pair consisting of a date of occurrence relating to the time simulated and a process. The Simula processes have four possible states: active, suspended, passive and terminated. The time schedule is of course classified by increasing dates of occurrence of events, the process present at the head of the list being considered active and the others suspended. The time schedule management which makes it possible to insert or execute processes is effected with the 'activate' and 'reactivate' instructions and their associated formats. The generic syntax of the activate instruction is as follows:

```
activate process        [at date]
reactivate              [delay duration]
                        [before process]
                        [after process]
```

The formats specified with the process make it possible to identify various time schedule management techniques. If no format is specified it means the immediate activation of a process (equivalent to: activate ... at time, activate ... delay (0)). The first two formats use 'at' and 'delay', which make it possible to determine the date of occurrence of the process which is being activated and so make an insertion in the ordered list which constitutes the time schedule. The last two formats specify insertions in the time schedule relating to other processes. A process may be suspended and later reactivated at the subsequent date. In this case the process of the next time schedule is activated. The sequence 'reactivate myself delay duration' or 'reactivate this myself delay duration', being frequently used in simulation, may be replaced by calling up a more concise procedure 'hold(duration)'. The durations specified for the 'hold' may follow a statistical distribution fed by pseudo-random numbers.

An example of Simula code for a machining process is given below.

```
PROCESS machining class
  begin
     real turning_duration ;
     while true do
     begin
        turning_duration := negexp (turning) ;
        activate transport after turning_duration ;
        hold (turning_duration) ;
     end
  end machining
```

◁ B.6 ModSim III

B.6.1 History of ModSim (Bryan, 1989) (now ModSim III)

The ModSim language is the result of a contract between the CACI software company and the American Army, more especially with the AMIP (US Army Improvement Program).

MODSIM III is the marketed version of ModSim, the objectives of which, set by the AMIP, were as follows:

- object orientation,
- modular development,
- direct support for expert systems,
- implemented as a translator to a target range (the C language),
- complete syntax validation by the translator.

Two objectives were not achieved. The objective of cooperation with expert modules was deferred and carried forward to the parallel version of the language; likewise ModSim does not use a translator but a compiler generating C, thus it is possible to bind programs with C or C++. In this approach it is possible to write functions directly in C or C++ to associate them with the ModSim code and to compile them as forming part of the program. The choice of C as target must be capable of allowing relatively easy transfer to various computers.

B.6.2 Modelling with ModSim III (Herring, 1990)

The ModSim II language is a general language based on a Modula-2 syntax and supporting an object-oriented approach. It allows single and multiple inheritance, polymorphism and dynamic binding, data abstraction and encapsulation. Typing is static which ensures good security for developers but does not provide them with sometimes useful programming flexibility when prototyping.

The overloading of operators, genericity and persistence are not mentioned. Since objects are concerned with the same subject, they may be grouped together in a module. Object attributes are protected and may be queried or modified by the object methods. Data may be specified as private to an object by means of the keyword PRIVATE, so it is impossible to gain access to this data from outside the object. All the objects are allocated and deallocated dynamically (no static allocation is effected for the objects).

Constructions peculiar to discrete event simulation were introduced into the MODSIM III language. They are the fruit of the 30 years of experience of CACI in this domain. The language therefore separates two categories of methods: the methods preceded by the keyword TELL and those preceded by the keyword ASK. In the case of ASK these are instant methods in relation to the simulation time. They behave like call-ups and procedures having access to the attributes of the object in which they are described. The TELL methods are asynchronous and may consume simulation time. When a TELL method is called up, the caller may immediately continue execution without waiting for the end of the execution of this method. This method is deferred in an orderly manner and then processed when control has moved on to the synchronizing kernel which decides the time for starting this method. We give an example of MODSIM III code in Figure B.2:

It is possible to create subclasses of the 'ProcessObject' object in order to have several concurrent activities and so be able to model a system with a process approach. These activities may operate synchronously or asynchronously. It is possible to interrupt the activities of other objects or within one and the same object.

```
TYPE
GraphicObject = Object
    x, y         : REAL;
    colour       : INTEGER;
    ASK METHOD InitXY (IN x, y : REAL) ;
    TELL METHOD MoveTo (IN destx, desty : REAL) ;
    PRIVATE
    Class        : INTEGER;
END OBJECT;

MachineObject = OBJECT(GraphicObject);
    CycleTime    : REAL;
    ASK METHOD InitTpsCycle( IN Tps : REAL);
    OVERRIDE
        TELL METHOD MoveTo (IN destx, desty : REAL) ;
        TELL METHOD Load(IN NumberOfComponents, Class : INTEGER);
    TELL METHOD Unload(IN NumberOfComponents, Class : INTEGER);
END OBJECT;
```

Figure B.2 MODSIM III object with inheritance and redefinition of a TELL method.

The base construction used to increase simulation time is associated with the keyword **WAIT**. Three forms are possible:

- WAIT DURATION: This instruction means the suspension of the method executed during the interval of simulation time specified in the parameters.
- WAIT FOR: Object TO Methods (parameters,...): With this WAIT instruction format, you activate a method of a specified object, but it is necessary to wait until the object has completed the execution of this method before going on to the other instructions. With this form of wait, objects may synchronize their activities.
- WAIT FOR ObjectTrigger TO Fire: This WAIT instruction format uses objects of the predefined TriggerObject class. These objects have a Trigger method which, for example, makes it possible to test a set of conditions in order to implement a special decision logic. The firing of this Trigger method by another method allows all the objects waiting on this WAIT to continue their life cycle.

Each WAIT instruction may include an output to interruption. The objects may interrupt their methods while awaiting a WAIT, and in this case instructions after the keywords ON INTERRUPT are executed. The code below illustrates the foregoing.

```
TELL METHOD Machining (IN ClassOfClient ; Client) ;
        VAR
                MachiningTime: REAL ;
        BEGIN
                MachiningTime := ASK Client TO GiveMachiningTime ;
                WAIT DURATION MachiningTime
                        OUTPUT ("Machining completed") ;
                ON INTERRUPT
                        OUTPUT ("Machining interrupted !") ;
                END WAIT ;
END METHOD ;
```

B.6.3 Editing of results in the form of graphics and animation

As regards the graphic outputs, MODSIM III has an interface with the SIMGRAPHICS software which has a graphic editor to produce the background, and which proposes two types of service for displaying graphic results:

- It is possible to link the variables of the simulation model to graphs such as: histograms, pie charts, curves, and so on.
- As regards animation, it is possible to associate an icon with an object of the program, and so move the images in terms of the change in certain attributes of objects. This is important to guarantee that the visual operation is consistent with the model written in MODSIM III.

The fact of proposing an interface for SIMGRAPHICS also allows a certain degree of interaction with the simulation and animation in progress. Interactions are performed by means of dialogue boxes which make it possible to input values which may modify the current data of the simulation.

When a program is run, the dialogue boxes may appear and so give the user the possibility of taking some action on the evolution of the simulation. This type of function is interesting for the dynamic control of a simulation in progress.

B.6.4 Simulation and parallelism with ModSim (Bryan, 1990)

A simulation is very often greedy for calculation time. It is therefore normal for this to be a privileged field for the application of parallelism techniques. The fact that simulation is effected by means of communicating encapsulated objects allows their allocation to any processor available in a distributed architecture. Each object becomes active and has its own local simulation clock and may execute its own control flow. One part of this control flow is independent of the other objects and one part requires synchronizing with other objects. According to Brian (1989), MODSIM II is executed concurrently with an operating system based on Time Warp. In the case of MODSIM II this means the Time Warp mechanism is applied to synchronize the simulation and execution of objects on different processors. The fact of using an optimistic technique involves the appearance of 'Rollback' (Jefferson and Sowizral, 1985; Gafni, 1988). On the other hand it therefore becomes necessary to put a number of restrictions on the MODSIM II code:

- There must be no global data.
- Only the TELL methods may be used, otherwise the processors would have to await the return of the control of an ASK method. Parallel processing is more important if only asynchronous methods are used. This philosophy is very close to the actor models.
- The object is hierarchically the largest entity of a parallel MODSIM II program; modules are therefore no longer there.

◁ B.7 QNAP2

B.7.1 History

The QNAP2 software (Queuing Network Analysis Package II) is performance evaluation software designed at the beginning of the 1980s (Potier, 1983; Potier and Veran, 1984; Simulog, 1991). This software is now embedded in user-friendly environments such as MODARCH, MODLINE.

It allows discrete event simulation and Markov analysis and also supplies a set of exact or approximate analytical methods based on the theory of queuing networks. It proposes a language derived from ALGOL using blocks which serve to specify and describe the model studied. The entities of a model are declared in a block '/DECLARE/' and the stations of a queuing network are described in '/STATION/' blocks. The control parameters are supplied in '/CONTROL/' blocks and the execution scripts are given in '/EXEC/' blocks. The QNAP2 language may be considered as based on objects from 1990, when version 6 appeared.

The portability of this software is excellent because it is written in Fortran 77 which makes it available from the PC to the CRAY. This portability has allowed us to have QNAP on a NeXT station in less than a day. We are only presenting the simulation aspect, which makes it possible to construct an abstraction of reality (the model) and make it evolve in terms of time. Many problems very often require simulation, sometimes due to lack of knowledge of mathematical tools, sometimes due to their non-existence, but also frequently for ease of use. Updating of QNAP2 with new functions is regularly proposed by the Simulog company, which is a branch of INRIA (we are currently using version 9). Simulog is a software firm specializing in simulation and optimization.

B.7.2 A few elements of the QNAP2 language (Pistre, 1991)

INTRODUCTION Constructing a network of queues consists of assembling complex entities such as queues, servers, resources and clients in order to represent the organization and behaviour of the physical system studied as faithfully as possible. In QNAP2, any data manipulated in a program belongs to a type which defines the set of values that this data may assume as well as the operators that may be applied to it. The types manipulated in the QNAP2 language are:

- scalar types,
- tables,
- object classes
- references (or pointers).

The scalar types and references are non-structured types, while the tables and object classes are structured. The scalar types are INTEGER, REAL, BOOLEAN and STRING, and it is not possible to create new ones. On the other hand the programmer can define object classes, in addition to the three types of objects predefined in QNAP2 corresponding to the basic elements of a queueing network, QUEUE, CUSTOMER and CLASS, and a type of object peculiar to synchronizing, FLAG.

QNAP2 uses the notion of a queuing network station. A station consists of a single queue and one or more servers making it possible to define and render services.

The services defined by the stations make it possible to define parallel processes. A station will be identified by the name of its queue. We must therefore declare the queue associated with a station as being an object of the type QUEUE. The notion of queuing network clients in QNAP2 allows a great number of possibilities, depending on the nature of the system modelled. They may be parts to be machined, processes in a data processing system, information or files in an administrative system, and so on. A client is defined implicitly as an object of the type CUSTOMER. For the purpose of representing the concept of client classes within a network of queues (not to be confused with the object classes of the object model), there exists the predefined object type CLASS. This type of object is used to manipulate populations of clients who have the same behaviour in the matter of distribution, service time, priority, routing rules, and so on.

The predefined FLAG object type designates a flag, a tool dedicated to the synchronizing of parallel processes. In fact, in a model, it is sometimes necessary to translate parallelism conditions between several clients of one and the same network. The flags (FLAG) have therefore been implemented to allow modelling by simulation of parallel activities.

Another basic synchronizing mechanism is implemented by means of stations of a special type which play the role of semaphores. With these two basic mechanisms and the possibility of defining user objects, it is interesting to construct more powerful tools such as Hoare's monitors.

OBJECTS
AND THEIR
ATTRIBUTES

A class of QNAP2 objects is defined by an identifier and by a list of attributes associated with objects of this class. We use the term type of object and also class of objects incorrectly because QNAP2 does not directly propose methods within objects and does not take into account the principle of encapsulation. A list of formal parameters may also be declared following the identifier of a class with a view to a static creation of objects. For example, we may declare the class MACHINE which possesses three attributes (a queue, a service time and a pointer to the next queue).

```
/DECLARE/ OBJECT MACHINE;          & Class identifier : MACHINE
               ENTRY QUEUE;        & MACHINE queue
               REAL M_SERV;        & Service time
               REF QUEUE M_NEXT    & Pointer to the next queue
```

The object attributes may be:

- scalar elements (INTEGER, REAL, BOOLEAN and STRING),
- tables,
- pointers,
- objects of other known types (predefined or declared in the same block/DECLARE/).

Since QNAP2 uses an interpreter, it is possible to add new attributes to classes of objects defined by the user, or to predefined types of objects (QUEUE, CLASS, FLAG, CUSTOMER). The attributes associated with a particular type of object may be declared in any order. An attribute is declared by giving the identifier of the object or class type, followed by the type of the attribute and the name of the attribute. For example, we declare QUEUE INTEGER I to specify I as a new integer attribute (INTEGER) for the queues (QUEUE). Attributes may not be initialized at the time of declaration of the object type, or even on the occasion of their declaration. The attributes of an object type must all be declared before the first creation of an object of this type. For the predefined object classes, QUEUE, CUSTOMER, CLASS and FLAG, there is a list of predefined attributes to which a programmer may add new attributes according to his or her own needs (which offers very interesting flexibility). With QNAP2, it is possible to qualify an attribute by the name of a class just as in C++ or in Simula, with the notation '::'. This notation is also used to gain access to the attributes of a class derived from a superclass.

```
name_class::name_of_object.name_of_attribute
```

THE REFERENCES (OR POINTERS)

A reference may point to any variable of the same type created in a program. The type must be known at the time of declaration of the reference. Since the QNAP2 object classes do not directly define integrated methods, it is necessary to use references to functions or to procedures to offset this weakness.

The declaration syntax of a reference is as follows: we associate with the keyword **REF** the identifier of the object type to which the reference refers. The constant **NIL** is a value of a reference which points to nothing (default value).

```
REF CUSTOMER RC;  & RC:  Reference to objects of the type
                           CUSTOMER
REF QUEUE RQ;     & RQ:  Reference to objects of the type QUEUE
```

In the first example which follows, the initial client of station Q1, created by the declaration INIT = 1, dynamically generates a new client by means of the instruction NEW (CUSTOMER). The address of the client so created is stored in the reference RC. The reference RQ points to station Q2. The instruction TRANSIT (RC, RQ) allows the passage of the client created dynamically to station Q2. The following example makes it possible to recover a reference to an object of the class MACHINE.

```
/DECLARE/      QUEUE Q1,Q2;        & Q1 and Q2 of type QUEUE
               REF QUEUE RQ;       & Initialized implicitly at NIL
               REF CUSTOMER RC;    & Initialized implicitly at NIL
/STATION/      NAME = Q1;          & Description of the station Q1
               TYPE = SINGLE;
               INIT = 1;
               SERVICE = BEGIN

                                   RC: =NEW(CUSTOMER)
                                   RQ: =Q2;
                                   TRANSIT(RC,RQ);
                                   ...
                                   END;

/DECLARE/      REF MACHINE R_MAC1; & Reference to the object MACHINE
               MACHINE MAC1;       & Instance of the object MACHINE
```

```
/STATION/      NAME              = ...
               TYPE·             = SINGLE;
               SERVICE           = BEGIN
                                 R_MAC:MAC1; & R_MAC points to MAC1
                                 ...
                                 END;
```

The dummy type ANY allows the declaration of references designated to point to objects, the type (or class) of which is to be defined explicitly at the time of declaration, but may be defined subsequently (in the description of the service or in a block '/EXEC/' of the QNAP2 program). References declared on the type ANY may therefore point to objects of any type (QUEUE, CLASS, CUSTOMER, FLAG, or types defined by the programmer), but not to the scalar types (INTEGER, REAL, BOOLEAN, STRING).

INHERITANCE   Inheritance in QNAP2 is single (no multiple inheritance). The subclasses have attributes which are peculiar to them, and statically inherit attributes from their superclasses. The QNAP2 syntax consists of declaring the name of the superclass, then the keyword OBJECT followed by the name of the subclass. In the example which follows a robot class derives from an OBJ_PROD (for production object); QNAP2 identifiers are unfortunately limited to eight characters.

```
OBJ_PROD OBJECT ROBOT;
        ENTRY   QUEUE, BREAKDOWN;
        FLAG    START;
        REAL    T_BREAKDOWN, T_REPAIR;
END;
```

For each QUEUE attribute of an object, a description of its service is given. The attribute name of a station object is a string of characters consisting of an asterisk (character '*'), followed by the name of the class and a full stop, followed by the name of the station. Such a station is qualified as a 'queue template' in the QNAP2 language. In the example, * ROBOT.FAILURE designates the station describing failures which all the objects of the ROBOT class will possess.

```
/STATION/ NAME          = *ROBOT.FAILURE;
          INIT          = 1;
          SERVICE       = BEGIN
                              EXP(T_BREAKDOWN);
                              BLOCK(ENTRY);
                              UNIFORM(0.76 * T_REPAR, 1.55 * T_REPAR);
                              UNBLOCK(ENTRY);
                              END;
          END;
```

THE CREATION   Objects (not including the objects of type CUSTOMER or any class making
OF OBJECTS   reference to the type CUSTOMER) may be created statically. For that the description associated with the object class must describe a list of formal parameters making it possible to initialize the object attributes at the time of its creation.

```
/DECLARE/        OBJECT   MACHINE(M_SERV, M_PAN, M_REP);
                 QUEUE    ENTRY, M_SEM, M_BREAKDOWN;
                 REAL     M_SERV, M_PAN, M_REP;
              END;


/DECLARE/        MACHINE(0.5, 0.6, 0.7) MAC1;
                 MACHINE(0.7, 0.8, 0.9) MAC2;
```

The dynamic creation of objects in QNAP2 is made possible by using the function NEW, which creates an object and refers a pointer to this object. An example is given below.

```
/DECLARE/        REF MACHINE     MAC1,MAC2;
                 REF CUSTOMER    RC;
                 QUEUE           A;
/STATION/        NAME    = A;
                 INIT    = 1;
                 SERVICE = BEGIN
                               RC   := NEW(CUSTOMER);
                               MAC1 := NEW(MACHINE,0.5,0.6,0.7) ;
                               MAC2 := NEW(MACHINE,0.7,0.8,0.9);
                         END;
```

The DISPOSE procedure is provided to allow the destruction of objects created dynamically with the function NEW. The syntax is:

```
DISPOSE (ref_object);
```

THE QNAP2 MACRO-INSTRUCTIONS

QNAP2 has a macro-instructions preprocessor which is used to facilitate the writing of sequences of instructions frequently used (algorithmic sequences or sequences of the QNAP2 control language). The definition of a macro-instruction begins with $MACRO, specifying the name of the macro-instruction and the list of formal parameters if there is one. The names of macro-instructions need not be declared. The definition of the macro-instruction may contain any sequence of instructions, but must not contain a definition of other macros. The definition of a macro ends in the instruction $END. A macro-instruction may be defined anywhere in a QNAP2 program. Calling up a macro-instruction is equivalent to copying the whole definition of the body of the macro, in which the formal parameters are replaced with real parameters. A macro-instruction may be called up anywhere in a QNAP2 program. Macro-instructions will allow us to create several instances of a class. The example below defines a GENMACH macro-instruction which, for example, groups together the initialization instructions of an instance of a machine class.

```
$MACRO GENMACH(NAME_MACH, SERV)
       /EXEC/ NAME_MACH.M_SERV := SERV;
$END
```

The macro-instruction is called up by linking the character '$' to the name of the macro, and by giving a list of the real parameters for the object to be created. The QNAP2 instruction below makes it possible to create a machine M1 with a service time of 30 units of simulation time.

```
$GENMACH (M1, 30);
```

B.7.3 Other features of the QNAP2 language

The QNAP2 language has plenty of other features which have not been described in this short introduction, particularly the exception objects, the debugging tools and above all the statistical functions (Badel *et al.,* 1991). A polymorphism mechanism associated with the inheritance of QNAP2, the addition of methods within objects, encapsulation, dynamic classification and delegation can all be implemented in QNAP2, in particular by means of references to procedures and functions (version 9). It is this which we have partly presented in Chapter 6 and which is given in detail in Hill (1993).

◁ B.8 Bibliographical references to the tools and simulation languages presented

B.8.1 GPSS

Gordon G. (1962). A general purpose system simulator. *IBM Systems Journal,* **1**

Gordon G. (1978). *System Simulation.* Hemel Hempstead: Prentice-Hall

Gourgand M. (1990). DEA Computer Science Course, modelling option. Computer Science Laboratory at the Blaise PASCAL University, Clermont-Ferrand II, France

McHaney R. (1991). *Computer Simulation: A Practical Perspective.* Academic Press

Schmidt B. (1980). *GPSS-FORTRAN.* Wiley

Schriber T.J. (1989). Perspectives on simulation using GPSS. In *Proc. 1989 Winter Simulation Conference,* pp. 115–27

Schriber T.J. (1991). *An Introduction to Simulation Using GPSS/H.* Wiley

B.8.2 MODSIM II

Brian O.F. (1989). MODSIM II – An object-oriented simulation language for sequential and parallel processors. In *Proc. 1989 Winter Simulation Conference,* pp. 172–7

Gafni A. (1988). Rollback mechanism for optimistic distributed simulation systems. Distributed Simulation 1985, *SCS,* **19**(3), July 1988, San Diego, pp. 61–7

Herring C. (1990). ModSim: A new object-oriented simulation language. SCS Multi-conference on OO Simulation, San Diego, pp. 55–60

Jefferson D. and Sowizral H. (1985). Fast concurrent simulation using the time warp mechanism. Distributed Simulation 1985. *SCS* **15**(2), January 1985, San Diego, pp. 63–9

B.8.3 SIMAN

Pegden C.D. (1982). *Introduction to SIMAN.* Systems Modeling Corporation.

Pegden C.D. and Sturrock D.T. (1989). Introduction to SIMAN. In *Proc. 1989 Winter Simulation Conference*, pp. 129–39

Pegden C.D., Shannon R.E. and Sadowski R.P. (1990). *Introduction to Simulation Using SIMAN.* Maidenhead: McGraw-Hill

Poorte J.P. and Davis D.A. (1989). Computer animation with Cinema. In *Proc. 1989 Winter Simulation Conference*, pp. 147–54

Zeigler B.P. (1976). *Theory of Modeling and Simulation.* John Wiley

B.8.4 SIMULA

Bezivin J. (1984). Simulation and object-oriented languages. *Bigre* No. 40, November 1984, pp. 194–211

Birtwistle G., Dahl O., Myhraug B. and Nygaard K. (1973). *SIMULA Begin.* New York: Petro Celli/Charter

Dahl O.J., Myhraug B. and Nygaard K. (1968). *The Simula Common Base Language.* Publication S-2, Norwegian Computing Center, Oslo

Kirkerud B. (1989). *Object-Oriented Programming with Simula.* Harlow: Addison-Wesley

Masini G., Napoli A., Colnet D., Leonard D. and Tombre K. (1990). *The Object Languages.* Paris: InterEdition

Meyer B. (1988). *Object Design and Programming.* Paris: InterEdition

Pooley R.J. (1986). *An Introduction to Programming in SIMULA.* Oxford: Blackwell Scientific

Stroustrup B. (1986). *The C++ Programming Language.* Harlow: Addison-Wesley

B.8.5 SLAM/SLAMSYSTEM

Hammesfahr R.D.J., Sigal C.E. and Pritsker A.A.B. (1989). *SLAM II Network Models for Decision Support.* Hemel Hempstead: Prentice-Hall

O'Reilly J.J. and Lilegdon W.R. (1987). *SLAM II Quick Reference Manual.* Pritsker and Associates Inc.

O'Reilly J.J. and Nordlund K.C. (1989). Introduction to SLAM II and SLAMSYSTEM. In *Proc. 1989 Winter Simulation Conference*, pp. 178–83

Pritsker A.A.B. (1986). *Introduction to Simulation and SLAM II.* Hemel Hempstead: Prentice-Hall

Pritsker A.A.B. (1989). *SLAMSYSTEM Total Simulation Project Support.* Pritsker Corporation

Pritsker A.A.B. (1990). *Papers, Experiences, Perspectives.* Systems Publishing Corporation

B.8.6 QNAP2

Badel M., Eyraud S. and Duong D. (1991). The new simulation facilities in QNAP2. European Simulation Symposium. *SCS*, Ghent, Belgium, pp. 5–10

Hill D.R.C. (1993). Enhancing the QNAP2 object-oriented simulation language for manufacturing modelling. In *Proc. 1993 European Simulation Multi-Conference*, June 7–9, Lyon, France

Pistre C. (1991). The QNAP2 language and the object-oriented approach. Draft Engineer Report, CUST, Blaise Pascal University, Clermont-Ferrand II, France

Potier D. (1983). New User's Introduction to QNAP2. *INRIA Technical Report no. 40*, October

Potier D. and Veran M. (1984). QNAP2: A Portable Environment for Queueing Systems Modelling. *INRIA Research Report* no. 314

Simulog (1991). *QNAP2: Reference Manual*. 1 rue James Joule, 78182 St Quentin en Yvelines Cedex

GLOSSARY OF TERMS

Abstract class: A class which is not intended to have representatives (instances) and which is an abstraction generally used to factorize by inheritance a set of characteristics common to several subclasses.

Abstraction: Mental operation consisting in concentrating on one or several notions of a system or an element, ignoring the aspects which are not significant concerning a context and an objective.

Accessor: See access method.

Accessor method: Category of method designed solely to gain access to the internal data of objects. *Principles of Software Engineering* keenly advise their use if direct access is physically possible.

Acquaintance: Protected attribute of an actor used as a reference to a friend known to the actor which is in fact another actor.

Action model: The action model is a translation of the knowledge model into a mathematical formalism or into a programming language. It may be used directly and supplies performance of the system modelled without resorting to direct measurement.

Action model verification: Ensuring that the program or mathematical formulation is operationally correct and that it properly translates the choices and hypotheses made.

Active resources: Entities which have a certain autonomy with respect to the system to which they belong. Their state may develop independently of the other entities which make up the system.

Actors: Active objects which are the components of a concurrent system communicating by sending messages.

Aggregate: Complex object consisting of other objects having the following special feature: the destruction of an aggregate also involves the destruction of the objects which make up this aggregate. (See the nuance with macro-object.)

Aggregation: A merging of objects to form a complex aggregate object. (See composition and aggregate.)

Attributes: Data associated with each object (instance of a class) and which compose the static characteristics of the instances. The attributes may be objects of other classes or references to other objects.

Base class: A class from which another class is derived. (Syn: superclass, parent class or ancestor class).

Behaviour: Way in which an object acts and reacts, in terms of change of states or communication by message. The behaviour is determined by all of the methods which an object may execute.

Category: (1) Terminology introduced by Bard J. Cox with the Objective-C language. This is a modular concept by which all the classes which deal with one subject are grouped together into the same family. To be associated with the notion of a subsystem of M2PO objects. (2) See the category theory (Math.)

Child class: See derived class.

Class: Abstract description in terms of data and behaviour of a family of objects. If representatives of this family of objects exist, they are called 'instances of the class'.

Class method: Method peculiar to a class and not to the instances. Synonymous with factory method. Class methods may be called up independently of instances and must be considered as the methods of the metaclasses.

Class variable: Variable which is shared by all the instances of a class (and not duplicated like the other instance attributes). It is a metaclass attribute.

Cloning: Copying of one actor from another. There is no class/instance relation in an actor model.

Compatibility: Aptitude of software to combine.

Composability: Possibility of combining a software component with others in order to obtain a new, more complex component.

Composition: Merging of objects to form a complex macro-object. (See: aggregation.)

Constructor: The constructors are methods intended to create and initialize the new instances of a class. They may be overloaded and also be linked up in accordance with the inheritance tree in order to avoid code duplications.

Container: Data structure containing heterogeneous or homogeneous objects. A chained list of miscellaneous graphic objects, a tree of production objects, and a stack of user interface objects are containers. It is possible to provide the containers from generic data structures which only handle a single class of object (homogeneous objects). For example, a generic table may generate complex number objects or integers, but not integers and complex numbers simultaneously.

Continuity: This is a mechanism for sending messages proposed by the actor model according to which the final addressee of a message is not necessarily the first recipient. The final addressee is specified as an acquaintance in the message which is evaluated before being transmitted to a third party. These successive transmissions are known under the concept of continuity.

Coupling: Degree of relationship between the various components of software. Highly coupled components use their respective services very frequently, and components which are not highly linked only use the services of the other components to a very low degree.

Data abstraction: Principle by which a data type is specified by all of the operations which apply to it and which control and limit the consultations and modifications.

Data member: See attributes.

Decisional model: The function of a decisional model is to supply information making it possible to take a decision intended to modify the system.

Deferred class: In this kind of class at least one method is purely virtual, and such classes are used as the basis for the design of other classes.

Delegation: This is the technique of sharing information used by the actor model. When an actor cannot deal with a message, it 'delegates' it to another actor which is its proxy.

Derived class: Class which is defined as being an extension or a specialization of another class called a base class or superclass, by means of the inheritance mechanism.

Description model: The purpose of a description model is to supply as good a relation as possible between the inputs and outputs of the system and in particular to specify the relative influence of the various input variables.

Destructor: Method used implicitly or explicitly at the end of the life of an object so as to automatically take a certain number of management actions such as memory release in respect of the object concerned.

Dynamic binding: A technique making it possible to bind procedure (method) calls to corresponding code at runtime and not on compilation (allows the implementation of polymorphism).

Dynamic inheritance: (1) Implementation technique of inheritance allowing a sharing of characteristics between subclasses without having to duplicate these characteristics (frequently used to inherit methods). (2) Faculty of updating the inheritance graph during execution.

Dynamic typing: Occurs when the developer is not obliged to specify a precise object type when declaring an identifier. The type depends on the dynamic content of a variable more than the declaration of the container.

Efficiency: A software system is said to be efficient if it uses the available time and space resources to the best possible advantage.

Encapsulation: Encapsulation is the process consisting, on the one hand, of grouping together the code and data within one and the same entity and, on the other, of preventing direct access to the data of an object.

Explanatory model: The function of an explanatory model is to supply a more or less conformist representation of an existing system or system to be built, highlighting certain of its properties and possibly making it possible to deduce others.

Extensibility: Facility for adapting software to specification changes.

Facet: Descriptor of an attribute. An attribute may possess several facets, and each may define a special feature of the attribute (constraint, commentary, associated code).

Factory method: See class method.

Function members: See methods.

Genericity: Possibility of parametrizing software components by types or classes. (Syn: Parametrized class.)

Information hiding: Principle making it possible to hide from the user of a software component the details of its implementation. Only the essential interface is visible and accessible.

Inheritance: Relationship between classes allowing a subclass to have attributes and share methods previously defined in a superclass representing a generalization of the subclass (itself considered as a specialization of the superclass).

Inheritance graph: Abstract structure representing the inheritance relationships between different objects.

Instance: An instance of a class is a variable constructed in accordance with the mould specified by the class. (Syn: object.)

Instance method: See Syn: method.

Instance variable: See attributes.

Instantiation graph: Abstract structure giving the relationships which link the classes to their instances.

Instantiation: Operation by which a class produces one or several instances.

Intelligibility: Intelligible software must have good legibility of its source code and it must also be understandable at other levels (analysis, design).

Interface: Complete description of all the methods of a class which are accessible through an external element. (Syn: Protocol.)

Knowledge model: This is a formalization in a natural or graphic language of the structure and functioning of a system.

Macro-object: Assembly of various objects to form a new object called a macro-object.

Member: Elementary component of an object, whether an attribute or a method (Stroustrup, 1986).

Message: The message is the only communications support between objects. The arrival of a message causes the execution of a method of an object. Each message has a method selector, possibly with arguments. The destination object is either specified or implied if an object calls on one of its own methods.

Metaclass: Concept used in models where the classes are also considered as objects. A metaclass is a class which describes the structures of another class considered as an object (an instance of a metaclass). This choice makes it possible to extend the concepts of objects and to approach the 'anything is an object' idea. To unify the model there exists a single metaclass at the highest level of the instantiation graph, common to all the other metaclasses. (See class method.)

Metadata: Data describing other data.

Method: Procedure, function or operation associated with instances or classes and which is actuated on receipt of a message.

Method selector: Method identifier which may contain the number and type of the arguments.

Modifiability: A system which allows easy modification of its structure without altering its complexity possesses good modifiability.

Modularity: Suitability of a system to be decomposed into an organized set of parts called modules. (Booch, 1991).

Mother class: See base class.

Multiple inheritance: Feature allowing a subclass to inherit from more than one superclass.

Object: Instance of a class. Entity encapsulating a state (the values of the attributes of the object) and a behaviour (the methods of the object).

Object-oriented analysis: Operation by which the mind, in order to fully understand a system, carries out a detailed study leading to the identification of objects which make up the system, and to a description of their structures as well as the relationships which link them together.

Optimizing model: The purpose of an optimizing model is to supply the optimum values of the command variables with regard to certain objectives, bearing in mind the input variables.

Overloading: Principle making it possible to give different meanings to the same identifier, whether for functions, operators or virtual methods.

Overriding: Consists of specifying in a subclass a new implementation of a polymorphic method (bearing the same name as one of the methods declared in the superclass which already possesses an implementation). Priority in execution is given to the new definition which replaces the old one and which may possibly refer to it (Syn: substitution.)

Parametric overloading: Overloading using the arguments signature to distinguish the methods.

Parametrized class: Class in which the types may be parametrized. Types are given as parameters at the moment of creation of the instances. (Syn: Genericity.)

Passive resources: Entities which do not take part directly in the processing but which are essential for the active resources to carry out their operations. The passive resources constitute in general critical resources.

Persistence: Property of an object enabling it to survive its creator program (for example storage on disk of an object created in memory at the end of the execution of a program).

Polymorphism: Feature making it possible to associate several implementations of methods (in accordance with the classes of the inheritance graph) with a single identifier. Polymorphism is implemented by dynamic binding, and gives the code that uses it as much power as flexibility.

Procedural abstraction: Principle making it possible to consider a set of low-level operations ending up with a definite effect such as a single entity or procedure which can be used directly.

Protocol: All the accessible methods of an object. Certain internal methods may be private and not form part of the protocol (Syn: interface.)

Proxy: Acquaintance of an actor to which unknown messages are delegated. (See delegation and acquaintance.)

Reliability: To be reliable, software must be able to be used safely (without unexpected blockages, with the possibility of resuming in the event of errors,...) by means of a consistent design, robust coding and serious tests.

Repetition inheritance: Phenomenon occurring when a class inherits several times from one of its superclasses following a multiple inheritance.

Reusability: This is the capacity of a software component or an analysis or design result to be used again in a context different from the application which brought about its creation.

Robustness: (1) (Software engineering): aptitude of a piece of software to operate even under abnormal conditions. (2) (simulation): the robustness of an action model allows relative confidence in the results supplied when the conditions in which those results were obtained are fairly different from those present at the time of validation. A model is robust when it depends relatively little on the modelling assumptions made to implement it.

Script: Procedure which describes the behaviour of an actor.

Signature: Set of information making it possible to identify a method by combining the name of the method with the list and types of arguments (Syn; selector, arguments signature).

Simulation: Simulation consists in bringing about the evolution of an abstraction of a system in time in order to assist in understanding the operation and behaviour of the system and to apprehend some of its dynamic characteristics with a view to evaluating various decisions.

Static typing: Occurs when the type of each identifier must be declared before compilation.

Static binding: The binding of procedure (method) calls with their corresponding code is done at compile time.

Static inheritance: Implementation technique of inheritance by duplication of the common characteristics between subclasses (frequently used to inherit attributes).

Strong typing: A language is said to be strongly typed if the type of each expression must be known at compile time.

Structural validation: A model is structurally valid, not only if it supplies satisfactory results, but if its internal structure corresponds to the operating structure of reality.

Subclass: Class derived by inheritance from a parent class.

Superclass and abstract superclass: See base class and abstract class.

Typing: Assignment of a class to an object in order to restrict the mixing and changing of category.

Validation of a knowledge model: Ensuring that the knowledge you have of the system (from the system inputs up to its operating logic) is correctly represented and has a sufficient level of accuracy and abstraction proportional to the set of objectives.

Validation of an action model: Consists in ensuring that a model supplies, in its application framework, consistent results which are sufficiently precise compared with those expected.

Validity: Capability of software to perform exactly the tasks defined by its specification (Meyer, 1988).

Virtual method: Polymorphic method which will be called up only with the dynamic binding technique. Such a method is defined only by an interface (list and type of arguments, and type of result). The implementations are only given in the subclasses. (Syn: deferred method.)

BIBLIOGRAPHY

Agha G. (1990). Concurrent objet-oriented programming. *Communication of the ACM*, 33 (9), 125–141

Agha G. and Hewitt C. (1987). Concurrent programming using actors. In *Object-Oriented Concurrent Programming*. pp. 37–54. MIT Press. Computer series.

Aho A., Hopcroft J., and Ullman J. (1989). *Structures de données et algorithmes*. Paris: InterEdition.

Ajmone M.M., Conte G., and Balbo G. (1984). A class of generalised stochastic Petri nets for the performance evaluation of multiprocessor systems. *ACM Transactions on Computer Systems*, May, 2 (2), 93–122

America P. (1987). POOL-T: A parallel object-oriented language. In *Object-Oriented Concurrent Programming*. pp. 199–220. MIT Press Computer Series.

AT&T *C++ Language System Release. 2.0.* Reference Manual.

Ayache J., Courtiat J., Diaz M. and Juanole G. (1985). Utilisation des réseaux de Petri pour la modélisation et la validation des protocoles. *TSI*, 4 (1) 51–71

Ayache M. and Ou-Halima M. (1992). *Représentation et identification des objets: modèle et méthode.* INFORSID Conference.

Clermont-Ferrand, France, 19–22 May, pp.43–62

Bailin S.C. (1989). An object-oriented requirements specification method. *Communication of the ACM*, 32 (5), 608–23

Balci O. and Sargent R.E. (1981). A methodology for cost-risk analysis in the statistical validation of simulation models. *Communication of the ACM*, 24 (4). 190–7

Balci O. and Withner R.B. (1989). Guidelines for selecting and using simulation model verification techniques. In *Proc. 1989 Winter Simulation Conference*, pp. 559–68

Banks J. (1994). Software for simulation. In *Proc. 1994 Winter Simulation Conference*, pp. 26–33

Banks J. and Carson J.S. (1984). *Discrete Event System Simulation.*

Barbier F. and Jaulent P. (1992). *Techniques Orientées Objet et CIM.* Eyrolles.

Barnes J. (1988). *La programmation en Ada*. Paris: InterEdition.

Barnichon D. (1990) Modélisation et simulation de systèmes de production: problèmes de spécification et d'ordonnancement. *Doctoral Thesis*, Université Blaise Pascale. Clermont-Ferrand II

Barnichon D. and Gourgand M. (1990). Modelling and scheduling a flexible line using a Petri net–SIMAN coupling. International Conference on Operations Research, Vienna, Austria, 23–26 August

Barnichon D., Caux C. and Gourgand M. (1990). Methodology for manufacturing system performance anlysis using a SIMAN–Petri nets coupling. European Simulation Symposium, Gand, Belgium, 8–10 November, pp. 148–52

Bazjnac V. (1976). Interactive simulation of building evacuation with elevators. In *Proc. 9th Annual Simulation Symposium*, March, Florida, USA, pp. 15–29

Beck K. and Cunningham W. (1989). A laboratory for teaching object-oriented thinking. In *Proc. 1989 OOPSLA Conference,* pp. 1–6

Bel G. and Dubois D. (1985). Modélisation et simulation de systèmes automatisés de production. *APII AFCET*, 19 (1), 3–43

Bell T.E. (1969). *Computer graphics for simulation-problem solving*. Rand Corporation, Santa Monica, CA

Bell P.C. and O'Keefe R.M. (1987). Visual interactive simulation: History, recent developments and major issues. *Simulation*, 49 (3), 109–16

Bezivin J. (1984). Simulation et langages orientés objets. *Bigre*, No. 41, November, 1–18

Bezivin J. (1987a). Some experiments in object-oriented simulation. In *Proc. OOPSLA 1987*, Orlando, USA, pp. 394–404

Bezivin J. (1987b). Time Lock: a concurrent simulation technique and its description in Smalltalk-80. In *Proc. Winter Simulation Conference*, Atlanta, USA, pp. 394–404

Bezivin J. (1988a). An evaluation environment for concurrent object-oriented simulation. In *Distributed Simulation*. pp. 149–154. SCS. San Diego, CA.

Bezivin J. (1988b). Langages à objets et programmation concurrente: quelques expérimentations avec Smalltalk-80. *Bigre + Globule*, No. 59, pp. 176–87

Bezivin J. and Imbert H. (1982). Adapting a simulation language to a distributed environment. 3rd International Conference on Distributed Systems, Miami, USA, pp. 596–603

Bezivin J. and Cointe P. (1991). Le modèle objet: un carrefour d'innovations dans le domaine des langages et des systèmes informatiques. *AFCET Interfaces*, May/June, 34–8

Bezivin J., Lanneluc J. and Lemesle R. (1994). Representing knowledge in the object-oriented lifecycle. TOOLS PACIFIC 94, pp. 21–30. Prentice-Hall

Birtwistle G.M., (1979). *DEMOS, a System for Discrete Event Modelling on Simula*. MacMillan Computer Science series.

Birtwistle G.M., Dahl O., Myraug B. and Nygaard K. (1973). *SIMULA Begin*. New York: Petro Celli/Charter.

Birtwistle G.M., Hill D., Lomov G., *et al.* (1984). JADE: A simulation and software prototyping environment. In *Proc. SCS Conf*, La Jolla, pp. 77–83

Blaha M., Premerlani W. and Rumbaugh J. (1988). Relational database design using an object-oriented methodology. *Communication of the ACM*, 31 (4), 414–27

Blaha M., Eddy F., Lorensen W., Premerlani W., and Rumbaugh J. (1991). *Object-Oriented Modelling and Design*. Prentice-Hall

Boehm B. (1986). A spiral model of software development and enhancement. *Software Engineering Notes*, 11 (4), 23–34

Boehm B. (1988). A spiral model of software development and enhancement. *IEEE Computer*, 21 (5), 61–72

Bonetto R. (1987). *Les ateliers flexibles de production*. HERMES

Booch G. (1987). *Software Engineering with Ada*, 2nd edn. New York: Benjamin/Cummings

Booch G. (1991). *Object-Oriented Design with Applications*. New York: Benjamin/ Cummings

Booch G. (1992). *Conception Orientée Objets et applications*. Paris: Addison-Wesley. (Translation of Booch, 1991).

Booch G. (1994a). *Object-oriented analysis & design*. Menlu Park, CA: Benjamin/ Cummings

Booch G. (1994b). Scenarios. *Report on Object Analysis and Design*, 1 (3), 3–6

Brams G. (1983). *Réseaux de Petri théorie et pratique*, Vols I and II. Paris: MASSON

Bresenham J.E. (1965). Algorithm for computer control of a digital plotter. *IBM System Journal*, 4 (1), 25–30

Breugnot D., Gourgand M. and Kellert P. (1990). SIGMA: An intelligent and graphical environment for the modelling of flexible assembly-systems. In *Proc. of the European Simulation Symposium 1990*, Ghent, Belgium, 8–11 November, pp 225–30

Breugnot D., Gourgand M., Hill D.R.C. and Kellert P. (1991a). Object-oriented animation for flexible manufacturing systems simulation results. In *Proc. of TOOLS 4*, Paris, pp. 283–95

Breugnot D., Gourgand M., Hill D.R.C. and Kellert P. (1991b). GAME: An object-oriented approach to computer animation and flexible manufacturing system modelling. In *Proc. 24th Annual Simulation Symposium*, New Orleans, IEEE/ACM/SCS, pp. 217–27

Breugnot D., Gourgand M. and Kellert P. (1991c). Les problèmes de terminologie dans la modélisation des systèmes de production. Terminology Work in Subject Fields conference. TTC 91,12–14 November, Vienna

Breugnot D., Gourgand M., Hill D.R.C. and Kellert P. (1991d). User-friendly object-oriented modelling for flexible manufacturing systems. European Simulation Multi-Conference, Copenhagen, Denmark, pp. 106–11

Brian O.F. (1989). MODSIM II An object-oriented simulation language for sequential and parallel processors. In *Proc. 1989 Winter Simulation Conference*, pp. 172–77

Brunner D., and Henriksen J. (1989). A general purpose animator. In *Proc. 1989 Winter Simulation Conference*, pp. 147–62

Buchanan G., Korson T. and Vaishnavi V. (1991). OMRB: Object Modelling Resource Base, a support tool for object-oriented analysis. In *Proc. TOOLS 4 Conference*, March 1991, Paris, pp. 215–24

Budd T. (1991). *An Introduction to Object-Oriented Programming*. Reading, MA: Addison-Wesley

Budd T. (1992). *Introduction à la programmation par objets*. Paris: Addison-Wesley. (Translation of Budd (1991))

Burger P. and Gillies D. (1989). *Interactive Computer Graphics*. Harlow: Addison-Wesley

Buzacott J.A. and Yao D.D. (1986). Flexible manufacturing systems: a review of analytical models. *Management Science,* 32 (7)

Campagne J.P., Peyron J. and Temani M. (1985). Structuration des bases de données techniques autour de nomenclatures et gammes-mères en vue de l'élaboration automatique de gammes. *APII AFCET*, 19 (4), 343–57

Caromel D. (1990). Concurrency and Reusability from Sequential to Parallel. *JOOP*, September, 34–42

Castellani X. (1991). Le modéle de la méthode MCO d'analyse et de conception des systèmes par objets. In *Proc. INFORSID Conference 1991*, pp. 395–429

Caux C., Gourgand M. and Hill D.R.C. (1991). Petri net simulation and animation in a graphical object–oriented environment. In *Proc. ISSM Parallel and Distributed Systems Conference*, Trany, Italy, pp. 359–62

Chen P. (1976). The entity relationship model – Toward a unified view of data. *ACM Transaction on Database Systems*, March

Christerson M. and Jabson I. (1995). A growing consensus on use case. *JOOP*, March/April pp.15–19

Coad P. and Yourdon E. 1991. *Object-Oriented Analysis*. 2nd Edn. Yourdon Press Computing Series

Coleman D., Arnold P., Bodoff S., *et al.* (1994). *Object-Oriented Development: The Fusion Method*. Prentice-Hall

Cook W., Hill W. and Canning P. (1990). Inheritance is not subtyping. POPL '90, pp. 125–35

Cook S. and Daniels J. (1994). *Object-Oriented Modelling with Syntropy*. Prentice-Hall

Coplien J. (1992). Programmation avancée en C++. Paris: Addison-Wesley

Coquillard P. and Hill D.R.C. (1995). Object-oriented simulation of Scots Pine growth interaction. In *Proc. Summer Computer Simulation Conference*, Ottawa, Canada

Courtois P. (1985). On time and space decomposition of complex structures. *Communication of the ACM*, 28 (6). 596–608

Cox B.J. and Novobilski A.J. (1991). *Object-Oriented Programming, An Evolutionary Approach*, 2nd Edn. Reading, MA: Addison-Wesley

Dahl O.J. and Nygaard K. (1966). Simula - an ALGOL Based Simulation Language. *Communication of the ACM*. Vol 9. (9) pp. 671–678.

Dahl O.J., Myhrhaug B. and Nygaard K. (1968). The Simula Common Base Language. *Publication S-2*, Norwegian Computing Center, Oslo

Davis S.R. (1992). C++ objects that change their types. *JOOP*, July/August

Dean H. (1991). Object-oriented design using message flow decomposition. *JOOP*, May, 21–31

DeMarco T. (1979). *Structured Analysis and System Specification*. Englewood Cliffs, NJ: Prentice-Hall

Desfray P. (1989). Définition d'un modèle de conception par objets à partir du modèle Entité/Relations. Deuxièmes journées internationales: Le génie logiciel et ses applications. Vol. II, pp. 569–85. Toulouse

Desfray P. (1990). A method for object oriented programming: the class/relationship method.

In *Proc. TOOLS 2 Conference*, November, Paris, pp. 121–31

Desfray P. (1994). Object Engineering the Fourth Dimension. Harlow: Addison-Wesley

Dixneuf P. and Aubert JP. (1990). Une méthode de conception et de programmation par objets. *Génie Logiciel et systèmes experts*. June, No. 1, 32–42

Ducournau R. and Habib M. (1989). La multiplicité de l'héritage dans les langages à objets. *TSI*, 8 (1), 42–62

Duke R., King P., Rose G., and Smith G. (1991). The Object-Z Specification Language Version 1. *Technical Report no 91–1*. Version 1, May, University of Queensland

Edwards M. and Henderson-Sellers B. (1990). Object-oriented systems life cycle. *Communication of the ACM*, 33 (9), 143–59

Ellis M. and Stroustrup B. (1990). *The Annotated C++ Reference Manual*. Reading, MA: Addison-Wesley

Ferrari D. (1978). *Computer Systems Performance Evaluation*. Prentice-Hall

Fishman D.S. (1978). *Principles of Discrete Event Simulation*. Wiley

Flitman A.M. and Hurrion R.D. (1987). Linking discrete-event simulation models with expert systems. *Journal of the Operational Research Society* 38, 723–56

Flory A. (1987). *Bases de données conception et réalisation*, 2nd edn. Paris: Economica

Flory A. (1991). Les objets dans les systèmes d'information. *INFORSID Conference*, Paris

Flory A. and Ayache M. (1993). CASsiopE: A three-dimensional model for object-oriented design. INDO-FRENCH Workshop on Object-oriented Systems, Goa, India

Gall J. (1986). *Systemantics: How Systems Really Work and How They Fail*, 2nd edn. Reading, MA: Addison-Wesley

Gamma E., Helm R., Johnson R. and Vlissides J. (1994). *Design Patterns Elements of Reusable Object-Oriented Software*. Reading, MA: Addison-Wesley

Gilb T. (1991). *Principles of Software Engineering Management*. Harlow: Addison-Wesley

Gilman A.R. and Billingham C. (1989). A tutorial on See Why and Witness. ISTEL Incorporated. In *Proc. Winter Simulation Conference*, pp. 192–99.

Gipps P.G. (1986). The role of computer graphics in validating simulation models. *Mathematics and Computer in Simulation*, 88, 285–89

Goldberg A. and Robson D. (1983). Smalltalk-80. Reading, MA: Addison-Wesley

Gordon G.M. (1962). A general purpose system simulator. *IBM System Journal*, 1

Gordon G.M. (1978). *System Simulation*. Prentice-Hall

Gorlen K. (1987). An object-oriented class library for C++ programs. *Software Practice and Experience*, December, 17(12), 889–922

Gourgand M. (1984). Outils logiciels pour l'évaluation des performances des systèmes informatiques. *PhD. Thesis*, Blaise Pascal University, Clermont-Ferrand II, France.

Gourgand M. and Hill D.R.C. (1990a). Petri Nets to Occam2 translation techniques. In *ISMM Parallel and Distributed Computing and Systems*, pp. 319–24. New York

Gourgand M. and Hill D.R.C. (1990b). Petri Nets modelling on transputers with OCCAM2. *SCS European Simulation Symposium*, Ghent, Belgium, pp. 143–8

Gourgand M. and Kellert P. (1991). Conception d'un environnement de modélisation des systèmes de production. 3rd International Industrial Engineering Conference, Tours. March

Gourgand M. and Hill D.R.C. (1992). Object-oriented modelling and design methodology for simulation animation. In *Proc. European Simulation Conference SCS*, June, York, pp. 256–61

Gourgand M., Hill D.R.C., Kellert P. and Tourron P. (1992). Environement orienté-objet d'animation de systèmes de production sur

station de travail UNIX. Congrès Interface des mondes réels et virtuels. March, Montpellier, France, pp. 333–45.

Graham I.M. (1992). Interoperation: Combining object-oriented technology with rules. *Object Magazine*, 2 (4), 36–43

Graham I.M. (1993). Migration using SOMA: A semantically rich method of object-oriented analysis. *Journal of Object-Oriented Programming*, 5 (9)

Graham I.M. (1994). *Object-Oriented Methods*, 2nd edn. Harlow: Addison-Wesley.

Graham I.M. (1995). *Migrating to Object Technology*. Harlow: Addison-Wesley.

Grant F.H. (1989). Tutorial scheduling manufacturing systems with FACTOR. In *Proc. 1989 Winter Simulation Conference*.

Green M. and Sun H. (1988). Interactive Animation. *IEEE Computer Graphics and Applications*, 8 (6), 52–65

Harris W. (1991). Contravariance for the rest of us. *JOOP*, Nov/Dec., 10–15

Heitz M. (1987). HOOD, une méthode de conception hiérarchisée orientée-objet pour le développement de gros logiciels techniques et temps-réels. *Bigre* 57, December, Journées ADA France: Le parallélisme en ADA

Henderson-Sellers B. and Edwards J.M. (1994). *Book Two of Object-Oriented Knowledge: The Working Object*. Prentice-Hall

Hewitt C.E., Bishop P. and Steiger R. (1973). A universal modular ACTOR formalism for AI. 3rd IJCAL Conference, Stanford, CA, pp. 235–45.

Hewlett Packard/Apollo documentation (1988). *Programming with System Calls for InterProcess Communication*.

Hewlett Packard documentation (1988). *Programming with Domain/OS Calls*.

Hill T.R. and Roberts S.D. (1987). A Prototype Knowledge Based Simulation Support System. In *Simulation*. Vol 48. No 4. pp. 152–161.

Hill D.R.C. and Junqua A. (1990). GAME: un outil orienté objet pour l'animation de simulation de systèmes flexible d'assemblage. Rapport d'Ingénieur et de DEA. Université Blaise Pascal. Clermont-Ferrand II. France.

Hill D.R.C. (1991–93). La modélisation par Objets. Cour d'analyse et de conception par objets en année d'Ingénieur au CUST. Université Blaise Pascal. Clermont-Ferrand II, France

Hill D.R.C. (1992). Etude de quelques concepts pour une analyse et une conception par objets. INFORSID conference, Clermont-Ferrand, France, 19– 22 May, pp. 307–326

Hill D.R.C., Laize E. and Ruch S. (1992). Etude d'outils de simulation et d'animation. *Rapport TEMPUS JEP* 2605–92/2.

Hill D.R.C. Gourgand M. (1993). A multi-domain tool for object-oriented simulation animation. TOOLS 10, Versailles, France, 8–11 March, pp. 181–195

Hill D.R.C., Gourgand M. and Kellert P. (1993). Object-oriented simulation animation builder. 26th Annual Simulation Symposium, IEEE/ACM/SCS, 29 March-1 April, Washington, USA

Hill D.R.C. (1993a). Enhancing the QNAP2 object-oriented simulation language for manufacturing modelling. In *Proc. 1993 European Simulation Multi-Conference*, June 7–9, Lyon, France

Hill D.R.C. (1993b) *Analyse Orientée Objets et Modélisation par Simulation*. Paris; Addison-Wesley

Hill D.R.C. (1994). Object-oriented simulation: Application to manufacturing systems simulation. TOOLS Europe 1994 Tutorial. 95 pages

Hill D.R.C., Pastre J., Coquillard P., and Guegnot J. (1994). Design of an ecosystem modelling environment: Application to forest growth simulation. In *Proc. CISS 94*, Zurich, pp. 538–43

Hill D.R.C., Coquillard P., Vaugelas J. and Meinez M. (1995). Preliminary results of the caulerpa taxifolia simulation in the North Mediterranean Sea. In *Proc. EUROSIM*, Vienna

Hill D.R.C. (1995). Verification and validation of ecosystem simulation models. In *Proc. Summer Computer Simulation Conference*, Ottawa, Canada

Hoare C.A.R. (1978). Communicating sequential processes. *Communication of the ACM*, 21 (8), 666–77

Hodgson R. (1991). The X-Model, a process model for O-O software development. Actes des quatrièmes journées internationales: Le Génie Logiciel et ses applications. December, Toulouse, France, pp. 713–29

Hollocks B.W. (1984). Practical benefits of animated graphics in simulation. In *Proc. Winter Simulation Conf.*, pp. 323–28

Hullot J.M. (1983). CEYX, A multiformalism programming environment. IFIP Conference, Paris, France, September and Rapport INRIA 210.

Hurrion R.D. (1976) The design use and required facilities of an interactive computer simulation language to explore production planning problems. *PhD. Thesis*, University of London

Hurrion R.D. (1989). Graphics and interaction. In *Computer Modelling for Discrete Simulation*. Wiley

Hurrion R.D. and Secker R.J.R. (1978). Visual interactive simulation, an aid to decision making. *Omega*, UK, 6 (5), 419–26

IGL Technology (1989). *SADT un langage de Communication*. Paris: Eyrolles

Jacobson I. (1987). Object-oriented development in an industrial environment. In *Proc. OOPSLA Conference*, ACM, December

Jacobson I., Christerson M., Jonsson P. and Overgaard G. (1992). *Object-Oriented Software Engineering: A Use Case Driven Approach*. Harlow: Addison-Wesley

Jacobson I. (1994). *Business Process Reengineering*. Harlow: Addison-Wesley

Jefferson D. and Sowizral H. 1985. Fast concurrent simulation using the time warp mechanism. In Distributed Simulation 1985. *SCS* Vol. 15, No 2, January, San Diego, CA. pp. 63–9

Jochem R., Bals P., Rabe M. and Sussenguth W. (1989). An object-oriented analysis and design methodology for computer integrated manufacturing'. In *Proc. TOOLS 2,* Paris, France, pp. 269–80

Johnson R.E. and Zweig J.M. (1991). Delegation in C++. *JOOP*, Nov Dec., 31–4

Jordan P., Keller K., Tucker R. and Vogel D. (1989). Software storming: combining rapid prototyping and knowledge engineering. *In IEEE Computer,* 22 (5), 39–51.

Kallel G., Pellet X. and Binder Z. (1985). Conduite décentralisée coordonée d'atelier. *APII AFCET*, 19 (4), 371–87

Kellert P. (1987). Modélisation de systèmes complexes avec QNAP2. *Thesis*, Blaise-Pascal University, Clermont-Ferrand II, France.

Kellert P. (1992). Définition et mise en ouevre d'une méthodologie orientée objets pour la modélisation des systèmes de production. INFORSID Conference, Clermont-Ferrand, France, 19–22 May, pp. 415–36

Kieffer J.P. and Khrifech L. (1989). Systèmes-experts en ordonnancement d'atelier: difficultés de mise en oeuvre et propositions méthodologiques. 7th Artificial Intelligence and Recognition of Shapes Conference, AFCET-INRIA, Paris, pp. 287–95

Knuth D.E. (1975). *The Art of Computer Programming*. Vols 1–3. Reading MA: Addison-Wesley

Kobayashi H. (1978). *Modelling and Analysis*. Reading, MA. Addison-Wesley

Kristen G.J.H.M. (1994). *Object-Orientation, the KISS Method from Information Architecture to Information System*. Harlow: Addison-Wesley

Law A.M. and Carson J.S. (1979). A sequential procedure for determining the length of steady state simulation. *Operations Research*, 27, 1011–36

Law A.M. and Kelton W.D. (1982). *Simulation Modelling and Analysis*. 2nd ed. McGraw-Hill

Lehman M.M. (1980). *Programs, programming and the software life cycle. Report 80/6*. April 15, Dept of Computing and Control, Imperial College of Science and Technology, London

Le Moigne J.L. (1977). La théorie du système général Théorie de la modélisation. *Systèmes Décision*. Universitaires de France.

Leopopoulos V. (1985). Loric, un simulateur de RdP écrit en MacLISP. *INRIA Report 371*, Rocquencourt, France

Leroudier J. (1980). La simulation à événements discrets. *Monographies d'Informatique de l'AFCET*, Edition Hommes et Techniques.

Lewis J. (1988). Hashing for dynamic and static internal table. *IEEE Computer*, 18 (5), October, 45–8

Liberherr K. and Holland I. Assuring good style for object-oriented programs. *IEEE Software*, 6 (5), 38–48

Liberman H. (1987). Concurrent object-oriented programming in Act1. In *Object-Oriented Concurrent Programming*, pp. 9–36. MIT Press. Computer Series.

Lippman S.B. (1992). *L'essential du C++* 2nd edn. Paris: Addison-Wesley

Martin C., Ergin B., Kouloumdjian J. and Pinon J.M. (1991). Méthode de conception par objets pilotée par les événements. Le génie logiciel et ses applications. December, Toulouse, pp. 761–73

Masini G., Napoli A., Colenet D., Limardo D. and Tonbre K. (1988). *Les Langages á Objets*. Intereditions

Mellor S. and Shlaer S. (1988). *Object-Oriented System Analysis: Modelling the World in Data*. Englewood Cliffs, NJ: Yourdon Press

Mesarovic M.D., Macko D. and Takahara Y. (1970). *Theory of Hierarchical, Multilevel Systems*. New York: Academic Press

Meyer B. (1988). *Object-Oriented Software Construction*. Prentice-Hall

Meyer B. (1990). Conception et programmation par objets. Paris: InterEdition (Translation of Meyer (1988))

Miles T., Sadoeski R. and Werner B. (1988). Animation with CINEMA,. In *Proc. 1988 Winter Simulation Conference*, pp. 180–87

Minsky M.L. (1968). *Matter, Minds and Models*. MIT Press

Mitrani I. (1982). *Simulation Techniques for Discrete Event Systems*. Cambridge University Press

Molloy M.K. (1982). Performance analysis using stochastic petri nets. *IEEE Transactions on Computers*, C31 (9), September

Nance R.E. and Overstreet C.M. (1985). A specification language to assist in analysis of discrete event simulation models. *Communication of the ACM*, 28 (2), 190–201

Neighbors J. (1981). Software construction using components. *PhD Thesis*. Dept of Information and Computer Science, Irvine, University of California

Nerson J.M. (1992). Applying object oriented analysis and design. *Communication of the ACM*, 35 (9),63–74

Nerson J.M. (1995). Un Aperçu de la méthode BON (Business Object Notation). *L'objet*. 1 (1), 5–13

Nijssen G.M. (1986). La méthode d'analyse IA-NIAM. *Revue Génie Logiciel* 4, Paris

Norre S. (1993). Problème de placement de tâches: méthodes stochastiques et évaluation des performances. *PhD Thesis*, Blaise Pascal University, Clermont-Ferrand II

O'Reilly J.J., Nordlund K.C., (1989). Introduction to SLAM II and SLAMSYSTEM. In *Proc. Winter Simulation Conf*, pp. 178–83

Ozden M.H. (1991). Graphical programming of simulation models in an object-oriented environment. *Simulation*, 56 (2), 104–16

Palme J. (1977). Moving Pictures show simulation to user. *Simulation* 29b, 240–49

Parnas D. (1972). On the criteria to be used in decomposing a system into modules. *Communication of the ACM*, 15 (12), 1059–62

Pegden C.D. and Sturrock D.T. (1989). Introduction to SIMAN. In *Proc. 1989 Winter Simulation Conference*, pp. 129–39

Pierrval H. (1990). Les méthodes d'analyse et de conception des systèmes de production. Hermes-Technologies de pointes.

Pooley R.J. (1986). *An Introduction to Programming in Simula*. Oxford: Blackwell Scientific

Popper J. (1973). La dynamique des systèmes, principes et applications. Paris: Editions d'Organisation

Potier D. (1977). Modèles à files d'attente et gestion des ressources dans un système informatique. *Thesis*, Grenoble.

Potier D. (1983). New User's Introduction to QNAP2. *INRIA Technical report*. N°40. October

Pritsker A.A.B. (1986). *Introduction to Simulation and SLAM II*. Prentice-Hall.

Roche C. and Laurent JP. (1989). Les approches objets et le langage LRO2 (KEOPS). *TSI*, 8 (1), 21–39

Rochfeld A. (1991). Modèle externe de données et modèle externe objet. *La génie logiciel et des applications*, December, Toulouse, pp. 775–89

Rochfeld A. (1992). Les méthodes de conception orientées-objets. INFORSID conference, Clermont-Ferrand, pp. 563–94

Rodde G. (1989). *Les systèmes de production, modélisation et performances*. Edition HERMES

Rolland C., Foucault O. and Benci G. (1988). Conception de systèmes d'information. La méthode REMORA. Paris: Eyrolles.

Rumbaugh J. (1994). Getting started: Using use cases to capture requirements. *JOOP*, September, 8–23

Rumbaugh J. (1995). OMT: The functional model. *JOOP*, March April, pp. 10–14

Sangbum L. and Carver D. (1991). Object oriented analysis and specification: a knowledge base approach. *JOOP*, January, 35–43

Sargent R.G. (1979). Validation of simulation models. In *Proc. 1979 Winter Simulation Conference*, San Diego, CA, pp. 497–503

Sargent R.G. (1984). A tutorial on Verification and validation of simulation models. In *Proc. Winter Simulation Conf.*, pp.115–21.

Sedgewick R. (1985). *Algorithms*. Reading, MA: Addison-Wesley

Shannon R.E. (1975). *System Simulation: The Art and Science*. Prentice-Hall

Shannon R.E., Mayer.R. and Adelsberger H. (1985). Expert systems and simulation. *Simulation*, 44 (6), 275–84

Shannnat R.E. (1986). The use of graphical models in model validation. In *Proc. 1986 Winter Simulation Conference*, pp. 237–41

Shlaer M. and Mellors S. (1992). *Object Life Cycles: Modelling the World in States*. Yourdon Press

Simon H.A. (1991). Sciences des systèmes, Sciences de l'artificial. AFCET systèmes. Paris: Dunod

Simulog. (1991). *Queueing Network Analysis Package 2: Reference Manual*. 1 rue James Joule. 78182 St Quentin en Yvelines, France.

Smith R.L. and Platt L. (1987). Benefits of animation in the simulation of machining and assembly lines. *Simulation*, 48 (1), 28–30

Sommerville I. (1988). *Le Génie Logiciel et ses applications*. Paris: InterEdition

Sommerville I. (1992). *Le Génie Logiciel*. Paris: Addison–Wesley

Song A.L. and Pooley R. (1992). An editing and checking tool for stochastic Petri Nets – ESP. SCS Simulation Multiconference, York, UK, pp. 228–32

Stroustrup B. (1986). *The C++ Programming Language*. Paris: Addison-Wesley

Stroustrup B. (1992). *Le langage C++*, 2nd edn. Paris: Addison-Wesley

Tankoano J., Boudebous D. and Dernaime J. (1991). PETRI-S: un simulateur de systèmes de production automatisés décrits à l'aide de réseaux de Petri interprétés colorés. *APII*, 25 (1), 1–31

Tardieu H., Rochfeld A. and Colleti R. (1985). La méthode MERISE tome 1: Principes et outils. Paris: Edition d'Organisation

Taylor R.P. and Hurrion R.D. (1988). An expert advisor for simulation experimental design and analysis. In *Proc. Multi-Conference on AI and Simulation CSC*, San Diego, CA.

Ten Dyke R.P. and Kunz J.C. (1989). Object-oriented programming. *IBM System Journal*, 28 (3), 465–78

Thalmann D. and Magnenat N. (1985). Controlling evolution and motion using the CINEMIRA-2 animation sublanguage. In *Computer Generated Images*, pp. 249–59. Springer

Tours (1991). Le Génie Industriel. 3ème Congrès International. Tours, France, 20– 22 March 1991, Vols 1 and 2

Vallette R., Thomas V. and Bachman S. (1985). SEDRIC: un simulateur à événement discrets basé sur les réseaux de Petri. *APII*, 19 (5), 423–36

Vince J. (1992). How real can a real-time world be? SCS European Simulation Multi-Conference, June, York, UK, Late papers pp. 3–20

Von Bertalanffy L. (1987). *Théorie générale des systèmes*. Paris: Dunod

Walden K. and Nerson J.M. (1995). *Seamless Object-Oriented Architecture: Analysis and Design of Reliable Systems*. Prentice-Hall. The Object-Oriented Series

Wasserman A., Muller R. and Pircher P. (1990). The object-oriented structured design notation for software design representation. *IEEE Computer*, March, 51–63

Wasserman A.I. (1991). From object-oriented analysis to design. *JOOP*, September, 46–50

Wiener R., Wirfs-Brocks R. and Wilkerson B. (1990). *Designing Object-Oriented Software*. Prentice-Hall

Wirfs–Brock R. and Johnson R. (1990). Surveying current research in object oriented design.

Communication of the ACM, 33 (9), September, 104–24

Yourdon E. (1989). *Modern Structured Analysis*. Yourdon Press. Computing Series.

Zeigler B.P. (1976). *Theory of Modelling and Simulation*. Wiley

Zeigler B.P. (1984). *Multi-faceted Modelling and Discrete Event Simulation*. London: Academic Press

Zeigler B.P. (1990). *Object-Oriented Simulation with Hierarchical Modula Models: Intelligent Agents and Endomorphic Systems*. London: Academic Press

INDEX

A

a posteriori modelling 7
a priori modelling 8
abstract class 42, 125, 234
abstract data type 32, 33
abstract superclass 42
abstraction 4, 29, 35, 59, 119, 124, 219
abstraction levels 49, 119
acceptance tests 178
acquaintances 57
action model viii, 2, 3, 12, 94, 96
active resources 4
actor models 55, 57, 58, 60
address of overloaded function 237
agent 117
aggregate 113
aggregation 49, 59, 84, 87, 107, 108
AGV 148, 176
analytical methods 3
analysis by constraints 12, 13
analysis methods 65, 66, 67, 101
ancestors 42
animation process 155, 175
animation xi, 11, 129, 130, 131, 132, 133, 136, 138, 145, 146, 165, 249, 254, 256, 262
ARENA 128, 252
argument signature 53, 229
assembly language 30
association 108
attributes 34, 90

B

base class 41, 219
black board 56
BON 79

C

C++ xi, xii, 55, 69, 147, 156, 157, 158, 190, 198, 211, 215, 218
categories 89
circulation flow diagram
class attributes 42
class methods 42
class variables 42
classification 40, 45, 59, 89, 126
CLOS 257
co-routines 56, 258
communication 87, 126
compatibility 28
completeness 92
complex systems vii, ix, 1, 4, 20, 26, 84
complexity 92
composability 38
composition 49, 59, 88, 107
concurrency 55, 56
connection 109
consistency 64, 77, 93
constrained genericity 41
constraints 106, 110
constraints on inheritance 46
construction inheritance 44

constructor 222, 226
continuity 39
continuous approach 254
continuous simulation 4
copy constructor 243
coupling 92
CRC 80, 85
CSP 206

D

data abstraction 36
data analysis 14, 16
data flow 65, 81
data member 219
database viii, 14
decisional subsystem 18, 174
decomposability 39
delegation 57, 104, 195, 269
delete 239
derivation 41, 225
derived class 41
descendants 42
design methods 65, 66, 67, 101
destructor 223
differential copying 57
discrete flow systems vii, 15
dispatch table 196
domain analysis 84, 94, 95, 98, 100, 124
dynamic analysis 12, 13
dynamic aspects 115, 125, 151, 214
dynamic binding 51, 60
dynamic classification 50, 104, 105, 116, 117, 195, 269

dynamic entities 249
dynamic inheritance 50, 115
dynamic typing 40, 59, 150

E

effectiveness 27
Eiffel 69, 147, 257
empiricism 125
encapsulation 34, 36, 37, 59, 219, 269
entity/relationship 15, 18, 19, 20, 78, 170, 173, 212
event approach 254
exceptions 244
experimental conditions 9
experimental framework 94, 99, 252
experimental model 253
expert software 144
exploratory programming 46
extended Petri nets 104
extensibility 28

F

FACTOR/AIM 257
factory methods 42
flow circulation diagrams 122, 123
flow elements 125, 174, 175
formal analysis 12, 13
fountain model 63
friend class 240
friend functions 240
functional decomposition 65, 81

G

generation of code 179, 189, 193, 200, 215
genericity 40, 109, 241, 261
GPSS 14, 248, 249

H

heuristics 125
hierarchical approach 137
hierarchy 40, 59
HOOD 71, 72
hypertext 162

I

IDEF 110
IEE 255
incremental 81
informal analysis 12, 13
information modelling 65, 81
inheritance (simple) 41, 43, 44, 59, 84, 87, 107, 176, 195, 224, 267
inheritance exception 46
inheritance graph 34, 149
inline 221, 242
instance attributes 42
instance card 102
instance diagrams 103, 112
instance methods 42
instance variables 42
instances 34
instantiation 87
integration tests 178
integrity 28
intelligibility 28
interface 31, 35, 85
internal behaviour 120, 160, 177, 212
internal validity 11
IPC 152
iterative process 81
iterator function 246

K

KISS 119
knowledge model viii, 2, 3, 17, 18, 94, 96, 126, 134

L

life cycles 61, 62, 63, 64, 120
logical subsystem 18, 148, 172, 174, 184

M

M2PO xi, 83, 98, 100
macro-instructions 268, 269
macro-place 121, 159
macro-transition 121, 122
macro-objects 113
maintenance 5, 97
manufacturing systems 43, 110, 168, 169, 215, 253

Markov model 181
Markovian analysis 16, 181
measurements 6
mechanism 90, 96, 126
member functions 219
message 34, 37, 38, 56, 59, 83, 121
message flow diagram 103, 104, 117, 118, 159
metaclass 42
metadata 42
method lookup 197
methods 34, 91, 221
MHEX 255
modelling cycle 93, 214
modelling environment 14, 15, 16, 18, 20, 22
modelling method viii, 14
modelling process 2, 93, 94, 99
modifiability 27
MODSIM 14, 128, 260
Modula-2 260
modularity 28, 38, 39
module 31, 32, 223
Monte Carlo simulation 4
MOO 78
MOOD 78
multiple inheritance 47, 48, 107, 227
multiple polymorphism 53, 54

N

network of blocks 252
network of queues 264
networking viii, 14, 16
new 239
NeXT 54, 97, 147
NeXTStep 55, 97, 115, 163
notion of model 1
notion of object 33

O

object model 25, 35, 124
Object-Z 114
Objective C 55, 199, 257
Objectory 74, 75, 77, 96
OCCAM 205, 207, 209
OMT 70, 72, 73, 74, 77
OOA 67, 68, 69, 70
OOD 68, 69, 71
OOSD 80
OOSE 74, 75, 77
operator= 238
operator[] 238

OSM 75
overloaded function 237
overloading 53, 236
overloading operators 237
overriding (redefinition) 53

P

Parallel processing 263
parallelism 263
parametrized metaclasses 41
parametrized overloading 53
passive resources 4
performance evaluation viii, 14, 263
persistence 54
persistent objects 55, 60, 113
Petri nets 120, 121, 125, 159, 161,
     167, 200, 208, 210, 216
physical subsystem 18, 154, 171
pipeline mode 56
pointers to members 245
polymorphic messenger 198
polymorphic method 51, 59, 150
polymorphism 51, 52, 53, 54, 195,
     229, 236
portability 28
post-processor 138
predictive validity 11
presentation of results 132, 136
primitiveness 92
private 220
procedural abstraction 36
procedural approach 113
process approach 56, 254
PROLOG 144
protected 220
protection 39
protocol 36
prototype 179
prototyping 46, 81
proxy 57
public 220, 227
pure virtual function 234

Q

QNAP2 vii, xii, 14, 154, 167, 180,
     181, 182, 183, 184, 186, 188,
     189, 204, 248, 263
queuing network 184, 264

R

random numbers 259
rapid prototyping 46
readability 28
redefinition 53, 233
references 235, 236
relationships 86
reliability 29
REMORA 78
repeated inheritance 48
resources 4, 250
responsibility 113
reusability 28, 59, 92, 99, 211
reuse 29
robustness 28
ROSS 116, 248

S

SADT 71, 118
scenario 104, 119
scheduling 5
script 57
selective inheritance 46, 47
sensitive analysis 11
Sim++ 248
SIMAN xii, 14, 128, 205, 206, 252,
     253
SIMULA ix, 14, 83, 131, 193, 194,
     218, 257
simulation animation 138, 139
simulation languages 248
simulation of Petri nets 201, 202, 203
SLAM 14, 128, 254, 255
SLAMSYSTEM 128, 254, 256
Smalltalk 56, 248, 257
software components 28, 29, 164
software engineering 26, 59, 99
specification viii, 66, 200
spiral life cycle 62, 63
static analysis 12, 13
static aspects 106, 125, 214
static members 243
static typing 40, 59
station approach 3
statistical results 131
statistics viii
streams (C++) 242
structural validity 11
subclass 41
subroutine 31
substitution 54, 233
subsystem 111, 120, 125, 147
sufficiency 93

superclass 41
symbolic analysis 12
synchronizing kernel 261
Syntropy 79
system 1, 2, 17

T

tasks (C++) 243
templates 241
TESS 255
testing of classes 178
testing of subsystems 178
textual notation 105, 112, 113, 125
this 238, 239
Time Warp 263
tracability 75, 214
transaction approach 3, 125
transaction flow 249
transactions 104, 122, 249
transformation of time 140
transient behaviour 131
transient results 132
transputer 209
Turing test 1
typing 39

U

unit tests 178
UNIX 141, 152
use cases 76

V

V model 61, 81
validation viii, x, 1, 9, 10, 13, 21, 99,
     129, 132, 134, 135
validity 28
validity of events 10
validity of repetitiveness 10
verifiability 28
verification viii, x, 1, 9, 12, 13, 21,
     99, 129, 133, 134, 135, 257
virtual functions 229, 230, 231, 232,
     233, 246
virtual reality 11
visual interactive simulation 135,
     138, 139, 142, 144, 163, 165

W

waterfall model 61, 81

X

X model 62